D1556290

FRANK FLETCHER

FRANK FLETCHER

1870–1954

A Formidable Headmaster

JOHN WITHERIDGE

MICHAEL RUSSELL

First published in Great Britain 2005
by Michael Russell (Publishing) Ltd
Wilby Hall, Wilby, Norwich NR16 2JP

Typeset in Sabon by Waveney Typesetters
Wymondham, Norfolk
Printed and bound in Great Britain
by Biddles Ltd, King's Lynn, Norfolk

Indexed by the author

ISBN 0 85955 292 6

CONIVGI CONIVNCTISSIMAE
QVAE
DVOBUS CVM DOMVS CARTHVSIANAE PRINCIPIBVS
LAETA PATIENSQVE VIVEBAT

Contents

Preface

Not choosing but being chosen by their subject is a common experience of biographers and it is certainly my experience of Sir Frank Fletcher. Of my twenty-eight predecessors at Charterhouse he seemed to me from the start to stand out as the most engaging. He had come to the school after some difficult years as I had and his example of courage and determination in bringing reform was an inspiration. There were other echoes too. At Cambridge I had specialised in nineteenth-century ecclesiastical history and I was fascinated to discover that Fletcher had known and been influenced by some of the titans of the Victorian Church. Before Charterhouse he was Master of Marlborough where I started my teaching career. He was a mentor and friend of two Archbishops of Canterbury and was acquainted with another four: after Marlborough I served as Chaplain to Archbishop Robert Runcie at Lambeth Palace.

I am indebted especially to the Fletcher family for the memories they have been so ready to share. Fletcher's nephew, Jim, and his nieces, Cicely and Barbara, gave me invaluable information, and Robert Cornish showed me what remains of the family's industrial heritage: he also proved an enthusiastic and perceptive critic of every chapter.

Members of the Governing Body of Charterhouse deserve thanks for their encouragement of a headmaster who must at times have seemed to know more about the school's past than its present.

I began by writing to 400 Old Carthusians who had been at Charterhouse under Fletcher and received over 200 replies, for which I am most grateful. The fact that my correspondents were all over eighty must say something for the start to life that Fletcher's Charterhouse had given them!

My debt to my friends and colleagues at Charterhouse is considerable. Theo Zinn sowed the seed of this biography by lending me his intriguingly annotated copy of Fletcher's memoirs. Richard Thorpe (now a distinguished political biographer) taught me how to approach the craft of which he is a master. His detailed comments on my draft chapters have been characteristically full of knowledge and anecdote.

Angela Bailey sketched the map, Jim Freeman assisted with everything classical, Ian and Britta Stenhouse reproduced the photographs, and Matthew Armstrong read the final draft and made this a better book than it might have been.

The staff of libraries and archives have been invariably welcoming and patient, not least at the London Library: I am grateful to the late Peter Bennett and John Russ at Rossall; John Jones and Alan Tadiello at Balliol; Rusty Maclean at Rugby; my former colleague Terry Rogers at Marlborough; Ernst Zillekens, Sarah Pritchard and Ann Wheeler at Charterhouse. My thanks go too to another former colleague, Melanie Barber, and her successor, Clare Brown, at Lambeth Palace Library; and to Robin Darwall-Smith at University College, Oxford; John Plowright at Repton; Simon Blundell at the Reform Club; Ruth Drysdale at the Surrey History Centre; Margaret Ecclestone at the Alpine Club; and Geoff Lucas, Secretary of the Headmasters' and Headmistresses' Conference.

I am indebted to Patrick Derham, Headmaster of Rugby; to two former Masters of Marlborough, John Dancy and Roger Ellis; and to Martin Evans, the doyen of Marlborough housemasters.

John and Ann Scott deserve thanks for revealing the fact that they live in the Fletchers' final house and for introducing me to Dorothy Humphries, who grew up in the Fletchers' household.

Acknowledgement is made to the following who have kindly given permission to quote or reproduce illustrations: The Masters and Fellows of Balliol and University Colleges, Oxford; The Governing Bodies of Charterhouse and Rugby School; The Master and Council of Marlborough College; The Principal and Council of Rossall School; Carcanet Press Ltd; The Classical Association; Martin Gibbs; Richard Perceval Graves; David Higham Associates; The Trustees of Lambeth Palace Library; John Murray Publishers; Times Newspapers Ltd; and Hugh Wilkinson.

My secretaries, Helen Laurie, Katherine Stevenson and Sue Cook, added the burden of this biography to their workload and have been cheerful and uncomplaining in their tolerance of the author's unreasonable demands.

Last, but most important, my thanks go to my family for their patience with what must have seemed at times an obsession. My wife, Sarah, has, as always, borne the brunt and it is very properly to her that the book is dedicated.

JOHN WITHERIDGE

The Fletcher Family Tree

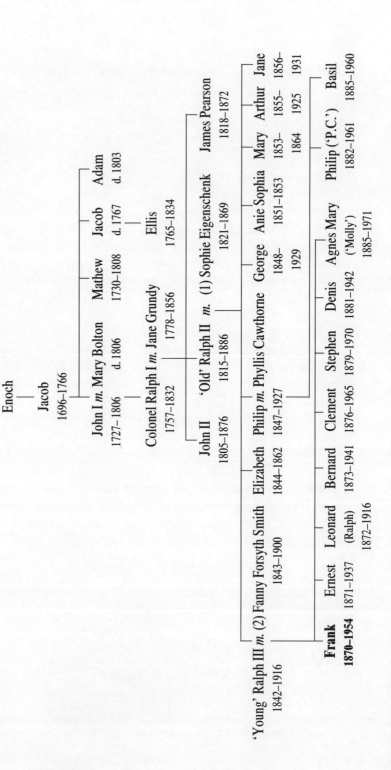

I
Origins

In his address at Sir Robert Birley's memorial service in the chapel at
Eton, Oliver van Oss described how in 1935 Birley came to follow
Frank Fletcher as Headmaster of Charterhouse.[a] 'At thirty-two', he
said, 'Robert Birley was appointed to succeed the most formidable
headmaster in England.' Fletcher was indeed an extraordinary scholar,
teacher and headmaster. He lived too in interesting times and places and
among fascinating people. Born to a prosperous and philanthropic family of Lancashire colliery owners, he won scholarships first to Rossall
School and from there to Balliol College, Oxford. Here he joined a
remarkable generation of undergraduates which coincided with Benjamin Jowett's last years as Master. Fletcher won firsts in mods and
greats (the two parts of the Oxford classics degree) and a hockey blue.
After two terms as a tutor at Balliol, and determined not to fulfil any
expectations that he would join the family firm, Fletcher went to teach
at Rugby, at a time when memories of Thomas Arnold were still tangi-
ble and revered. 'He had won most of the classical prizes and could have
chosen almost any career and reached the top of it as Lord Chancellor
or Archbishop of Canterbury or as a distinguished civil servant. He had
chosen schoolmastering and had gone to Rugby.'[1] Among his pupils
were R. H. Tawney and William Temple who both followed Fletcher to
Balliol and came to share the same radical social concerns.

Although personally devout and already ambitious to become a
headmaster, Fletcher resisted the still customary qualification of holy
orders. Nonetheless, he was appointed Master of Marlborough in 1903
aged thirty-three, the youngest and the first lay headmaster of a major
public school, and one founded for the sons of Church of England
clergy. The appointment occasioned a leader in *The Times* which later
described Fletcher, in a vivid turn of phrase, as the 'one lay apple in the
clerical dumpling'.[2] One of his senior prefects (whom he later

---

[a] Robert Birley died in 1982. He was Headmaster of Charterhouse from 1935 to 1947 and
was appointed Headmaster of Eton in 1949 after two years as an education adviser in
post-war Germany. Oliver van Oss had been his Lower Master at Eton before becoming
Headmaster of Charterhouse in 1965.

appointed to the staff) was Geoffrey Fisher, William Temple's successor as Primate of All England and another lifelong friend. 'Always for me he is the Master', confided Archbishop Fisher in his address at Fletcher's memorial service in 1954, 'and I the eager and clumsy pupil.'³

After eight successful years at Marlborough Fletcher was summoned to Charterhouse to rescue a school in decline. He raised its sights, guided it through the First World War, built its great memorial chapel, and ruled it for twenty-four years with a characteristic mixture of tradition and innovation, discipline and kindliness. Fletcher bequeathed to Birley what was again one of the finest schools in England. Two years later, he was the first headmaster to be knighted for his services to education.

Frank Fletcher was born on 3 May 1870 at home in the village of Howe Bridge twelve miles to the north-west of Manchester. The year before, his father, Ralph, had married his second wife, Fanny, a naval officer's daughter. Frank was the first of seven sons, followed by a daughter born fifteen years after Frank who was her godfather. The Fletchers had been pit proprietors for a hundred years and Ralph's was the fourth generation to have mined in south Lancashire. The family were revered and respected as paternalistic and enlightened employers: 'Their name was, and remains, a synonym for fairness and justice, for simplicity of life and for a sense of responsibility for all in their employ.'⁴ This benevolent tradition was fostered as much by Frank's father as by any member of the family: 'He was a first-class man of business; the prosperity and reputation of the collieries are due in large measure to his wise and just management.'⁵

Fletcher's earliest memories were dominated by the Howe Bridge coal pit. His home, The Hindles, once a farmhouse, was only 500 yards from the mine. It was a substantial ivy-clad red-brick house, long and narrow with a large, adjoining cobbled yard. On the far side six draught horses were stabled and were led out early each morning to pull the carts which carried coal from the pithead to local depots. Also in the stable block were kept the family's pony and trap and there is an enchanting photograph, taken in about 1885, showing Frank's mother seated, Frank standing behind, a nanny and various siblings out for a walk and ride.⁶ Looking back, Fletcher recalled the horses and the sounds of the winding-engines, drawing men and coal up the lift shaft from dawn till dusk. He remembered too the thunder of steam trains passing close to the side of the house along the line from Wigan to

Manchester: the station was just a hundred yards from The Hindles. He never forgot the blackened hands and faces of the men, women and youths who trudged past his house on their way home from the pit, their clogs clattering on the cobbles. And with a certain boyish pride Fletcher remembered the parish pump, erected in 1862 and called 'The Colonel' after his notorious great-grandfather.

Colonel Ralph Fletcher was the grandson of Jacob with whom the family's history begins. Of the Fletcher patriarchs we know that Enoch begat Jacob in 1696 and that Jacob had four sons, John, Mathew, Jacob and Adam. The first Jacob was a yeoman farmer and coal merchant with a small upland estate at Crompton Fold near Bolton, six miles north-east of Howe Bridge. Jacob's fields happened to overlay substantial seams of coal with sufficient outcrops to make surface or shallow 'delving' possible. Increasing demand soon rendered coal more profitable than crops and by his death in 1766 Jacob had made a modest fortune. Two years later, Jacob's eldest son John started mining a few miles south at Atherton. Two pits were sunk in 1769 by Messrs Fletcher and Fyldes who mined there until 1775. In 1776 John Fletcher and Thomas Guest began negotiations with the lord of the manor, Robert Vernon Atherton Gwillym. They agreed a ninety-nine-year lease on all workable coal within the boundaries of the town. Under the terms of the lease the Atherton family was to receive royalties of one shilling for every 'pit load' of thirty baskets of coal (the coal sold for tuppence a basket). Unlimited coal was also to be provided for their Palladian manor house, Atherton Hall.

John Fletcher's brother, Mathew, brought to the family's burgeoning investment in coal remarkable skills as a hydraulic and mining engineer. Five miles to the east of Atherton lies the small village of Clifton, surrounded by a rich coalfield. Shallow mining began there close to the River Irwell as early as the mid-seventeenth century and shafts were sunk in the 1740s. The first deep mine in the valley represented a major undertaking. In order to sink the pit to a depth below 300 feet Heathcote engaged Mathew Fletcher who was still in his teens. He soon encountered a serious problem with water: the deeper the seam the greater the flooding. Conventional drainage methods proved inadequate and this Wet Earth Colliery was forced to close in 1750. But Mathew was not defeated and brought in the millwright, James Brindley, who was to make his name as the Duke of Bridgewater's brilliant canal engineer. Brindley suggested using waterpower to operate a pump, and construction began in 1752. A weir had to be built across

the Irwell which helped to create an enterprising siphon system requiring a channel to be cut under the rock of the riverbed, an 800-yard
tunnel and a huge wooden waterwheel which ran for over a century
before being replaced by a turbine. Although Brindley deserves the
lion's share of the credit for this ingenious scheme, Mathew Fletcher's
role must not be overlooked. Brindley was based in Staffordshire and
was busy with a variety of other projects, leaving Mathew to supervise
the work at Clifton. The drainage system proved successful and in the
1760s Mathew's colliery and estate interests began to expand and he
was able to build himself an imposing residence, Clifton House. He was
already a magistrate like his brothers and by the turn of the century he
had risen to the position of deputy lieutenant.

In the early 1780s Mathew applied waterpower to his nearby
colliery of Botany Bay, using it here for winding coal up to the surface.
He did this by extending Brindley's feeder stream to Wet Earth eastwards towards Botany Bay. In 1790 he started work to deepen and
widen the course of the stream to create what became known as
Fletcher's Canal. It linked Mathew's two pits and allowed his coal to be
transported to Manchester via the new Manchester, Bury & Bolton
Canal which Mathew had helped to build and which Fletcher's Canal
joined at Clifton junction.[b] Work on the canal was finished in 1795 and
had 200 narrow barges in operation, each carrying as much as ten 14
hundredweight boxes of coal. Their narrow shape lent them the grim
sobriquet 'starvationers'.

Mathew died in 1808 and his estate passed to his nephew Ellis. Since
1804, with his sinking of a downcast shaft at the Wet Earth Colliery and
his installation of a steam winding-engine, Ellis had been showing signs
of his uncle's innovative and enterprising characteristics. He is commemorated today (somewhat unjustly) by 'Fletcher's Folly', a high
chimney built in splendid isolation on the hillside (and well away from
the steam-engine) so as not to spoil the view from Clifton House. It was
connected to the boiler by two long underground flues and, as the number of boilers increased, the chimney had to be heightened. In the 1890s
it was replaced by a second and more practical chimney built at the pit.

Ellis's cousin Ralph (John Fletcher's son) was the Fletcher referred to as
'The Colonel'. He was born in 1757 and died aged seventy-four in

---

[b] Mathew Fletcher was the driving force behind the Manchester, Bury & Bolton Canal
Company, formed in 1790; the canal opened in 1796.

1832. His life is the best documented and most controversial of the Fletchers. His imposing portrait, painted in classical style, shows a man of power and prosperity: formal, efficient, commanding, but not without a touch of sympathy in his expression.[7] Opinion is divided between historians who regard him as a cruel, callous, even sinister opponent of social justice, and those who see him as a man of his time and class, reactionary and repressive, but concerned for the public good and (like many of his contemporaries) fearful that England, like France, might come to suffer a revolution.

Ralph married Jane Grundy in 1805: he was forty-eight, she twenty-seven. Ralph's father died the following year, and Ralph and Jane moved into the family house and home farm, The Hollins, on the road to Little Lever just south-east of Bolton.[c] Three years before, his father's partner had sold Ralph his share in the Atherton colliery. During the thirty years of his stewardship investment continued, both at his Ladyshore pit on the canal bank at Little Lever and at Atherton. Here the company diversified, making bricks and running coke ovens which were highly efficient. The ovens used small pieces of coal which were difficult to sell to produce coke which found a ready market in Atherton's textile and nailmaking industries. Atherton, however, was becoming isolated by the canal boom and the pit owners faced a major problem in transporting their coal. In 1799 the Duke of Bridgewater extended his canal to Leigh, just a few miles from Atherton, and by 1818 coal from the Atherton mines could be taken by horse tramway to be loaded onto barges. In time, canal barges gave way to steam trains, and ten years later Ralph owned a siding off the Bolton to Leigh railway, the second railway to be built anywhere in the world.

Ralph's interests were not confined to coal, bricks and coke. He invested too in Lancashire's burgeoning cotton mills, and there is at least a supposition that he helped to finance Samuel Crompton's invention in 1779 of the spinning mule, a hybrid of Hargreaves's spinning jenny and Arkwright's water-frame. Crompton was a Bolton man and his ostentatious tomb can be seen in the graveyard of the parish church. But it belies his circumstances and he died penniless. By contrast, investors, manufacturers and employers were growing rapidly rich and powerful. Ralph Fletcher enjoyed all the advantages of wealth and a position in Lancashire society as head of what was by now an established and

---

[c] The Hollins was leased from the Earls of Bradford and passed on to Colonel Ralph's sons and grandsons.

successful family. The new manufacturers were soon joining the squires
and parsons on the bench of county magistrates and in 1797 Ralph was
elected one of 'His Majesty's Justices of the Peace for the county pala-
tine of Lancaster'. He exercised his legal responsibilities with vigour and
determination, even ensuring that his brother magistrates put his own
workmen in prison when they struck for an advance of wages.

Ralph Fletcher had served for several years as a captain in the Bolton
volunteers. In 1798 he was promoted to the rank of major, and in 1803
he rose to the position of colonel-commandant. Five years later he took
command of the Bolton militia. These local units, raised by compulsory
ballot, acted essentially as a police force. Constabularies then (and the
Colonel had established one in Bolton in 1806) were primitive and
unreliable. It was not until 1829 that Robert Peel's new police force was
organised in London, and it was another twenty years before the force
had extended across the country. So matters of internal order, civil
strife, industrial disturbance and riot all concerned the militia. Their
function was to repress minor outbreaks and to keep order in serious
cases until regular troops could be summoned. Again, Colonel Ralph
took his duties seriously and was 'offered a baronetcy by the Government of the day (and denounced by the Opposition) for his services as a
county magistrate and colonel of militia, and very wisely declined the
honour'.[8]

Colonel Fletcher's commemorative tablet in Bolton's parish church
was erected by public contribution and describes 'many years of difficulty and danger' through which he 'faithfully served his King and his
Country'. And dangerous and difficult times they were. As the industrial revolution tightened its grip, the demand for coal to power the new
mills and engines, factories and forges, seemed limitless. In 1770 the
nation's coal production was 6,000,000 tons – by 1830 it had almost
quadrupled to 23,000,000.[9] This offered enormous opportunities to
the colliery owners but placed appalling burdens on the miners. At least
until the Coal Mines Act of 1842, children as young as four were toil-
ing, often alone, in cramped subterranean cavities and passages. 'Many
of these children never saw the daylight for months at a stretch: it was
dark when they descended the pit, dark below and dark when they
ascended.'[10] From the age of six, children took their places with the
women, pushing, dragging and carrying coal from the place where it
was hewn to the main roads of the pit or the bottom of the shaft. Risks
to life and limb through falling, suffocating, burning or drowning were
manifold and fatal accidents were frequent.

The suffering of children labouring in the mines for a pittance may have been the worst example of life in the new industrial age but work in the mills and factories was almost as squalid and wearisome. 'Talk of *vassals*! Talk of *villains*! Talk of *serfs*! Are there any of these, or did feudal times ever see any of them, so debased, so absolutely slaves, as the poor creatures who, in the "enlightened" north, are compelled to work fourteen hours a day, in a heat of eighty-four degrees, even who are liable to punishment for looking out at a window of the factory!'[11] Indignation like William Cobbett's and demands for freedom and justice were becoming violent and vociferous. Soon orators were inciting riots, luddites were destroying machines, workers' associations were organising strikes, rabble-rousers were demanding reform. The French Revolutionary wars had inflated prices and stirred up in the hearts of both gentry and entrepreneurs a paranoia that in England too the mob would rise and the guillotine would follow. 'The state of the country is very alarming,' wrote Richard Hodgkinson in 1819. 'All sense of Morality and Religion seems totally to have forsaken the great Mass of the People. Led by appetite and passion alone they are ripe for all the horrors of a French Revolution, and Bloodshed, Rapine and Plunder form the general topic of familiar Conversation.'[12]

Hodgkinson enjoyed a business and social relationship with the Colonel who would have shared the same fears and anxieties. He certainly lacked any sympathy for the cause of industrial or political reform and in 1815 he threatened his own miners with transportation to the colonies for any breach of colliery rules. In addition to his membership of the Protestant Church & King Club, Fletcher was a pillar of Bolton's ultra-conservative Pitt Club, a powerful group of men who shared a deep admiration for the late Prime Minister's distaste for reform. As a magistrate he showed himself a formidable opponent of machine breakers. In 1812 a mill was burned down just north of Atherton and four luddites, including a boy of fourteen, were hanged at Lancaster prison. Fearful of a reaction to the severity of the sentences, Fletcher wrote to London demanding that more soldiers be sent to Bolton.

Although not the only magistrate or commanding officer to do so, Fletcher was notorious for his employment of spies whom he cynically referred to as 'missionaries'. 'From the Public Record Office, Bolton appears to have been the most insurrectionist centre in England, from the late 1790s until 1820. But it is by no means clear whether this was because Boltonians *were* exceptionally revolutionary in disposition; or

because Bolton suffered two unusually zealous magistrates – the Rev.
Thomas Bancroft and Colonel Fletcher – both of whom employed spies
on an exceptional scale.'[13] Spies were deployed in the battle against the
early trades unions, and were used either to gather intelligence or to act
as *agents provocateurs*. They were well paid (in 1805 Fletcher sent a
bill for £123 to the Home Office to pay agents who had been watching
a weavers' combination) but their work was perilous and discovery of
their identity could be fatal.

Fletcher's most infamous actions as a magistrate occurred on 16
August 1819 at what became known sardonically as Peterloo.[d] 1818
had seen a large strike in Lancashire which had encouraged workers in
their pursuit of better conditions and fair pay. 'Mass meetings were
taking place at the end of the year, and the cries were for universal
suffrage and the repeal of the Corn Laws.'[14] The threat of political
violence and even revolution pervaded the impoverished towns and
villages of Lancashire. '"There is scarcely a street or a post in the Land
that is not placarded with something seditious," wrote "Bolton
Fletcher".'[15]

The Lancashire reformers decided to hold a great meeting on St
Peter's Fields, an open space on the outskirts of Manchester. The popular radical Henry Hunt was to be the main speaker. It was to be an
orderly demonstration of men, women and children: the organisers
were so determined to show that working people were not a violent
rabble that only the aged and infirm were allowed to carry sticks. 3,000
marched from Middleton, 3,000 from Rochdale, and as many as
60,000 people assembled in their best Sunday clothes, with banners
flying and bands playing. The days before had been full of rumours and
though the magistrates remained uneasy, they decided that the meeting
could not be considered illegal. To prevent any interference Hunt
offered to give himself up before the meeting but his offer was refused
and the demonstration was allowed to proceed unhindered.

The majority of those who took part had their hearts set on immediate and mundane concerns (shorter hours, for example, and a decent
wage) but Hunt and others clamoured for parliamentary reform,
demanding universal suffrage, vote by ballot and annual parliaments.[e]

[d] And the heroic host no more shall boast
  The mighty deeds of Waterloo,
  But this henceforth shall be the toast,
  The glorious feats of Peterloo!
[e] Manchester, though by then one of the largest (and most impoverished) towns in
England, was unrepresented in Parliament.

This proved too provocative for the authorities, and while Hunt was addressing the crowd, the magistrates decided that the meeting was illegal after all and sent in a contingent of militia to arrest him. What happened next is unclear. Certainly, mounted soldiers forced their way through the crowd to the platform and Hunt allowed himself to be arrested. Then, either through panic at being surrounded by so many people, or through vindictiveness, the cry was raised, 'Have at their flags!', and the cavalry struck out with their sabres. Alarm and confusion followed but the field was cleared. 'There remained only dead and wounded men and women, mutilated banners, women's bonnets, torn shawls. Among 80,000 unarmed and closely packed people, many of them women and children and old persons, mounted horsemen with drawn swords had been let loose. Over 400 people were wounded, 113 being women. Eleven died, including two women and a child. Of the wounded over a quarter were injured by the sword.'[16]

Inevitably, in a fraught and fast-moving conflict like this, details are far from clear. The fact that the Prince Regent and the government of Lord Liverpool thanked the magistrates for their prompt and efficient measures for the preservation of the public peace makes it uncertain whether fault lay with over-zealous magistrates acting on impulse or with the government which had ordered the authorities to be on their guard. Neither Colonel Fletcher's precise role nor even his presence at Peterloo is certain. However, given his seniority (he had by then been a justice of the peace for twenty-two years and had commanded the Bolton militia for eleven) it seems more than likely that he was the magistrate described later as forcing his way through the crowd in the wake of the cavalry. He is supposed then to have read the Riot Act near the hustings. The inquiry afterwards was long, heated and complex. Whether or not the Act was read at this point was hotly disputed though Lord Castlereagh (then Foreign Secretary) said that the magistrate was sent in for that very purpose. 'The best or the worst that could be brought out of the incident in cross-examination was the rather ludicrous spectacle of an irate Col. Fletcher berating and belabouring some of the crowd with his cane across their backs, telling them to go away. He did not, the witness maintained in spite of searching questions from the radical counsel, seem to be hurting them!'[17]

Colonel Fletcher's association with Peterloo meant that for the rest of his life he remained the radicals' 'arch-fiend', 'their deadly antagonist, the enemy of liberty, the violator of civil rights and the despoiler of domestic peace'. On the other hand, 'those who held that reform meant revolution regarded Colonel Fletcher as one of the saviours of society.'[18] He was certainly held in high esteem by many of his contemporaries, and an annual Colonel Fletcher commemoration took place in Bolton until well into the nineteenth century. 'His death had occasioned the deepest grief to an affectionate family;' wrote his obituarist in *The Gentleman's Magazine*, 'the most unfeignedly to a numerous circle of friends & acquaintances; & a severe loss to the public, for whose benefit his valuable life was principally spent. In 1797, he undertook the arduous situation of a magistrate. In times of difficulty & danger, he was always at his post, & mainly contributed, by his foresight & firmness, to the repression of violence, & the preservation of the public peace.' The Colonel died, significantly, in the year of the great Reform Act, 1832. Society was changing and so too the Fletcher family whose later members, driven in part by guilt over Peterloo, were inclined to support the champions of social justice and reform, not oppose them.

It was, of course, incumbent upon a man in Colonel Ralph's position to provide for his sons the kind of education and opportunities befitting a gentleman. His second son, Ralph, Frank Fletcher's grandfather, started at Bolton Grammar School but in 1831 moved to Sedbergh School in Westmorland to join the sixth form. Under the reforming headmastership of Henry Wilkinson, Sedbergh was enjoying a good reputation for discipline and scholarship. Ahead of his time, Wilkinson promoted the study of mathematics as well as classics, both of which he taught himself. The school enjoyed the prestige of an early foundation and a distinguished founder, Roger Lupton, Provost of Eton, who had established it in 1525 as a small chantry school close to the site where he had been born.[f] Ralph Fletcher fitted well into the Sedbergh and Wilkinson mould, and won a scholarship in mathematics to St John's, the Cambridge college closely connected with the school's foundation and where Wilkinson had been a fellow. Ralph's Cambridge career was a success. As a boy he had learnt to row on his great-uncle's canal, and at Cambridge he pulled the stroke oar in the college boat at the head of the river and rowed too for the university against London. He was classified twenty-ninth wrangler[g] in 1838 and was later called to the bar at Lincoln's Inn, although he never actually practised as a barrister.

After Cambridge Ralph set off for Europe on his grand tour. There

[f] Roger Lupton is commemorated at Eton by a chantry chapel and the familiar clock tower.
[g] A Cambridge undergraduate who is awarded first class honours in mathematics.

he met Sophie Eigenschenk who was to become his first wife and Frank Fletcher's grandmother. They married in 1841 at the British embassy in Paris. Sophie added a romantic strain to the Fletcher blood: she was French, of German descent, and the granddaughter of Antoine Eigenschenk, the clarinettist in the orchestra at the court of Louis XVI at Versailles. She was a Roman Catholic but brought up her children as Anglicans. French was spoken at home at The Hollins, though in later life Frank's father refused to speak it and was said to harbour a particular prejudice against French imports! By contrast, his brother Philip spoke French fluently and would often dress in gallic fashion.

Despite a start to life undreamt of by earlier generations of Fletchers, Ralph's destiny lay in the mines. In 1840 the family firm became known as John Fletcher & Others, John being Ralph's elder brother and the Others being Ralph, his younger brother James Pearson, and a cousin, John Langshaw. The company's work was concentrated on developing the mines around Atherton and on sinking a series of new deep pits. During these decades, and in keeping with rapidly rising demand, massive tonnages of coal were extracted from under Atherton. Manpower increased and the latest machinery was introduced to speed production. At the same time widespread concern was growing about conditions in the pits, and in 1842 the Mines Act followed a royal commission. Under the Act all women and girls, and all boys under the age of ten, were banned from working underground. This reform was long overdue, though its introduction was not always welcomed by those it sought to help. 'Colliers who could no longer employ their wives, daughters and under-age sons as drawers, door minders or for other menial and arduous tasks, saw the Act as a threat to family income and security. Worse off still were those women who were the sole providers for their families. For them and their kin the Act was disastrous, unless there was alternative unskilled employment available.'[19] The Fletchers were compassionate and conscientious in implementing the Act's demands, and women and girls were employed instead as 'pit brow lasses', whose job was to sort and clean the coal.

Ralph Fletcher was an educated, cultivated man and alongside his work he maintained his interest in music. He donated and played the organ in the parish church of Atherton and started the first choir in 1853 with his son Philip as one of its founder members. He also compiled the Atherton Psalter which was published in 1855 as an attempt to improve the style of chanting. Following family tradition

Ralph became a magistrate in 1859. After Sophie's death he married again, aged fifty-six, and had two more children.

The eldest of Ralph's and Sophie's eight children, Frank Fletcher's father, was also (and confusingly) named Ralph. Since for many years father and son had worked together in the company, the miners referred to the son as 'Young' Ralph. Before going to Rossall (his father had contributed to its foundation in 1844) Young Ralph had attended a Church school in Atherton and he remained grateful for the education he received there. 'He believed in Church schools, of which he was an active and generous supporter, and kept a vigilant eye on all measures by which they might be affected. He was also a leading authority on problems of religious education, a subject which he had made peculiarly his own.'[20]

Young Ralph started in the firm in 1859. In 1867 the coal lease was renewed with the same four partners as in 1840. Abraham Burrows[h] had joined the firm and was then in charge of sales, with Young Ralph as general manager. In 1872 his uncle James Pearson died and John, his other uncle, retired, so Abraham Burrows and Young Ralph joined the board. Two years later, after John Langshaw had also retired, the name of the firm was changed to Fletcher, Burrows & Company and the partners were Abraham Burrows and the Ralph Fletchers, father and son. Burrows's strict non-conformist business ethic further strengthened the Fletchers' commitment to providing fair and benevolent terms and conditions for their workforce. But, despite the company's concerns for safety and welfare, accidents were unavoidable in an industry as difficult and dangerous as mining. In the year and place of Frank Fletcher's birth, Arthur Lee, aged 36, was 'killed by the stemming which was blown out by a shot'; Robert Cowburn 'died after being hit by a windlass handle which he had let go of'; William Edwards, aged 33, 'died in a coal fall'; James Charleson, a miner aged 34, and Wm. Aldred, a waggoner aged 11, 'were killed by an explosion'; William Heald 'was killed after being caught by the engine brow rope while unhooking it from moving tubs'. Two years later, twenty-seven men and boys died in Atherton's worst pit disaster, when a huge gas explosion left twelve widows and thirty-seven fatherless children, and many other victims badly burned and maimed. Every year, as Frank was growing up, there were

[h] Burrows had first come into contact with the Fletchers when he sold Atherton coal in Liverpool, his adopted town. Later generations of both families worked together in running the pits and developing cotton mills.

fatalities in the mines which surrounded Howe Bridge. News of deaths and the accidents which had caused them added to the melancholy of his surroundings and the seriousness of life at home.

What became known as the Battle of Howe Bridge was waged in January 1881 when Fletcher was ten. Lancashire miners were striking over pay, working hours, and compensation for death or injury. Fletcher Burrows did their best to meet demands and by 26 January two thirds of the Atherton miners had returned to work. Other less fortunate miners demanded solidarity and as many as 3,000 men from Wigan arrived at the Howe Bridge pit demanding that the men working below be brought out. Rioting erupted, the militia were called in, the Riot Act was read. Frank's father was present throughout as, presumably, his great-grandfather had been at Peterloo: the cartoonist of the *Leigh Chronicle* shows him in top hat pointing a pistol and leading a charge of policemen, truncheons drawn. The circumstances though were very different from Peterloo and the actions of the authorities, draconian though they were, were justified. Nonetheless, it was a terrifying experience for all concerned with fierce fighting throughout the day.

On a happier note, Frank Fletcher's early years were marked by the building of a range of model amenities at Howe Bridge, most of which remain. Immediately opposite his house a church was built and consecrated in 1877. Just 300 yards or so from The Hindles, in the opposite direction to the pits, a block of red-brick houses for miners and their families, a school, several shops, and a miners' institute were built. The houses (with two rooms downstairs and two bedrooms upstairs) were erected in 1875 and were a marked improvement on the cramped and squalid housing in other areas of the coalfields. They were well designed in an almost Dutch style and built on a promenade along the road. Most remarkable of all was the inclusion of a three-storey bathhouse in the centre. Pithead baths had to wait until 1913 (when the first in Britain were built at Howe Bridge) but a considerable step forward was taken when the men were allowed a hot bath, free of charge, as soon as they returned home from work. The institute provided a place for meetings, a reading room and a bar, and has claims to being the first working men's club in England.[i] The fine, stone-built church of St

---

[i] The Fletchers' practical concern for their employees' welfare continued: in 1903, the first central rescue station was established at Howe Bridge; a fund was set up in 1914 to help families of miners who had joined the forces; in 1919, *Carbon*, a quarterly colliery magazine, was started and Christmas food parcels began to be distributed; in 1921, Briarcroft, Philip Fletcher's home, was donated as a social centre.

Michael and All Angels was in large part paid for by Frank's grand-father, while his father provided the endowment for the incumbent's stipend. Frank's brother Clement is recorded as the first to be baptised in its font though there is a suspicion in the family that the vicar managed to christen his own son just before! Young Ralph was one of the first churchwardens and both Fletcher benefactors are commemo-rated by handsome inscriptions.

Such a long and distinctive family background was bound to leave its mark on Fletcher's character, outlook and attitudes. *Alta pete*, 'aim high', is the family motto and Fletcher took it to heart. Responsibility, independence, hard work, straightforwardness, resilience, common sense – all these are strong traits that Fletcher derived from his roots. The way he understood and evaluated his home and heritage is suggested in his memoirs, *After Many Days*. His reactions are mixed but he tries to be fair and even-handed:

> There is about the district what H. G. Wells in a fine phrase has called the 'weird inhospitable grandeur of industrial desolation'. But it was not a good district for childhood and boyhood ... My family have been colliery owners for a century and a half. As such they must, I fear, share the responsibility for past deface-ments of the land: in this respect they were no worse, even if they were no better, than the other great industrialists of that time. At least they have never been absentee owners: they did not migrate from the neighbourhood where their money was made. To this day they live and work in the midst of it. I have been so long detached from their work that I hope that I may without boasting record my pride in the reputation borne by the family firm for the fairness and justice of their dealings, their care for the health and safety of their workers, and the friendly spirit which is well known to exist between employed and employers.[21]

For all Fletcher's consciousness of his family's history and achieve-ments in Lancashire, and for all the admiration and respect he undoubtedly felt for them, it is clear that his mind and heart were never much engaged or attracted by the place, the people or the enter-prise into which he was born, and in the midst of which he spent his first formative years. Fletcher was the eldest son (as his father had been) in a fifth generation of pit proprietors, and he had watched his father and grandfather working as partners in the family firm. A strong sense of what was expected of him was inescapable. But somehow Fletcher knew, even before he started at Rossall, that this was not to be, and Rossall convinced him.

2

Rossall

1882–1889

Given his father's active interest in local Church schools it is surprising that Frank Fletcher was sent away at the age of nine to one of the new preparatory schools. Fletcher's school, J. Thompson's at St Anne's-on-the-Sea in Lancashire, was typical of a development which occurred towards the end of the nineteenth century. Previously private tuition provided the preparation necessary for entry to the public schools and was usually offered by clergymen anxious to supplement their modest stipends. A few boys were taken into the vicarage or rectory and in some more ambitious cases a pupil room was added, allowing for the education of as many as twenty boys at a time. But by the turn of the century 400 preparatory schools had opened, modelled on the schools they served.

Less surprising is the choice of Rossall, which to Fletcher must have seemed as much a part of the expected scheme of things as a career in the mines. His grandfather had subscribed to its foundation in 1844 and had sent his sons there. Fletcher's father was a pupil when it had been open for barely a decade, and Frank was followed by all six of his brothers. Fletcher had shown promise at Mr Thompson's and, despite having mumps during the examination, he won a foundation scholarship worth seventy guineas a year which covered the fees entirely. This was welcome because Fletcher's father's income was not then considerable and by the time Frank started at Rossall there were seven children to support. Fletcher's memoirs start with 'a day in late September, 1882, when I arrived at Rossall as a new boy. I was only a little over twelve years old: but I travelled unaccompanied … I have a memory of a railway carriage full of boys and of myself as the one new boy among them, of a glimpse of the school buildings in the distance as the train drew near to Fleetwood, and a voice from one of the boys in the carriage, "There's the old pig-sty." Even at twelve years old I was shrewd enough to recognise that the description recoiled upon the speaker: but the sense of depression it produced on me at the time has remained in my memory.'[2]

The practice of sending boys as young as seven or eight away from home can seem cruel and callous. It means that 'successive generations passed ten of the most imaginative and impressionable years of their lives under influences other than those of their parents'.[3] It is though a justifiable custom if these influences have more to offer than those of home and family. 'Children leave home to go to school,' wrote Edward Thring, Headmaster of Uppingham. 'In theory they are sent to a place which is better than home, to be under men who train better than fathers and mothers ... Every boy who leaves home ought to go to a better than home place.'[4] That was certainly Fletcher's view, and not only in later life as a schoolmaster. Despite that first twinge of depression, and the physical hardships of boarding school, Rossall soon impressed itself upon him as a place which provided the intellectual and cultural stimulation and companionship he found lacking at home.

In chapter 2 of *After Many Days* Fletcher describes his 'Home Surroundings' (significantly the first chapter is on 'Rossall Memories'). He makes it plain that school was a welcome escape from the drabness and narrowness of life at Howe Bridge:

> It is a common criticism of the English public schools that being primarily and traditionally boarding-schools they involve a loss of home life, and of the possibilities of a kindlier, more cultured atmosphere and freer surroundings which this offers. Those who urge this objection need to be reminded that there is gain as well as loss. How many homes are really cultured? And what about the families who live in town streets or unattractive parts of the country, for whom the public school to-day affords a chance of escape into fresher air and healthier, more beautiful surroundings?[5]

Fletcher goes on to describe the 'sad work' the industrial revolution had made of south Lancashire. 'We used to wonder sometimes what the district had looked like a century earlier, when there were real trees, and the grass was green, not black, and the brooks were really brooks and not channels polluted by the refuse of mills and collieries.'[6] He also describes the limitations of his parents. His mother, he says, was delicate and eight children left her little time or strength for the things of the mind or for living her own life. Fletcher poignantly describes the delight he would feel when, in the company of strangers, she gave an impression of charm and graciousness. 'The way in which she brightened and blossomed out in congenial company–such as our neighbourhood seldom afforded–suggested what she might have been in less cramping surroundings, and with the wider education which girls receive to-day.'[7]

His father's education was similarly restricted: he had left school at seventeen to join the family firm and had not had his father's or his younger brother Philip's opportunities of a university education. 'He cared nothing for poetry ... he was more careful to prevent us from reading what he thought unsuitable than to suggest stimulating books.'[8] Fletcher's father had been left a widower in his early twenties and Fletcher's mother was his second wife. 'His youth had ended early ... he was old in experience, and the gap between his age and his sons' was wider than the years represented. He had ceased to play any games – if indeed he had ever played them – long before his sons were old enough to join in them: and he did not easily show sympathy with our interests or impart his own to us.'[9] Nonetheless, he was a devoted parent and though he did not often show his feelings, he took his parental responsibilities seriously and was proud of his children. He wrote a weekly letter to them all and continued to do so until his death. But 'some things he could not give us. I never found at home the stimulating conversation which is found in some families: it was a rare treat when a visitor came and talked of books and suggested wider ideas. And as school and college opened my mind to literary interests, I felt the want of them in the home circle.'[10]

The rapid growth in the power, prosperity and aspirations of the middle class (not to mention the expansion of the railways) in the early nineteenth century led directly to the founding of a number of new public schools. They were based very deliberately on the great boarding schools with medieval, Elizabethan or Jacobean origins: Winchester, Eton, Westminster, Rugby, Harrow, Charterhouse. Cheltenham, Marlborough, Rossall, Radley, Wellington and Clifton were all founded during the reign of Queen Victoria.

Marlborough (1843) followed Cheltenham (1841) and Rossall (1844) followed Marlborough. All three began as proprietary schools, with donors or shareholders who were entitled to nominate boys for entry. Fees were charged as in other schools but in practice donations had to help cover the costs. Cheltenham had high social ambitions while Marlborough was founded specifically for the sons of Anglican clergy and the poorer professional classes. Rossall's foundation was shaped and inspired by Marlborough's and it too set out to provide a public school education for the sons of parsons and laymen of modest means. It was to be 'The Northern Church of England Public School'.

The details of Rossall's foundation combine the exotic and romantic with the pragmatic and realistic, a mixture which Fletcher found appealing. 'The founding of a school at Rossall was due to the financial straits of Sir Peter Hesketh Fleetwood, the imagination of the Corsican Vantini, and the practical ability of the then Vicar of Thornton–with–Fleetwood, the Rev. St. Vincent Beechey.'[11] Sir Peter's family had lived by the sea at Rossall Hall since the end of the sixteenth century. Not content with the leisurely life of a squire (which he could not afford), Hesketh determined to create a new seaside town, to be called Fleetwood after his adopted surname. He invested large sums of money in an attempt to convert sandy wastes into a harbour and in employing the classical architect Decimus Burton to design a symmetrical network of streets and a collection of imposing public buildings. Hesketh had speculated on a boom for his town as soon as the railway arrived but he was soon disappointed and had spent all his reserves.

Monsieur Vantini was courtier to his compatriot Napoleon but when offered the choice he preferred to settle in England rather than join his master in exile on St Helena. He invested in railway hotels and devised an ingenious scheme for educating all England's children on the basis of insurance. He had reckoned that since half the children would have died before the age of twelve, the money saved would be sufficient to educate the other half who survived. When this grand design failed, Vantini proposed the founding of two schools near Fleetwood, one for 500 boys and one for 500 girls. To discuss his plans he held a public meeting at the North Euston Hotel (which he owned) and invited the Vicar of Fleetwood to be chairman. The Revd St Vincent Beechey was no humble parish priest but the twenty-first child of the court painter to King George III and Queen Charlotte. He derived his Christian name from his godfather, Admiral Sir John Jervis, who was created Earl St Vincent in recognition of his great naval victory in 1797. Rossall's *Centenary History* explains that 'after careful inquiry, Mr. Beechey took the chair, reduced Vantini's project to practical proportions by cutting down the 500 boys to 200 and "dropping the 500 girls into the Wyre," secured a resolution that a boarding school was required in the North of England and that Fleetwood was a very fit and proper place for its establishment. Vantini fades from the story and we rightly hail St. Vincent Beechey as our Founder.'[12]

Beechey's next step was to raise the money and secure the support of the illustrious and influential. Hesketh generously headed the list of subscribers with a donation of £500. Beechey persuaded the Earl of

Derby to be patron, the Duke of Devonshire to be vice-president, and the Bishop of Chester to be visitor. The council consisted of fourteen clergymen and ten laymen. It obtained from Hesketh a twenty-one-year lease on his seaside mansion with the option to purchase for £7,000 in the next ten years (the purchase was made in 1852). Beechey was in constant touch with the founders of Marlborough on matters of organisation and economy, and on whom to appoint as headmaster. The school opened on 22 August 1844 with seventy boys.

Of the many factors that shape the distinctive character of a school, geography is one of the most important. The great public schools derive much of their peculiar spirit from their location: Westminster seated at the feet of Abbey and Parliament; Eton colonising the banks of the Thames below Windsor Castle; Marlborough nestling between forest and down at the head of a Wiltshire market town; Charterhouse at first 'shrivelling in the purlieus of Smithfield',[13] then free to expand in its new parkland setting in Surrey. Rossall's position on the shore, exposed to the clouds, winds and waves of the Irish Sea, was as rare as it was rugged. The first captain of the school described how 'the choosing of the site was often held up to ridicule ... but to us, who could bear the winds and brunt the storm, it gave a hardening strength which has braced us up for life.'[14] When Fletcher arrived at Charterhouse as head-master and looked back on his own school days, he was struck by the comparison. 'Few contrasts could be greater than between the Surrey school set in its rich landscape on a hill crowded with trees, and the bleak, flat Lancashire coast, treeless and windswept, only defended from the sea by a sea-wall which was liable to be battered to pieces by the violence of the waves.'[15]

This vivid experience of schooldays by the sea is a common theme in Rossall's school songs and the poems of boys and masters:

> Of sounds which haunt me, these
> > Until I die
> Shall live. First the trees,
> Swaying and singing in the moonless night.
> (The wind being wild)
> > And I
> A wakeful child,
> That lay and shivered with a strange delight.

Second – less sweet but thrilling as the first –
The midnight roar
Of waves upon the shore
Of Rossall dear:
The rhythmic surge and burst
(The gusty rain
Flung on the pane!)
I loved to hear.[16]

Fletcher writes in similar vein in a Latin verse, *Carmen Boreale*, composed for the school's jubilee in 1894:

Pleasant is the quiet waves' slowing heaving motion,
Pleasant too the spectacle of the raging ocean,
Pleasant, when in noble wrath billows roll and thunder,
Safe upon the shore to stand, contemplate, and wonder.[a]

The peculiar rigours and romance of Rossall's setting have always left a deep and lasting impression on her pupils' memories and affections, Fletcher's included:

Most people who go to Rossall are impressed at first by the loneliness and the flatness and the bleakness: there is little conventional beauty about either buildings or situation. But Rossallians carry with them through life memories of noble waves breaking on the beach and filling the Square with foam; of brilliant sunsets streaming in through windows that looked out on the sea, of clean, fresh air and cloudless skies: of occasional views of the Lake hills seen across the head of Morecambe Bay, with every peak standing out clear against a June sunset; of winter evenings when the sea wind battered against the chapel windows, while within the chapel we sang the hymn for those in peril on the sea.[17]

By June 1844 twenty-five men had applied for the post of first Headmaster of Rossall and just four were short-listed. One was Headmaster of Uppingham, then (ten years before the creative headmastership of Edward Thring) still a small, local grammar school. Another was

---

[a] Fletcher's own translation of the third stanza of his verse:

Juvat unda placidis vix turbata ventis,
Juvat et spectaculum pelagi furentis,
Juvat iras fluctuum nobiles mirari,
Eque terra sospites mare contemplari.

J. C. Penrose, Thomas Arnold's nephew and pupil and, wrote Beechey, 'reported to be the best man who ever left Rugby'.[18] Given the great reforming work Arnold had accomplished at Rugby it seems surprising that Penrose was not appointed. But Arnold had died in office in 1842 and knowledge of his achievements, and his theories and methods of education, was not widely disseminated until the publication (also in 1844) of A. P. Stanley's *Life and Correspondence*.[b] Instead the council chose the Revd Dr John Woolley, Headmaster of King Edward VI School, Hereford. He and Stanley had been fellows of University College, Oxford and Stanley had told him about Arnold's educational ideals and practices. Woolley's emphasis on præpostors (prefects) derives entirely from Arnold. They were to be invested 'with certain powers, immunities and privileges, which may enable them effectually to co-operate with their masters, in the maintenance of necessary discipline, and in promoting a spirit of strict integrity, gentlemanly feeling, and Christian principles among their companions generally'.[19]

For all his quality of character and good intentions Dr Woolley proved 'a poor disciplinarian and a weak and indecisive headmaster'.[20] In his *Rossall School, Its Rise and Progress*, Beechey expressed his regret that 'the sixth form ruled him, instead of his ruling them, to the great humiliation of the assistant masters, who were a very superior and gentlemanly class!'[21] Dr Woolley resigned after five years in which numbers had reached 200 but by 1849 had fallen to 140. Nonetheless, in 1846 a small group of inspectors (including the poet William Wordsworth, whose grandsons were to be educated at Rossall) referred to the 'gentlemanly deportment and religious behaviour of the boys'.[22] The following year Queen Victoria and Prince Albert landed at Fleetwood on their way south by sea from Scotland. The first captain of the school presented a Latin address to Her Majesty, including the customary request for an extra holiday.

The next two headmasters, William Osborne and Robert Henniker, were both clergymen with strong academic backgrounds. Osborne was captain of the school at St Paul's and went up to Trinity College, Cambridge as senior classic.[c] Henniker was educated at Charterhouse

[b] Arthur Penrhyn Stanley had been a boy at Rugby under Arnold, to whom he remained devoted.
[c] Osborne was Craven Scholar and senior medallist at Trinity where his contemporaries included C. J. Vaughan who was at Rugby under Arnold and later Headmaster of Harrow. As Woolley learnt about Arnold's methods from Stanley, so Osborne learnt the same from Vaughan. Vaughan married Stanley's favourite sister.

and became a scholar of Trinity, Oxford where he gained a congratulatory first in classics and a second in natural science: he was also offered a fellowship which he refused.[d] Both were said to be men of charm and conviviality, and excellent teachers. However, Osborne had the strength of character to enforce discipline that Henniker lacked, making Osborne's tenure largely a success for the school and Henniker's a failure. Osborne appointed excellent staff, established organised games, provided scholarships, started the preparatory school, raised money for new buildings, introduced French, German and drawing into the curriculum, and increased the school roll to almost 400. But he stayed for a quarter of a century and his last years were marred by a series of disputes, disasters and general decline.

The school needed a man of considerable presence and talent to restore it and Beechey soon regretted his appointment of Robert Henniker. 'I couldn't be ignorant that the School was going down in his hands,' he wrote. 'In his general management, his want of dignity and lax discipline, he failed even more lamentably than Dr. Woolley.'[23] He was a kind and avuncular man, and certainly the new regime felt more compassionate and humane: prefects were prevented from caning while beating by masters was 'marvellously diminished'. One new housemaster even thought Rossall 'a paradise for small boys'! But a relaxed and easygoing school does not make for hard work or the will to win, and numbers fell with the school's diminishing reputation. Henniker left for a parish near Stroud where his wife died five years later. Tragically, Henniker died of an epileptic fit on his way to her funeral.

Fletcher's first headmaster was the Revd Dr H. A. James, Henniker's successor. He had been in post for seven years when Fletcher started in 1882, and he left four years later to be succeeded by Charles Tancock. A change of headmaster or housemaster is often unsettling but for a precociously thoughtful and reflective boy like Fletcher it can prove an advantage. 'During my last years', he wrote, 'I changed my headmaster and my housemaster: and the changes added to my experience.'[24] His attention was drawn especially to the headmaster's function and influence in a school, and he was able to observe the differences in character, style and approach of James and Tancock. Looking back, it seemed to Fletcher that he had learnt important and lasting lessons, and was

---

[d] Henniker was nearly appointed Headmaster of Charterhouse: instead the governing body chose William Haig Brown who moved the school from London to Surrey.

already beginning to glimpse his own future as a schoolmaster, and even as a headmaster. 'To the end of my days', he confided, 'I found myself using the experience and remembering the precedents of my own life as a schoolboy.'[25] The lessons continued when Fletcher went to teach at Rugby and James arrived in his second year to succeed John Percival as headmaster:

> It is no small part of a boy's education in a big school that he is forced, for his own comfort, to study the personality of the various masters whom he encounters. The experience gained lasts throughout life. It was my good fortune to be associated with H. A. James at two periods of my life: I observed him with the hero-worshipping eyes of boyhood in his last four years at Rossall, and with the anxious and critical eyes of young manhood during the earlier part of his Rugby headmastership. It is no depreciation of him to say that he succeeded at Rugby a greater man than himself: for John Percival was a headmaster of outstanding distinction. Nor again is it a depreciation of that genial and cultivated man who succeeded him at Rossall, C. C. Tancock, to say that he too was not of the calibre of his predecessor. Thus in each school I witnessed a change from the greater to the less great; I was in a position to observe the reactions of boys and masters to the change, and to judge my old headmaster in the double capacity of predecessor and successor.[26]

Fletcher remembered James as a man of warm affections, simple tastes and glorious prejudices. He was short and stout, with a long black beard and a strong resonant voice. By the time Fletcher arrived, James's reforms had taken root and Fletcher's generation felt the benefit. 'Rossall was what he had made of it: we felt that it was in a large measure his creation, that it represented his plan, the plan of one who knew what he wanted and meant to have it …We regarded him with awe, but it was an awe tempered with affection, and sometimes by amusement.'[27] 'That "hirsute and emotional Welshman", as someone once called him, with all his simplicity and limitations, was certainly a great figure: in some ways he was also a great man.'[28]

James was born in August 1844, the month and year of Rossall's foundation. After Oxford he taught temporarily at Marlborough, returned to Oxford for a short period as a fellow of St John's, and then went back to Marlborough as a housemaster. James's Marlborough years were critical to his achievements at Rossall. Not only were they schools with similar foundations, but Marlborough had forged ahead under the distinguished headmastership of George Cotton. Cotton had been a housemaster at Rugby under Arnold and had moved to Marlborough in 1852, bringing with him many of Arnold's methods and ideals. During James's first spell at Marlborough the headmaster was Cotton's friend and successor, G. G. Bradley, who had been a boy at Rugby in Arnold's and Cotton's time and had returned to teach there. James's second headmaster was F. W. Farrar who had taught at Marlborough under Cotton before moving to Harrow where the headmaster was C. J. Vaughan, another of Arnold's pupils. This Arnoldian triumvirate of Cotton, Bradley and Farrar not only raised Marlborough to the ranks of the best public schools but also (through their influence on James) ensured that Rossall prospered and won wide acclaim.

The Revd Darwin Wilmot moved from Rossall to Marlborough in 1874. He and James became friends and when Henniker resigned from Rossall, Wilmot encouraged James to apply. He was appointed (somewhat to his surprise) and began what he came to see as his most important and difficult work. 'Hardly had I applied,' he wrote, 'when there came rumours that the school was in a bad way alike intellectually, morally and financially.'[29] Immediately James set about reforming the school and no detail or dimension escaped his attention. Even before he arrived he had worked out exactly what reconstruction would be necessary to combine Rossall's original hostel system with new boarding houses, just as had happened at Marlborough in the 1860s and '70s. In both schools the boarding arrangements had not been based on separate houses as at, for instance, Rugby, Eton and Charterhouse, where boys of all ages live, eat and study under their housemaster's roof. Instead the hostel pattern is more centralised and collegiate, with one dining hall to feed the whole school and study and social areas for different age groups. Bradley and Farrar had adjusted this system at Marlborough by adding new 'out-college' houses. Although this may have weakened the sense of the common life of the school, it provided a closer community in each of the houses, and helped school discipline by means of divide and rule.[e] In

---

[e] After visiting Marlborough towards the end of Cotton's time, Edward White Benson (Wellington's first headmaster and later Archbishop of Canterbury) observed: 'One very great difference between Marlborough and Rugby and any other school where the *House System* properly so called prevails is in the oneness of interest throughout the school – and if there is any good in this, there is very great evil also. Rows and discontent of all kinds are smothered within one of the houses at Rugby, for all the members of the House have a pride in keeping their affairs to themselves and not exposing either their own set of boys or their own master to the animadversion of the rest. But at Marlborough disaffection spreads like fire.'

his chapter on Dr James in the school's *Centenary History*, Fletcher describes his organisation of the house system as 'his most permanent contribution to Rossall life ... He skilfully adapted life in separate "houses" or rather blocks, to the existing hostel arrangements. (In this he followed the Marlborough model, but with the important difference ... that every boy had a study throughout his school life) ... By instituting houses and housemasters he changed the whole life of the School. It was a fine piece of constructive organisation.'[30]

Fletcher's house was named Crescent and was the oldest and smallest. His housemaster was C. B. Ogden whom Fletcher described as 'a kindly housemaster who encouraged his boys to play hockey and taught some of us chess, at which he was an expert'.[31] There were thirty-five boys in Crescent in Fletcher's time and they slept in two dormitories, the one for the senior boys was separated into cubicles but each dormitory had only one bathroom with a single bath. Despite these privations every boy had or shared a study and there was a small library used for occasional house assemblies. It was the only room on the boys' side with any kind of fireplace: the housemaster, on the other hand, had 'a masterpiece in wrought iron of metallic fruits and grapes'![32]

At the end of Fletcher's second year a monitor named Robert Barnes was drowned in the sea. Popular, high in the sixth and making his mark in sport, Barnes was 'a boy with a keen sense of enjoyment in all he took up, of a ready good nature, always willing at a moment's notice to do any friend a favour or to undertake any duty he was asked'.[33] He had been down to bathe at noon in front of the sea-wall and he and another boy swam northwards along the shore. After 40 yards his companion returned while Barnes continued for a further 150 yards. Several pupils noticed him swimming back but then he disappeared. After two hours of frantic attempts to find him, his body was seen floating in shallow water. Every effort was made to resuscitate him but it was too late. In his memoirs Fletcher recalls

the sudden rumour that something had happened, the quick gathering of all the school on the shore, the one rowing boat and the swimmers who searched the sea for the missing boy; then suddenly the glimpse of something in an oncoming wave, the rush of his housemaster, T. Christie, into the water, and his return bearing the dripping, naked, inanimate body. Then the long effort at revival, which only ended when the school doctor, stooping over

the body, rose with a sad decisive shake of his head, and we realized that all was over.[34]

It is a vivid and moving account and Fletcher explains that 'the only
death which occurred at school during my seven years made a great
impression on a community which was small enough for all the
members to know one another'. Fletcher adds that he and the drowned
boy had sat next to each other in class and, in spite of the difference in
their ages, he thought of him as a friend. Yet curiously he confides: 'I
had no sense of personal loss: I remember thinking at the time that I
ought to grieve, and being secretly ashamed of feeling excitement and
interest instead of sorrow.'[35] Fletcher was fourteen at the time and there
are clear signs of immaturity in this confusion of emotions but the self-
controlled detachment which accompanies the confusion is a characteristic to be seen later in the adult Fletcher.

James was by all accounts a powerful and memorable preacher
whose sermons were full of fervour and sincerity. 'A man need not be
afraid to wear his heart on his sleeve,' he told the school, 'it is only
daws that will peck at it.'[36] Fletcher remembered the sermon James
preached after Barnes had drowned and how he spoke of himself as
'holding you all in my heart as I do'.[37] The captain of the school remembered James's first sermon as 'one of the best he ever preached to the
boys in that Chapel or in any other. Those who had ears to hear never
forgot it, sometimes spoke of it, and often thought of it. It brought our
religion into the everyday life of the School. Rossall was our city, and
we were the watchmen on guard ... "Rossall will be what you make it."
That was the burden of the discourse, and it was directed to one and
all.'[38] It was in the power and simplicity of James's preaching, the moral
idealism of his sermons, and indeed the supreme emphasis he placed on
chapel, that the influence of Thomas Arnold can be seen most clearly.
James's practical and earnest rhetoric, his appeal to the individual's
conscience and courage, and to collective pride in the school, are pure
Arnold:

> We too have a city – a city whose walls and towers many of you
> have learned to love as English boys alone love their school: a city
> which, from the humblest of its buildings to its grand wave-beaten
> beach and its limitless expanse of sea, many of you would not
> willingly exchange for any other ... Will you be among the watch-
> men on the walls? When you hear the evil word spoken, the
> wrong deed whispered of, when you see the bad habit growing

and spreading, the duty forgotten or neglected, speak from a
brave and honest heart the word of warning or reproof.[39]

Fletcher was promoted very early to the sixth form and was in the
upper sixth for his final four years. These were the school years he most
enjoyed, finding the work stimulating and feeling that at last he
belonged. In his first three years he had either been in class with boys
older than himself whose outlook was too grown-up for him, or with
boys of the same age whose intellectual interests were far behind. It was
the sixth form that fostered Fletcher's love of school and devotion to
Rossall. He valued the responsibilities and privileges that seniority
brought, as well as the friends who shared his interests, especially in
literature. 'I began to appreciate what the school meant for me and laid
the foundations of a loyal affection which neither time nor change has
effaced.'[40]

James's own scholarly teaching, the masters he recruited, and the
high standard of work he demanded had built up an outstanding upper
sixth by the time Fletcher joined it in 1885 at the start of James's final
year. James himself describes it as 'a really able Sixth Form, indeed the
ablest I have ever tried to teach'.[41] The form of eleven included three
Balliol scholars and an exhibitioner: F. Fletcher; H. Stuart Jones and
R. W. Lee who both became professors at Oxford; and R. D. Byles who
was ordained as a Roman Catholic priest and perished on the *Titanic*.
Two others won scholarships to King's, Cambridge, one to Trinity,
Oxford and one to Christ Church. This was a very remarkable record
for any school, and particularly one founded just 40 years before and
with only 300 pupils. 'I doubt', wrote Fletcher fifty years later, 'whether
any sixth form that I have known since could improve on it.'[42]

Classics dominated the curriculum and was still regarded as pre-
eminent and the subject most worthy of study by the cleverest boys.
From the start Fletcher exhibited a very considerable talent for learning and translating Greek and Latin. His memory and rigorous attention to detail were always formidable but he was also beginning to
show a more artistic flair for composition and the critical appreciation
of classical literature. This appreciation extended to English writers and
he and his friends read widely and enthusiastically. He mentions one
master, Leonard Furneaux, who ran a small literary society which met
weekly in his rooms and where boys read poetry to each other while
consuming copious quantities of tea and cake. Another master, Owen
Seaman, was also a member. He went on to become a writer of political

satire and later edited *Punch*, for which he was knighted. Furneaux was a housemaster for nearly thirty years and taught ancient history to the sixth. He had been a boy in James's house at Marlborough and had returned there to teach before James summoned him to Rossall as head-master's assistant.[f] Fletcher was introduced by this circle to the poetry of Robert Browning who was to remain his favourite poet. It was not a taste shared by the headmaster, as Fletcher discovered at a meeting of the essay society in the headmaster's dining room:

> We had decided to have a Browning evening, each member to read one poem. Enter the headmaster with an armful of Brownings, which he dumps upon the table. 'Someone tell me a piece to read: I never read Browning'. H. Stuart Jones promptly found the Solil-oquy of the Spanish Cloister ('Grr! there you go, my heart's abhorrence, water your damned flower-pots, do!') and suggested it as suitable. H. A. J. glanced at it for a moment and brusquely rejected it: 'Can't read that, man swears in the second line!'[43]

James was succeeded in 1886 by Charles Coverdale Tancock. When he died in 1922 Fletcher was asked to compose the Latin inscription for his memorial tablet in the chapel, as he was when James died nine years later. James is described as honest and courageous and Tancock as ener-getic and warm-hearted. Both men came from schools where Fletcher was to become headmaster – James from Marlborough and Tancock from Charterhouse. Tancock had married a local Godalming girl in the same year that he moved to Rossall and the school welcomed the arrival of a headmaster's wife after James's bachelor reign. He had made a great impression on Charterhouse during his time there and had 'perhaps done more to make Charterhouse what it is than any living man, save he who brought us here ... There was hardly a single school institution, whether in work or games, he did not patronise.'[44] Fletcher claimed that he learnt from Tancock the important lesson that a head-master can also be a friend. He was evidently a person of considerable warmth and kindness who 'should perhaps be best remembered for the humanizing and refining influence which he exercised during his ten years. A man of such Christian sincerity and honest transparency of purpose could not fail to win universal respect.'[45]

[f] In 1937 Fletcher preached the sermon in Rossall chapel at the dedication of the Furneaux memorial windows. He described Furneaux as 'not a scholar of the highest rank, but by his unfeigned enthusiasm, he inspired others with his great love of literature and learning'.

Tancock had revived the debating society at Charterhouse and he brought his passion for discussion and dispute to Rossall. Fletcher came to share the same enthusiasm both at school and at Oxford. The society at Rossall was restricted mostly to the sixth form, motions were wide-ranging, and discussion seems to have been remarkably astute and well-informed. The first debate Fletcher took part in was in November 1886, not long after Tancock's arrival. He spoke for the motion, 'That in the opinion of this House any proposal to give Ireland home rule for the present is absurd.'[46] The motion was carried. In June 1887 'F. Fletcher moved "That ... the present position of Classical and Modern knowledge, as taught in our Public Schools, should be reversed."'[47] Even allowing for the perversity of debate, the details of Fletcher's speech reveal a surprisingly radical and forward-looking point of view for a boy working for a Balliol classics scholarship:

> The hon. member said that he did not wish by any means to abolish the study of Classics altogether; he merely thought that they are put in too high a position. Dead languages and History occupy nearly all our time. Education is meant to prepare a man for life, not only to enlarge his mind. He took two views of the question, (a) utilitarian, (b) literary. (a) He complained that time was wasted on Classics which might be better spent on Modern History or Science. We have no more need for Greek or Roman History, than for Assyrian or Indian; German clerks are constantly used now as being much better linguists than English. (b) He said that though he would not disparage Demosthenes, or Æschylus, yet Shakespeare, or Dante, or Schiller was just as good. Vergil ought to be read for pleasure, not as a mass of troublesome moods and tenses. He did not mean to do away with Classics, but that they should be treated as French is now. Men ought to study problems of modern life.[48]

The motion was lost by eight votes. Other debates in which Fletcher spoke include the form of the English constitution, control over the press in England (Fletcher refers in his speech to the recent Whitechapel murders of Jack the Ripper), the equality of women with men, and the desirability of a Channel tunnel. On this proleptic subject Fletcher seems to have met his match: 'The hon. member, having launched his one argument went on for some time looking for a neat sentence to end his speech. At last he found a very suitable truism, and practically telling the House that if they thought the motion a good one they were to vote for it, and if they did not to vote against it, he sat down.'[49]

Fletcher won promotion to the upper sixth when he was fifteen and he became a monitor automatically on his sixteenth birthday. His memoirs record that again he reflected carefully on this experience of responsibility and learnt from it lasting lessons. He remembers the night of Queen Victoria's golden jubilee in 1887. Despite the excitement, the house captain was away playing cricket against Malvern and the housemaster had gone with him to watch the match. The house was left in the charge of a master who just happened to have rooms there.

> I was the senior monitor left, and had to maintain some semblance of order among boys mostly older than I was, who had not been accustomed to taking orders from me. I did what I could, more from pride than from conscientiousness; but the result was at best a creditable failure. However, the other boys, even while they did their best to defeat my efforts, respected me, I believe, for trying to do my job. On the whole I found the experience exhilarating.[50]

Fletcher's taste for leadership was rewarded in the following term when he was made head both of his house and of the school, positions he held for two years. 'I discovered on the first evening how much difference official position can make. Concealing my nervousness as best I could, I gave an order, wondering what would happen; it was immediately obeyed. I had no further difficulties with discipline: as King Lear observed, "A dog's obeyed in office."'[51] Mixed in with his diffidence there are clear signs here of a natural authority so essential to success in his chosen career. Further lessons for the future headmaster were learnt when his housemaster changed in Fletcher's final year. He describes the new man as 'a strict disciplinarian who was very unpopular with the school' but, nonetheless, 'a close personal friend of mine. Between him and the house I had a difficult course to steer: the experience was a practical lesson in diplomacy, and by no means without educational value.'[52]

Tancock had won a double first in classics at Oxford as James had. Like James he taught the sixth form and 'his notes on the Greek Testament and Ancient History were masterly and bore signs of immense trouble in their preparation.'[53] James, observed Fletcher, 'was more of a scholar, Tancock more of a thinker. James taught on a rigid system: every lesson he gave was carefully prepared … Tancock was more haphazard: he left more to the inspiration of the moment. Thereby he imparted less knowledge, but in some ways he taught us more: we saw the process of his mind; it was an education

"to watch
The master work, and catch
Hints of the proper craft, tricks of the tool's true play."[54]

Fletcher was fortunate in being taught first by James who laid sound foundations of knowledge and then by a different kind of scholar who took risks in interpretation and looked beneath the letters of a text to the spirit within. Fletcher remembered 'more about the books that I read with him, perhaps because under him you had to use your own mind in order to learn: from James it was possible to learn by rote.'[55] Fletcher also owed to Tancock his love of the epistles of St Paul, a writer (along with Browning and Plato) who was to remain a lifelong favourite.[g] 'It was from Tancock's teaching that I discovered that Paul was a man writing letters to his friends and not merely an apostle writing epistles.'[56]

This contrast of teaching styles bolstered Fletcher's very considerable academic ability and industry and helped him win the scholastic blue riband of an open classical scholarship at Balliol in November 1888. At prize day earlier in the year he had been awarded prizes for Greek, French and German, and in the higher certificate examination he alone at Rossall had gained distinctions in all six of his subjects (Latin, Greek, French, German, divinity and history). In his final editorial in the school magazine after three years as editor, Fletcher looked back on the changes and improvements in the school during his seven years. 'In the matter of work', he observed, 'we have covered ourselves with distinction lately. Seven years ago no Rossallian had ever won a Balliol Scholarship: we have now three Classical ones and one Mathematical to our credit.'[57]

Those seven years at school, and especially the four spent in the sixth form, were decisive and in Fletcher's case perhaps indeed the happiest of his life. The rugged charm of Rossall's setting; the academic, literary and cultural excitement the school provided; the companionship of like-minded friends; the exemplary dedication and devotion of the masters; the contrasting examples of two distinguished headmasters, teachers and scholars; the first successful exercise of leadership – all these provided opportunities impossible and unimagined at home. Rossall inspired in Fletcher a loyal and lifelong devotion, and with it the vocation of a schoolmaster.

[g] 'My masters', wrote Fletcher in 1908, 'are Plato, Browning and St Paul.'

3
Balliol
1889–1894

Those who have been to a good school often find university a disappointment. Sixth form teaching and discussion can seem so much more lively and stimulating than university lectures and tutorials. 'Strange how unmemorable any of my tutors at Oxford were compared with some of the teachers at Charterhouse,' scribbled Dr Theo Zinn[a] in the margin of his copy of Fletcher's memoirs. No one can have felt a deeper appreciation of his schooldays than Frank Fletcher but, thanks largely to his choice of college, Oxford was not for him an anti-climax. Instead Balliol introduced him to a much wider world whose people were as brilliant as they were various and idiosyncratic. The college made as deep an impression on Fletcher's affections as Rossall and it left a more profound and lasting impression on his intellect, outlook and opinions.

Fletcher's father had his doubts about Balliol. The long association of Benjamin Jowett with the college had given it 'a reputation for unorthodoxy alarming to one who both by family tradition and personal conviction was a devoted member of the Church of England'.[1] On the other hand, Balliol's academic pre-eminence was well known and long established, and the enviable distinction of a Balliol scholarship seems to have won him round. The scholarship was worth £80 per annum and although it did not go as far as the Rossall scholarship, this too helped to win his father's approval. The termly expenses for tuition were £8. 6. 8d plus £16 for 'establishment' (library, chapel, bedmakers, porters, gas, water, room rent and furniture). In addition, annual 'battels' (buttery, kitchen, shop, coal, messenger, milk and fines) were estimated at anything between £25 and £95. On top of this an undergraduate had to budget for a cap and gown, subscriptions to college clubs, books, clothes and boots. It was reckoned at the time that £200 a

---

[a] Zinn was among the last group of potential Charterhouse scholars whom Fletcher interviewed in 1935: he won the fifth foundation scholarship and went on to become head of classics at Westminster.

year would maintain a man in Oxford in comfort. Fletcher managed on considerably less but he had been brought up to live simply and to be strict and sparing with money.

By the time Fletcher went up to Balliol in the autumn of 1889 Jowett had been in residence as scholar, fellow and Master for over half a century. The last four years of his life coincided with Fletcher's time as an undergraduate, and although in his seventies by then and in poor health, Jowett's personality remained as influential if not as domineering. The college was what he had made it – distinctive in spirit, unrivalled in influence, supreme in intellect. Noël Annan, writing in 1999, describes how

> For a century and a half Balliol has been one of the most splendid colleges at Oxford or Cambridge. It sent a host of distinguished graduates into all walks of life; its successes in the schools were proverbial; its junior common room provided a scene of animated intellectual life which few other undergraduate societies could rival. It was a society with a history of academic distinction and the nursery of statesmen, pro-consuls, scholars, lawyers and men of letters. When Harrovians sang, 'the Balliol comes to us now and then', they acknowledged that a Balliol scholarship was prized higher by headmasters than that of any other college – because the winner would have had to have faced the stiffest competition. How did this come about? The answer is that it was the work of Benjamin Jowett.[2]

Jowett was an extraordinary man – industrious, fastidious, shrewd, snobbish, opinionated, taciturn, worldly and petulant. 'It is easy to describe his appearance,' wrote Cosmo Gordon Lang who had left Balliol three years before Fletcher arrived, '– the little figure with its black swallow-tail coat and white shirt-front and "choker", the ruddy chubby face with its rather fretful mouth "like a cherub out of condition", the chirpy voice. But how difficult to describe either his character or his influence.'[3]

Jowett attended St Paul's School but his family had fallen on hard times and, remarkable though it may seem, he lived alone in lodgings in the City Road. He was lonely, deeply ashamed of his poverty, and immensely intelligent. He too won a classical scholarship to Balliol where his tutor, Archibald Campbell Tait, was (like Lang) a future Archbishop of Canterbury. 'He was much more worthy to teach me,' confessed Tait twenty years later.[4] Indeed, so brilliant was Jowett that he was elected to a fellowship before he had graduated. In 1842 he became a tutor when Tait left to succeed Thomas Arnold as Headmaster of Rugby. Jowett was ordained in the same year and though ordination was necessary (his fellowship depended on it) it was not undertaken lightly. Jowett had been brought up in the low-church tradition and throughout his life he retained an evangelical's personal devotion to Christ and to the primacy of scripture. After a brief and luke-warm flirtation with the high church Oxford Movement of Newman, Pusey and Keble, the influence of Tait and his close friendship with his Balliol contemporary, A. P. Stanley, drew Jowett into the liberal camp epitomised by Arnold.

The controversial theological symposium, *Essays and Reviews*, published in 1860, made Jowett's a household name and had him condemned by all the bishops and 11,000 clergy, lending Balliol the kind of notoriety which worried Fletcher's father. Seven essayists contributed, including Frederick Temple who had been Tait's and Jowett's pupil and a fellow of Balliol and was by then Tait's successor-but-one at Rugby (he was also to be Tait's successor-but-one as Bishop of London and Archbishop of Canterbury). The intention of the authors was that 'theological subjects should be freely handled in a becoming spirit'.[5] In his own essay 'On the Interpretation of Scripture' Jowett insisted that the results of scientific enquiry and critical scholarship be taken seriously. 'The Bible ought to be treated as any other book would be treated, in its context and as expressing the mind of a particular author, an era, and a cultural setting.'[6] The bitterness of the attacks on 'septem contra Christum' seem to the modern mind extraordinary and misplaced. The friendship between Jowett, Tait and Temple was strained to breaking point. Jowett and Temple felt betrayed by Tait who as Bishop of London had condemned the book. Jowett felt betrayed by Temple because, under pressure from the Rugby governors, he distanced himself by asking his pupils not to read the book. It seemed to Jowett that they both lacked a genuine concern for truth.

Jowett now turned his back on public theological debate. He had been surprised and wounded by the violence of the outcry provoked by *Essays and Reviews* and he dedicated the rest of his life to Oxford, Balliol, and the herculean labour of translating, editing and interpreting the complete works of Plato. But Balliol was always Jowett's first love and he devoted himself to its members, interests and reform for nearly sixty years. As early as 1852 the royal commissioners were able to report that 'the most distinguished characteristic of this Foundation [is] that it is most peculiarly free from all restrictions which might prevent the election of the best candidates to its Headship, Fellowships, Scholarships, and even to its Visitorship. The result of this has been that Balliol, which is one of the smallest Colleges in Oxford ... is certainly at present the most distinguished.'[7] The fact that scholarships were competitive (and financially valuable) meant that Balliol attracted the brightest of applicants. Jowett was elected Master in 1870 and in a letter to Tait he wrote 'I am where I wish to be ... My desire here is not to be a leader of a party but to educate the young men or get them educated.'[8] To Jowett that meant encouraging hard work, character and ambition, and a way of thinking that was at once positively religious and open-minded. It meant cultivating the most able and well-connected undergraduates[b] while also promoting the cause of those who could not afford to attend the university.

When Fletcher arrived at Balliol Jowett had been Master for nearly twenty years. Who he was, what he stood for, and what he had achieved for the college were unmistakable. 'Jowett was Balliol', wrote Sir Leslie Stephen in 1897, 'and Balliol was Jowett.'[9] The culture and ethos of the college were as unique and distinctive then as they are difficult now to distil and describe. But the ingredients were these: a reforming, radical and progressive spirit; an emphasis on intellect, industry and earnestness; a liberal, questioning, broad church Anglicanism; a social, economic and political awareness which encouraged public service; and physical surroundings whose disregard for comfort or architectural grace seemed to mirror Balliol's highmindedness. The college buildings are strikingly Victorian, and although lacking the beauty and charm of Oxford's medieval quadrangles and cloisters, they are at least a vivid reminder of the modernising zeal that so inspired the college in the nineteenth century.[c] 'We have been credited', wrote Fletcher, 'with intellectual arrogance, or, as that most loyal of Balliol men, Lord Oxford and Asquith, phrased it, "a consciousness, even a

[b] The number of leading establishment figures produced by Jowett's Balliol was unrivalled: statesmen (Lansdowne, Asquith, Curzon, Grey, Milner, Samuel, Amery), an Archbishop of York and Canterbury, permanent under-secretaries, diplomats, law lords, headmasters, academics, and poets (Hopkins and Swinburne).
[c] The buildings facing Broad Street, including the Master's lodgings, were designed by Alfred Waterhouse in 1867, as was the hall ten years later. William Butterfield designed the chapel in his distinctive neo-gothic style in 1857.

sublime consciousness, of effortless superiority". But no one, I hope, has accused us of being proud of our buildings. If we ever allowed ourselves to boast, it was of the men, not the walls, of our city.'[10]

Fletcher is defensive of Jowett in his memoirs and it is clear that he held him in high esteem. He describes Jowett's notorious taciturnity (he would often sit or walk with an undergraduate in disconcerting silence, only to issue a barbed remark in response to his companion's embarrassed attempt to engage him in conversation). 'No doubt there was an element of the mischievous in him: he knew that people expected to be shocked by his utterances, and he sometimes played up to their expectations. But if he was provocative, it was in order to stimulate thought: if he was cutting, it was because he thought the occasion called for incisiveness.'[11] Fletcher is either being generous here or his experience of the Master was more favourable than others. The Liberal politician Herbert Samuel, who was an exact contemporary of Fletcher, records a breakfast party at the Master's lodge: 'An undergraduate, – "I see, Master, in this morning's paper that one of the Cunard liners has crossed the Atlantic in under six days; don't you think that rather remarkable?" The pause, and then Jowett in his high voice, "No, I don't think it remarkable."'[12] Fletcher puts some of this down to diffidence, and regards what was perhaps Jowett's sharpest comment to him as positive:

> He was shy (although not everyone recognized this) and I was shy ... On the occasion which I specially remember he asked me whether I was competing for any of the University composition prizes.
>
> 'No, Master. I thought I ought to be reading rather than writing.'
>
> His answer went straight to the mark. 'I suppose the fact is that it takes an effort to go in for a University prize, and you didn't feel inclined to make the effort.'
>
> The shrewd wholesome truthfulness of the reply justified it. Of course it killed the conversation: there was no possible answer to the indictment. But the temporary loss was more than compensated for by the permanent value of the lesson.[13]

Shyness may have been part of the problem but Jowett's inquisitorial, socratic approach to teaching and the search for truth can also be discerned. 'Whatever was advanced, his first impulse was always to deny.'[14] The severely rational caterpillar in *Alice's Adventures in*

Wonderland may well have been a caricature of Jowett, and certainly Lewis Carroll's[d] own drawing bears a definite resemblance:

> '... when you have to turn into a chrysalis – you will some day, you know – and then after that into a butterfly, I should think you'll feel it a little queer, won't you?'
>
> 'Not a bit,' said the Caterpillar.
>
> 'Well, perhaps your feelings may be different,' said Alice; 'all I know is, it would feel very queer to *me*.'
>
> 'You!' said the caterpillar contemptuously. 'Who are *you*?'
>
> Which brought them back again to the beginning of the conversation. Alice felt a little irritated at the Caterpillar's making such *very* short remarks, and she drew herself up and said, very gravely, 'I think you ought to tell me who *you* are, first.'
>
> 'Why?' said the Caterpillar.
>
> Here was another puzzling question; and as Alice could not think of any good reason, and as the caterpillar seemed to be in a *very* unpleasant state of mind, she turned away.[15]

Fletcher too was a man of few, carefully chosen words. When headmaster he would listen intently to a boy's or a master's plans and ideas before posing the inevitable question, 'Why?' He was impatient with small-talk or ill-considered remarks, and his silence or laconic reply would make his disapproval plain. In an otherwise normal conversation he might interject, 'That's a very silly thing to say.' He could also be ingenious and witty in a Lewis Carroll kind of way and was fond of quoting from *Alice's Adventures*. On one occasion the wife of a Charterhouse master was offered a cigarette by Fletcher and declined, saying that she had given up smoking. 'Altogether!' he remarked, 'How very weak!'

There were over 150 undergraduates at Balliol in Fletcher's time, making it the third largest Oxford college after Christ Church and New College. And Balliol was unusually mixed, even cosmopolitan. 'Young men were attracted to Balliol from every corner of the empire, and from other lands touched by British influence where the rulers wanted to learn something about the principles of liberal and constitutional government. C. E. Vaughan, who came up in 1873, recalled how,

[d] Charles Dodgson ('Lewis Carroll') was a contemporary of Jowett and a tutor at Christ Church.

already, the place was a medley of "Japanese and Scots, Hindoos and Frenchmen, Americans and Englishmen, Brahmins and Catholics, Nonconformists and high Anglicans, Jews and Gentiles ... sparks of nobility and artizans; a bazaar of all nations and languages, the whole world in miniature."[16] Shrimpton's caricature of *Oxford types: Balliol* presents an unsympathetic view of this diversity.[17] It shows an aristocrat on the left and a mature student on the right and between them a cockney from a London day school, a Brahmin, a Scot, and an undergraduate from China.

To make matters confusing, Fletcher overlapped for a year at Balliol with another Frank Fletcher. The latter was one of a number of poor and deserving young men whom Jowett prepared and provided for a Balliol education. The other F. F. started as a library assistant, became Jowett's secretary in 1886 and took his degree in 1890. He won the Gaisford Prize for Greek Verse and ended up as Professor of Classics at Exeter University.

Among Fletcher's friends and contemporaries at Balliol were Nugent Hicks who became Bishop of Lincoln; Amyas Waterhouse, the son of Balliol's architect; Henry Marten, who when Vice-Provost of Eton tutored Princess Elizabeth in constitutional history; John Wood, whose father became Headmaster of Harrow; and the maverick writer Hilaire Belloc whom the college register describes as walking the fifty miles from Oxford to Marble Arch in eleven and a half hours! Four of Fletcher's closest friends became tutors and fellows of Balliol, and Fletcher made a fifth. These were E. J. Palmer, later Bishop of Bombay; Cyril Bailey, a life-long friend of Fletcher who returned to Balliol in 1902 after six years as a fellow of Exeter College; A. W. Pickard-Cambridge who returned from Oriel and was later Professor of Greek at Edinburgh and Vice-Chancellor of Sheffield University; and Francis Fortescue Urquhart, the only non-classicist among them.

Fletcher notes that when Urquhart was elected a fellow the evangelical *Record* observed that 'the college which had long been known for its agnosticism had now set the seal to its apostasy by electing a Roman Catholic Fellow.'[18] Urquhart taught history and was a popular and cultivated tutor with a gift for friendship. He was nicknamed 'Sligger' which Fletcher explains as 'a corruption of "sleek one"' and suggests it was 'first given him on a reading party, I think at Bude, of which I was a member'.[19] Reading parties were very much a part of Balliol life. Jowett continued, even as Master, to take undergraduates away during the vacations and it was a practice followed by many of the fellows.

Urquhart had inherited a chalet which his father had built near Saint-Gervais in the French Alps. He started to host annual reading parties there in 1891 when an undergraduate, and continued to do so until three years before his death in 1934. Fletcher was present in 1894 and 1896 when he was teaching at Rugby. The chalet (nicknamed locally the Chalet des Anglais) was remote and reached from the station on foot along a mule-path. Mornings were spent reading; afternoons playing games, scrambling or walking; reading continued between tea and dinner, and the evening finished with talk and occasionally with cards.

Balliol's diversity of undergraduates was fine in principle but it tended to create cliques and coteries rather than the harmonious microcosm which was Jowett's ideal. To Fletcher the defect of Balliol 'was that there were too many sections. It was divided into several almost water-tight compartments; men might be contemporaries in college and yet quite unknown to one another. I recall a brief speech by Jowett at some college gathering, in which he said, "I am told that there is a phrase used in rowing to describe a boat where all the oarsmen have got together and work as one man. Such a boat is said to 'make.' I want the college to make." But that was just what it didn't. There was, I suppose, too much difference in origin and outlooks between the different types of men.'[20] Much of this separation was due to the mutual unease athletes and scholars ('bloods' and 'reading men') always seem to feel. Fletcher recognised that the situation would have been helped if only the all-rounders had made more effort to bridge the gap. He mentions Herbert Samuel (who went on to become Home Secretary), Patrick Duncan (who had a distinguished political career in South Africa), and Malcolm Jardine (captain of the Oxford cricket XI and later a successful barrister in India) as three such men who failed to break free of their own narrow circle of friends.

Even those who liked to debate or discuss learned papers had to choose between three exclusive college societies. The Dervorguilla was the most élitist of the three. It was started in 1871 and named after the wife of John de Balliol with whom she founded the college in the thirteenth century. The Brackenbury was Fletcher's choice. It was started six years after the Dervorguilla in honour of Hannah Brackenbury whose donations to the college had allowed for its extensive rebuilding in the 1860s and for the establishment of scholarships. During Fletcher's first term a third society was founded by a scholarly group who broke away from the Brackenbury. It was named after Matthew Arnold who had died the year before and had been a scholar at Balliol in the 1840s. Unusually, Fletcher belonged to both the Brackenbury and the Arnold but his chief loyalty was to the former. Members met in each other's rooms and drank coffee (not wine as at the Dervorguilla). 'It offered a happy combination of the social and intellectual, a society in which interesting subjects were debated among friends ... we of the Brackenbury could talk together pleasantly on a variety of topics, gaining at the same time knowledge of our friends, practice in speaking, and a good deal of intellectual stimulus.'[21] Among Fletcher's friends in the society were the four who, with Fletcher, became fellows and tutors at Balliol. By the end of his first year he was a non-official member of the selection committee, the following summer he was elected secretary, he was voted vice-president in December 1891 and then president six months later. This may seem a rapid rise but membership was small and elections for the officers were held at the end of every term. Meetings happened most Saturdays at 8 p.m. and debates generally alternated with papers followed by discussion. The ironic and satirical tone of the minutes suggests that humour, teasing and high spirits seasoned the intellectual stimulus. In April 1891, for example, Fletcher spoke for the motion, 'That the practice of debating is mentally and morally pernicious' (the motion was lost by nine votes to three). In June 'Mr Cunliffe moved that the House should pass a note of censure upon Mr Browne for surreptitiously withdrawing my chair, when I entered the room and tried to sit down, and thereby precipitating me with some violence on the floor'! In November the society debated the motion, 'That this House regrets the decay of the sense of humour.'

When Fletcher was vice-president he moved, 'That this House regrets that the present system of public school and university education does not adequately provide for all members of the community' (the motion was carried). Other subjects discussed or debated included modern philanthropy, the abolition of the House of Commons, the retention of the colonies, the influence of the modern stage, local government in Ireland, and the reorganisation of the German Army. The society's 300th meeting happened during Fletcher's term as president. It was marked by a combined debate with the Dervorguilla and the Arnold at which Mr Cunliffe moved 'That the Conservative party is the party of true Progress' (lost by twenty-five votes to twenty-two).

Despite Fletcher's enthusiasm for debating and his skill as a speaker he did not involve himself much in the Oxford Union. The Union's reputation as a nursery for the highest reaches of public service was well established but the Union was at a rather low ebb at the end of the nineteenth century and the best Balliol speakers preferred their own societies. Nonetheless, Fletcher did attend when invited to propose or oppose motions. On one occasion he proposed the extension of suffrage to women, and on another he led the opposition to a motion which declared Rudyard Kipling to be a great writer. In February 1890 Gladstone spent a week in Oxford and Fletcher was there when he paid his last visit to the Union. Throughout his long life he had been closely associated with both Union and University and held them in great affection and esteem. Gladstone was eighty-one and very much the Grand Old Man. He gave an erudite lecture on Homer and Assyria and proclaimed his devotion to Oxford, and his pleasure in coming back to the Union and finding that Sir Robert Peel's grandson was president. Members responded with enthusiasm and the Archdeacon of Oxford (one of the trustees of the Union and father of E. J. Palmer, Fletcher's friend and later colleague as tutor) hailed him as a 'characteristic Oxford man'.[22] 'When', wrote Fletcher, 'he quoted lines from Homer, and when in reply to a vote of thanks he said a few words about Oxford ("In one brief word, I love her") we got an echo of the old orator who had swayed multitudes.'[23]

By the end of Jowett's time as Master the senior common room was exceptionally strong and distinguished. There were ten fellows, six of whom were classical tutors. Among them was James Leigh Strachan Davidson who lectured in Roman history, was an enthusiastic expert on Cicero, and took great care of Evelyn Abbott who taught Greek history and had been a pupil of Jowett in the 1860s. During Abbott's last term as an undergraduate he had injured his spine and become paralysed and was now confined to a wheelchair and had to be hoisted up to his rooms. To Fletcher he was a 'heroic figure ... who bore his life-long infirmity with a courage and patience that were in themselves an inspiration ... I remember once, at one of the Master's at homes, when Abbott had wheeled himself out of the drawing-room, that Jowett turned to us and said, "There goes the most learned man in Oxford."'[24] He was co-author of 'Abbott and Mansfield', still the standard Greek primer, and wrote the second volume of The Life and Letters of Benjamin Jowett (1897). A. L. Smith (known as 'Smuggins') was the history tutor, and Master from 1916 to 1924. He was one of the first dons to involve himself in undergraduate sport, coaching generations of Balliol oarsmen, and amalgamating the various clubs at Balliol in order to make sport more affordable. Coming from a relatively poor background Smith had discovered that rowing was a way to find acceptance, and he valued sport above all as 'a solvent of social barriers in the college'.[25] Fletcher also mentions Paravicini, 'a fine Latin scholar, who taught little to men who did not want to work'; Sir John Conroy who taught science and 'exercised a friendly courteous influence over those of us who knew him'; and W. H. Forbes, 'an able scholar who had broken down in health from over work, and was in those days an excitable, eccentric, kindly figure'.[26]

Fletcher had three tutors during his four years as an undergraduate. First was W. R. Hardie, a don with a phenomenal memory whose reading parties were noted for hard work in the morning and golf in the afternoon. 'Much as I gained from Hardie's direct teaching I gained more from the intercourse of the reading parties, when he was working and we were working, each on his own, but with constant discussion of difficulties as they arose ... Those reading parties were by no means the least enjoyable part of our Oxford life ... they were a simple and delightful way of spending several weeks of the liberal vacations which Oxford allows.'[27]

Fletcher's second tutor was R. L. Nettleship whom he described as 'the greatest thinker that I ever encountered'.[28] His was perhaps the seminal influence on Fletcher, who remained devoted to him. Nettleship taught philosophy and, like Urquhart later, exercised a strong pastoral role among the undergraduates. Undogmatic and free-thinking, he was admired nonetheless for the exemplary Christian life he led. He was remembered most for his distinctive style of teaching which was reminiscent of Jowett's, and from which Fletcher learnt much. A. C. Bradley, the Shakespearean critic who had been a friend and contemporary of Nettleship at Balliol, described how, when discussing his pupils' essays, he 'attacked the matter as if it were something perfectly new, into which he was making his way for the first time'.[29] Fletcher explains that 'he was notorious for being constitutionally unwilling, almost unable, to give a definite answer to philosophical questions ... But if you were prepared to sit and listen, he would talk round the question until you got, if not an answer that could be put down in examination, at least a glimpse of the working of a great thinker's mind and of a method whereby this and other problems might be tackled. It is the function of the good teacher to sow seed, not to plant full-grown trees.'[30] Fletcher had encountered a similar approach at Rossall when taught by Tancock and these examples shaped his own style of teaching. 'The teacher must, of course, know his lesson: he should have a full well to draw out of.

But too detailed preparation may defeat his object: the over-prepared lesson easily loses its freshness. I know no higher praise of a teacher than what was said to me once of a Rugby colleague: "He didn't know so much, but he taught you just twice as much as he knew."'[31]

Tragically, Nettleship died of exposure in August 1892 while climbing Mont Blanc. 'He was only forty-five;' wrote Fletcher, 'but those who knew him count him as one of the great men that they have known.'[32] Jowett preached a memorial sermon in Balliol chapel on 16 October.[33] He referred first to his friend Tennyson who had died just ten days before. Nettleship he described as 'one of the best of men and one of the greatest teachers whom we have had at Oxford during the present generation ... I do not suppose that he will be forgotten by any of his pupils.' Nettleship is commemorated by a tablet in the chapel with an inscription by A. C. Bradley,[e] and by a music scholarship. Fletcher was chosen as the undergraduate member of the committee which founded it: other members included Bradley and Henry Scott Holland.[f] In his sermon Jowett had paid tribute to Nettleship's love of music and his 'great belief in its power as an instrument of education'.

Nettleship was succeeded as Fletcher's tutor by J. A. Smith. He was only six years older than Fletcher and had been elected a fellow just the year before. Intellectually gifted though he was (he became Waynflete Professor of Ethics at Oxford), his teaching was as yet undeveloped and Fletcher and his colleagues felt the draught after Nettleship. But Fletcher recalls that he was nonetheless a delightful and amusing companion.

Tennyson had been a regular visitor to the Master's lodge, as had Robert Browning, Fletcher's favourite poet. Browning was the first of Balliol's honorary fellows, elected in 1867 on Jowett's recommendation. Fletcher himself was elected in 1924 and he regarded it as the highest of honours. He certainly found himself in distinguished company: before him Archbishop Frederick Temple, Curzon and Asquith had been elected, and after him, Tawney and Beveridge and Archbishops Cosmo Lang and William Temple.

'The ideal object of an Oxford career is to imbue the student with the

e 'He loved great things and thought little of himself. Desiring neither fame nor influence he won the love of men and was a power in their lives; and seeking no disciples he taught to many the greatness of the world and of man's mind.'
f Scott Holland was an undergraduate at Balliol in the 1860s and later a canon of St Paul's and Regius Professor of Divinity at Oxford.

highest form of culture, to teach him the best that has been taught and written by the best minds on the highest subjects, and to enable him to play the best part in the great struggle of human life. A special and professional training should be only a secondary object of such a career.'[34] This 1887 description of the purposes of a liberal education could have been Jowett's. He would certainly have been in no doubt that the subject best suited to these ends was classics, still then the most popular and prestigious school. At Oxford, then as now, the classics degree fell into two parts: moderations ('mods') taken after five terms, and *literae humaniores* ('greats') taken at the end of four years of study. The mods course had been radically reformed three years before Fletcher started. The staple authors (Homer, Virgil, Demosthenes and Cicero) remained but, instead of specific passages being prescribed for translation and criticism, the texts were set in their entirety, for translation only. The purpose was a modern one: to promote breadth as well as depth. 'The aim was that candidates should be encouraged to read widely in these authors, but also to cultivate an understanding of Latin and Greek generally and of the style of these authors in particular, so that they would be able to translate those parts of them which they had not read.'[35] Mods was a rigorous and demanding examination but Fletcher easily fitted Macaulay's image of a scholar as a man who could read Greek and Latin with his feet on the hob and was awarded a first.

Greats combined classical literature, history, and ancient and modern philosophy, requiring a remarkable range, depth and application. Fletcher took the examinations in June 1893 and was again awarded a first. He is modest about what was undeniably a fine achievement: 'I have often thought that I did not deserve my first in Greats: for I was neither a good philosopher nor a good historian. But I was deeply interested, and had read the main books, especially Plato's *Republic* and Aristotle's *Ethics* and Herodotus with great care and thoroughness. Greats is the best examination in either Oxford or Cambridge, whatever class a man may be awarded in it.'[36] Fletcher's comments are revealing. From the start he had shown extraordinary acumen as a classical philologist but his intellectual interests were widening and developing, and he was willing to set aside the linguistic brilliance he had already proved in mods to embark on studies which fascinated him, but for which he did not feel he had a particular talent. As it was, his habits of concentration, industriousness and attention to detail overcame whatever weaknesses he may have had. Jowett would have approved: 'The object of reading for the Schools', he had written, 'is not chiefly to obtain a First Class, but to elevate and strengthen the character for life. I would say the means was, first, hard work; secondly, a real regard for the truth and independence of mind and opinion; thirdly, a consciousness that we are put here in different positions of life to carry out the will of God.'[37] Fletcher kept up his Latin and Greek by preparing for the university's classical scholarships (then almost the preserve of Balliol men), particularly the Ireland. Stuart Jones, who had been in the sixth form with Fletcher but had preceded him to Balliol in 1886, had won all three scholarships and Fletcher was determined to match him, winning the Craven in his second year, the Ireland in his third, and the Derby in 1894. 'He was', wrote his friend and contemporary, Cyril Bailey, 'without doubt the most outstanding classical undergraduate of his time; he had a great memory, a sensitiveness to style and a fine critical sense.'[38]

Although Fletcher was very much the serious-minded reading man and always made his studies a priority he did not neglect some of the other opportunities that Balliol, and to a lesser extent Oxford, had to offer. Debating was an important diversion but so too was sport. H. A. James had ensured, not least by his own example, that games were taken seriously at Rossall. He had in his day played for Monmouthshire and Fletcher recalled 'his appearance on the cricket field, where he always wore black flannels, bowled slow balls with a phenomenal break and on occasion made heavy scores against the school bowlers'.[39] James was also an enthusiastic fives player (as later was Fletcher) and when the gymnasium was built in Fletcher's second year, fives courts were included. With Fletcher's active encouragement, paperchases were revived and Fletcher was captain. But swimming in the sea and hockey on the beach were Rossall's distinctive sports and Fletcher excelled at the latter. Its elaborate rules, tenacious spirit and physical demands turned many Rossallians into leading players. Fletcher's brother Ernest played for England, while Frank played regularly for the Balliol XI and in 1893 was selected for Oxford and played in one of the first hockey 'blues' matches against Cambridge. In his article on Fletcher in *The Dictionary of National Biography* Cyril Bailey describes how 'in his last year he played in the university hockey team against Cambridge; trained on the sands of Rossall as an individualist he twice took the ball down the wing and scored a goal.' Again, Fletcher's own account is self-effacing: '... almost by accident I found myself in the Oxford team, and was fortunate enough to score two out of the three goals by which we beat Cambridge. Hockey was an easy game in those days: there was less combination and more individual work, and the main requisites were a good eye and pace.'[40]

The college divisions Fletcher complains of came most to the fore when the rowdier sportsmen had a victory to celebrate. In the 1880s bonfires became the fashionable way to mark an athletic triumph and they caused the authorities much concern. In 1881, for example, a vast bonfire in the quadrangle of Hertford College threatened to burn down part of the Bodleian which at the time was covered in wooden scaffolding.[41] Fletcher tells of a similar incident at Balliol ten years later: the vivid and dramatic picture he paints of the occasion, of Jowett's intervention, of the conflicting types of undergraduate, and of his own reaction and involvement makes the story worth quoting in full:

The popular captain of the college boat, F. N. Rogers, was going down that term, and a dinner was given him in Balliol Hall, attended by about half the college and some visitors from outside. After dinner the feasters proceeded to improve the occasion by making a bonfire in the corner of the back quad – a practice severely discouraged by the authorities, who were pledged to the insurance societies to prevent it. When the bonfire was well alight, and the revellers were dancing in a ring round it, Jowett, whose rooms looked out on the scene, came out and tried to stop the proceedings. The men were excited and ignored his orders. It was strange and rather alarming to see the old man, in cap and gown, going about among them, with the light of the fire on his white head, ordering them to go to their rooms. The only don who could be found in college was W. H. Forbes, a very inadequate person for the purpose: but he was fetched. A party of men, lacking fuel, tore up one of the wooden seats round the trees and began to carry it to the fire. Jowett was immediately in their path, and Forbes stepped forward to intercept them. One of them, a man of weak head easily affected by a little drink, began to hit him over the head. There was a cry of 'shame!' from an upper window, which was echoed by some of us watching below. As we ran forward protesting, I suddenly found myself collared from behind by a member of the Varsity rugger team who objected to my joining in the protest. He got my head into chancery: but he had been one of the diners and I hadn't, and I was steadier on my feet. In the wrestle which ensued I threw him, and went my way. Shortly afterwards I discovered to my great regret that his leg was broken.[42]

Nineteenth-century Oxford was a profoundly religious place, at least in the sense that religious issues and controversies mattered, and were argued and contested passionately and often acrimoniously. Oxford had been dominated in the thirties by the Catholic revival of the Tractarians and in the sixties by *Essays and Reviews* and Darwin's *Origin of Species*, and in every decade there were fierce arguments over university reform and its attempt to curb the Church of England's dominance. Religion was still as prominent and hotly debated at the end of the century when Fletcher and his friends were, as he put it, 'trying to discover for ourselves what we believed'.[43] There was much for them to choose from, much to confuse, and much to discourage.

In 1890 a third of all Oxford fellows were in holy orders: at Balliol there were only two. One was the chaplain, W. H. Fremantle, an Etonian aristocrat, who had been Jowett's pupil in the 1850s and remained deeply devoted to him, an affection which Jowett did not reciprocate. Jowett had asked him to return to Balliol as chaplain in 1882: he left with Fletcher twelve years later to become Dean of Ripon. Fremantle shared Jowett's liberalism and worked hard to convince others that Jowett's faith was sound and that Balliol was not the thoroughly secular place many supposed it to be. He wanted to influence the undergraduates but was not taken very seriously and he seems to have been more the subject of ridicule than respect.

Jowett was a regular attender at chapel services throughout his time as Master, administering the communion on Sundays and preaching to the college on the first and fifth Sundays of every term. Fletcher was usually there to hear his sermons and it is interesting to speculate on what influence and effect they may have had on him. Scott Holland had dismissed them twenty years before as 'just Platonism flavoured with a little Christian charity',[44] a judgement which seems unfairly severe. The sermons are admittedly more ethical and practical than doctrinal or spiritual, but Jowett's devotion to the Christ of the gospels is clear, as is his concern for his congregation. Fremantle reckoned that 'many of his sermons told, although somewhat indirectly, upon the conscience of young men.'[45] To Peter Hinchliff, 'he preached a religion of endeavour, of moral integrity, and of fulfilling one's obligations in life. But there is little or nothing of hope, of forgiveness or of redemption. For some it must have been a rather crushing religion.'[46] It is apparent too that the sermons are more encouraging to the intelligent layman than to anyone who might have been considering ordination. Fletcher was conscious of the extent to which the clergy still dominated Oxford and, more important, the common rooms, and certainly the headmasters' studies, of the public schools. For the career he had already chosen, holy orders, if not essential, were certainly to be recommended. But Jowett's sermons, and indeed the whole atmosphere of Balliol, discouraged him. His tutor, R. L. Nettleship, had rejected ordination when he was a scholar at Balliol. He wrote in 1868 to Edward Thring, his headmaster at Uppingham: 'I could not with a free conscience go into the Church as I am now or as I am likely to be for some time to come. To do such work requires a foundation of absolute certainty, and that I do not feel that I have.'[47] It was not that religion and theology were regarded at Balliol as unimportant or insignificant for everyday life – on the contrary. As such, Balliol's approach was positive and influential, but it was not compatible with the commitment and doctrinal orthodoxy that ordination demanded.

Early in his time at Balliol Fletcher had come under the spell of Charles Gore who was then in his thirties and principal of Pusey House in Oxford. He was destined to become, in Bishop Hensley Henson's words, 'the most considerable English churchman of his time, not the most learned, not the most eloquent, but so learned, so eloquent, so versatile and so energetic that he touched the life of his generation at more points, and more effectively, than any of his contemporaries.'[48] As a child Gore had reacted to his low church upbringing and turned to Anglo-Catholicism. At Harrow he was taught and influenced by Westcott, the Biblical scholar and future Bishop of Durham: 'Westcott began to open his mind to many truths – the moral value of exact scholarship; the insight to be gained from a religious study of history; the spiritual glories of simple living; love of the poor.'[49] Like Fletcher nearly twenty years later, Gore won the second classical scholarship at Balliol and then gained firsts in mods and greats. He was a pupil of Jowett but in his case the college's liberal and critical atmosphere did nothing to dissuade him from ordination. After brief periods as a fellow of Trinity College and vice-principal of the clergy training college at Cuddesdon, near Oxford, Gore was appointed the first principal of Pusey House, established to commemorate its namesake who had died the year before.[g] The house

---

[g] Edward Bouverie Pusey was Regius Professor of Hebrew at Oxford and Newman's successor as leader of the Oxford Movement. He was always Jowett's arch-rival.

was essentially Pusey's library and the priests who lived there acted as librarians, though they were also appointed to offer pastoral care to the undergraduates and, most important, to maintain the Tractarian tradition in the heart of Oxford. Understandably Fremantle regarded the place with a measure of resentment and suspicion: '... the Pusey House had been erected for the object of perpetuating the influence of Dr Pusey; and as Balliol was not esteemed an adequate place for young men who look forward to ordination, I found there was a constant influence which drew men away from us.'[50] Fletcher was certainly drawn there, and he records in his memoirs that 'the greatest religious force in Oxford at the time was certainly Charles Gore, then head of Pusey House. It was by no means only the High Churchmen whom he attracted and influenced ... I have grateful and pleasant recollections of his eloquent and inspiring sermons, of walks with him, of evenings as his guest at the Pusey House and, once at least, at Trinity High Table, of his humour and his earnestness and the personal interest and affection which he could spread over so many of his younger friends. He had taken the whole undergraduate world for his parish.'[51]

Lux Mundi, edited by Gore, was published a month after Fletcher started at Oxford. Like *Essays and Reviews* thirty years before, it was a theological symposium which met with the same virulent opposition. The essayists (who included Gore's friend Henry Scott Holland) tried to combine traditional Catholic orthodoxy with contemporary critical and scientific thinking. Gore's own essay on 'The Holy Spirit and Inspiration' was reminiscent of Jowett's contribution to *Essays and Reviews* and attracted the fiercest hostility. Professor Henry Liddon, on whose shoulder's Pusey's mantle had fallen, regarded the book as a *trahison des clercs* and felt especially betrayed by Gore. Fletcher was present when Liddon preached his last sermon in the university church. He 'watched Gore sitting with bowed head beneath the pulpit while Liddon with his beautiful face and perfect voice and delivery poured out his soul in what was practically a reasoned protest against what Gore had written.'[52]

Fletcher had lengthy discussions with Gore about his beliefs. The faith brought with him from home and school had been orthodox, uncomplicated and low church. Balliol and Oxford's religious controversies made him question what he had inherited and absorbed as a boy and were indeed to shape and determine both the nature of his faith and the level of importance he attached to it. Fletcher's Christianity was to prove a strong part of his life and work and he never seems to have doubted the essentials. But any intensity and passion his faith might once have had were dispelled, not least by the critical approach that Balliol taught him. Even Gore, who managed to maintain his fervour, kept a picture of Jowett on his study wall: 'When I feel I am stressing an argument too far', he would say, 'I look at Jowett and he pulls me up.'[53] Though Fletcher had considered ordination, not least (it has to be said) because of the career advantages it would bring, it was becoming increasingly unattractive to him, and indeed impossible if he was to preserve any kind of intellectual integrity. Ordination must have been the subject of many of Fletcher's conversations with Gore and there is a fascinating paragraph on the matter in *After Many Days* (if only the letter had survived):

> I have still in my possession a letter that Gore wrote me after a walk in which I had set forth the objections that I felt to ordination – the natural reluctance that a man must feel about binding himself to hold always certain definite beliefs. In his letter he laid down the principle that if a man could say 'I believe in the Incarnation and have every reason to think that I shall continue to believe in it,' he must offer himself for ordination with a clear conscience. But nowhere in his letter does he define what he means by the term Incarnation.[54]

Fletcher's objection to ordination (reluctance to bind himself to definite beliefs) is precisely Jowett's and Nettleship's. When Jowett asked himself the question, 'Why really great men are never clergymen?' he concluded that the truly great dislike being constrained by creed or dogma. They prefer (like Jowett himself) to question and reinterpret.[55]

Although Fletcher wrestled with ordination he remained intent on becoming a schoolmaster. Jowett had suggested the bar (he often did) but the law did not appeal. And, whatever the pressures, there remained no possibility in Fletcher's mind of joining his father, and now his brother Leonard, in the family firm. Their grandfather had died in 1886 when they were still at school, leaving their father as the chief Fletcher of Fletcher Burrows. The eldest of Frank Fletcher's brothers, Ernest, was now articled to a solicitor. Whether from persuasion or inclination, the lot fell to Leonard who went straight into the firm from school and was a mainstay until his early death in 1916. The 1890s were an especially difficult time for the coal industry and letters from home (and what Fletcher saw for himself during the summer vacation) could only have convinced him to stick doggedly to his calling. The miners' lock-out in 1883 was one of the first occasions when unions inflicted shortages on the public as a means of pressurising the government to intervene. The cause was the owners' demand for a ten per cent reduction in wages. It turned out to be a long and bitter struggle, involving over 300,000 miners in Lancashire, Yorkshire and the Midlands. After a month the Atherton miners and their families were beginning to experience real hardship and, with anxious strikers pleading for credit, trade slumped in the town. Soup kitchens were set up in Atherton and Howe Bridge, and by mid-October more than 14,000 meals were being served each week. The company also allowed miners to help themselves to coal from the waste-tips. Once again Fletcher Burrows's benevolence eased the situation and the Atherton miners remained peaceful. It was very different in other areas: in Pontefract, for example, troops fired on rioting miners, killing three and injuring many more. An agreement was at last reached in November but the damage had been done. Lost wages had caused considerable deprivation to the miners and their families, and coal production in the Atherton collieries fell from 560,000 tons in 1890 to 360,000 in 1893.

Knowing Fletcher's determination to teach, Strachan Davidson had offered to write on his behalf to the Headmaster of Eton, Dr Warre. Fletcher declined, fearing 'the size and magnificence of that great school: it seemed to pursue its majestic course unaffected by individual effort, and not to offer so much scope to an ambitious man.'[56] It was a shrewd and typically pragmatic assessment. Strachan Davidson wrote instead to John Percival at Rugby and on the strength of his letter Fletcher was appointed without an interview. He was to take up his duties at the start of the summer term 1894 and, in the two terms between then and completing greats, Fletcher stayed on at Balliol as a classical tutor, preparing men for mods. Among his pupils was Leo Amery who, like Fletcher, played hockey for the college and was president of the Brackenbury. Fletcher took pride in the fact that Amery was honourably mentioned for the Ireland during the first term he taught him and took a first in mods in the second. He became a fellow of All Souls and Secretary of State for India. Another pupil was Murray Coutts Trotter, later Chief Justice of Madras: he too was president of the Brackenbury and won the Hertford Scholarship and a first in mods.

Jowett was seventy-two when Fletcher went up to Balliol and his last years were dogged by illness. He was particularly unwell at the start of

Fletcher's third year, and when it came to his turn to preach, a characteristic message from the Master was read out instead: 'It has always grieved me to see how many lives have been wasted at Oxford ... the waste is caused by want of energy and industry, and by weakness of character, and by ignorance of the world.'[57] When at last Jowett recovered and resumed his place at dinner in hall the undergraduates greeted him with applause (they still do so whenever the Master dines on Sunday evenings). Jowett's last term was Fletcher's last as an undergraduate. Soon after it had ended he was invited to the lodgings after dinner to meet some of Jowett's influential friends. 'My last recollection of him is of the kindness with which he encouraged me to be hopeful about the result of Greats. That evening, I remember, he took me across the room and introduced me to Miss Tennant (now Lady Oxford), who was surrounded by a number of elderly M.P.s keeping up an animated conversation. Someone asked her whether Asquith or Balfour was the better talker. To my lasting regret I cannot remember which she answered.'[58] Jowett died, aged seventy-six, just before the next term began. Frederick Temple, then Bishop of London, officiated at his funeral in the chapel, assisted by Fremantle.

The election of the new Master occupied the first few weeks of Fletcher's time as a tutor. Strachan Davidson was the obvious candidate but some fellows favoured a more distinguished academic from outside the college. Edward Caird, another pupil of Jowett and Professor of Moral Philosophy at Glasgow, seemed the ideal candidate and in the end the fellows elected him as the first lay Master of Balliol. The 1899 college history records: 'When the Fellows left the Chapel after the election and the result was announced to the undergraduates assembled in the Front Quad, Frank Fletcher murmured:

''Tis better to have Caird and Strachan
Than never to have Caird at all.'[59]

He had spoken truer than he intended: Caird and Strachan Davidson proved a productive and amicable partnership and Strachan Davidson succeeded Caird as Master in 1907.

As at Rossall Fletcher had scarcely wasted a moment of his time and had taken every advantage that Balliol had to offer. The college left its distinctive and indelible mark, especially on his modes of thought and habits of mind, and for this he remained deeply indebted. In his memoirs Fletcher recalls Caird's first speech to the college and he adds his own tribute: 'In his strong Scots accent he referred to the "dues of nurrrture" which Plato said a man owed to the city which bred him. "Now I", he said, "owe dues of nurrrture to Balliol."' Fletcher concludes, 'I also owe dues of nurture to her; since I have no better way of discharging the debt, may these chapters of affectionate reminiscence be accepted as part payment.'[60]

4
Rugby
1894–1903

Rugby's headmaster, John Percival, was bold and imaginative in his choice of teachers. 'He brought a steady flow of new masters – young, active men with brains-straight from the University. He had no belief in "previous experience"; he liked to get men fresh and train them.'[1] It was a successful approach, creating a talented and dedicated staff and a prodigious supply of eminent headmasters. Frank Fletcher was a typical appointment and was recruited two years before he was to start in 1894. He was staying alone in the Engadine when a letter arrived from Strachan Davidson, offering the post on behalf of Percival. Rugby had enjoyed half a century of renown and five fruitful years under Percival, and Fletcher recognised this as an excellent opportunity. 'I had no real doubt about acceptance of the offer: but I realized that the decision was important and took twenty-four hours to consider it. It was during a lonely walk up a mountain near St. Moritz that I made up my mind ... Never before had I been alone on a high mountain top; it is at once an exhilarating and humbling and almost frightening experience. I recall now ... that it was in such surroundings that I took what proved to be one of the most important decisions of my life.'[2]

Rugby School was founded in 1567 by Lawrence Sheriffe, a member of the Grocers' Company who had served Princess Elizabeth and acquired property near London and in his home town of Rugby. It was to be a small, free and local grammar school. The school moved to its present site in 1750 and began to achieve a national reputation under the headmastership of Thomas James (1778–94). By the time Thomas Arnold became headmaster in 1828 there were 350 boys in what was by then 'one of those which Dr. Johnson called "the Great Schools"'.[3] Arnold's famous reforms and a series of distinguished successors (including two future Archbishops of Canterbury) established and extended the school's importance and its reputation for religious and moral seriousness, academic distinction, and sporting enterprise.

The end of the nineteenth century and the beginning of the twentieth was a golden age for the public schools. Britain was an unrivalled power in the world, proud and confident, and the public schools educated Britain's élite. And the élite was expanding fast to include new occupations created by the Industrial Revolution, and here Rugby proved particularly attractive. Even in Arnold's time the mass of boys had been 'the sons of gentlemen of moderate fortune',[4] and the school's emphasis on moral character appealed to those who disapproved of the indolence and indulgence associated with nobility. A friend of the educationalist J. H. Simpson (who started at Rugby in 1897) admitted to him that 'one of my greatest regrets is that I was not a boy at Rugby about the year 1900':

> There was a point in his remark. Anyone who was at Rugby at that time, and is interested in the history of education in this country, may well feel that it was a particularly happy conjunction of school and period. It was a great time – probably the greatest – for the public schools, and Rugby could claim, although it was never the way of Rugby to be too loud in its claims, that more than any other school it had preserved the principles which raised the public schools to the pre-eminence that they enjoyed at the end of the nineteenth century.[5]

Rugby when Fletcher arrived was certain of the excellence of its purpose and its ability to achieve it, though with such an assurance went a certain complacency and conservatism. Nonetheless, this was undoubtedly a propitious time and place for Fletcher to begin his career, and sure foundations were laid for the future.

Teaching is the most important and vital part of any schoolmaster's responsibilities. No matter what other contributions he might make to the pastoral or extra-curricular life of a school, if a master is not a success in the form-room he will not win respect from pupils or colleagues. With a brilliant degree and two terms' teaching experience at Balliol, Fletcher's academic credentials were second to none, and his subject was classics which dominated the curriculum. He was allowed some sixth form teaching but the majority of his time was spent with the most junior and least able forms. He began as form-master of the lowest but one and in subsequent years he took the two forms next above it, 'moving up in order of seniority according to the Rugby custom'.[6] As a classical master Fletcher taught Latin, Greek, English, divinity and history. His form-room was in New Big School (now the school's theatre) opposite the entrance to the headmaster's house. In Fletcher's time it was indeed a new building: it was completed in 1886. The architect was William Butterfield who was responsible for many of Rugby's buildings. Thirty years before he had designed the controversial chapel at Balliol which bears the same Butterfield trade-mark of elaborate multi-coloured bricks and slate. On the ground floor were three large form-rooms and upstairs was Big School itself where the whole school could assemble for morning prayers, concerts, speeches and examinations.

At first Fletcher made the same mistakes as any new teacher. He was only ten years older than his pupils and he assumed that an intimate and fraternal approach would win all the order and concentration he required. The boys would enjoy his company as much as he would enjoy theirs. But it was not to be and discipline soon proved a problem:

> I was raw and untrained, ignorant of the very elements of form-teaching, and I am ashamed, looking back, to realize how little I recognized my own ignorance. It took me some time to make the salutary discovery, and to learn how much there was to learn about the technique of form-teaching ... I immensely enjoyed my first teaching experiences. So I believe, for a different reason, did my form; it was not until some time later that I learnt from a friendly colleague that they thought they were having the best of it. After that they didn't. But I had started with the idea that formal discipline was unnecessary, that boys should be allowed to sit where they pleased and more or less talk when they pleased. Later I discovered that the ordinary rules of discipline were not arbitrary or meaningless, but the results of practical experience. I was 'very very young'.[7]

Fletcher's initial approach was surprisingly modern and very different from the way he had been taught at Rossall. Nearly five years being tutored and then tutoring at Balliol made him forget the difference between schoolboys and undergraduates. But lessons were learnt which were to shape both the way he taught and what he was later to expect of his staff at Marlborough and Charterhouse.

Fletcher always preferred to teach the sixth form: it was a privilege that he later found one of the chief attractions of being a headmaster. In those days boys reached the top of a school almost as soon as they were able and might remain in the sixth form for three or four years, as Fletcher had. Those who were less accomplished left school when they had attained their potential: of eighty boys who entered Rugby in 1897 only twenty-four reached the sixth form. The sixth was divided at Rugby into two divisions, lower bench and upper bench, and from the beginning Fletcher taught Greek and Latin composition to the latter, 'a more strenuous but much more interesting job'.[8] However, at the end of his second term Percival cut back on Fletcher's sixth-form teaching to allow him to spend more time with his junior form. He wrote to explain his reasons for this change, saying that senior masters had reported that Fletcher's form-teaching and discipline were not going well and they needed his full attention. But it was not for long and when, four years later, the master of the upper bench, George Smith, left to become Headmaster of Merchiston Castle School in Edinburgh, Fletcher took over his work and gave up his form. Now, in addition to teaching Latin and Greek to Rugby's most senior and ablest pupils, Fletcher taught English literature to 'specialists' who were preparing for university scholarships in mathematics or natural science, a task which brought him into contact with the brightest of the non-classicists. He observed in 1937 that:

> The unhappy divisions which now tend increasingly to divide specialists in the various subjects were not such watertight compartments in those days; there was no School Certificate, and Greek was still necessary for admission to Oxford or Cambridge. I like to remember that I interpreted Shakespeare and Plato's *Apology* to boys who afterwards distinguished themselves as scientists, and argued about the Epistle to the Ephesians with the late Vice-Chancellor of Cambridge, Will Spens, who is as well known now for his theology as for his science.[9]

The teaching was rigorous and demanding and the reading extensive and detailed, but Fletcher relished it all, feeling as stretched at times as he had been by his students at Oxford. Percival was a harsh taskmaster, insisting that every lesson began with questions and written answers on the work prepared for it. 'Under him one was moving towards noble ends along a sure road; but he did force the pace till one almost dropped from fatigue. After the first weeks of term one was always submerged under papers – Intermediates, Long List Latin Proses, Grammar Papers, General Intelligence Papers – apart from the ordinary paperwork of a large form. And he would listen to no plea for mercy. He was working just as feverishly himself.'[10]

Percival 'wanted to see the whole day mapped out and to know what every boy was doing at any moment ... He was so sure that Satan would find some mischief to fill any empty corner of the time-table, that he sought to leave no empty corners.'[11] The day began with chapel at seven-thirty (seven in the summer), followed by an hour's lesson before breakfast. Between breakfast and lunch were four more hours of work, part spent in school and part in preparation. On three days a week there were two more lessons before tea, and again each lesson lasted an hour. On every day except Saturday boys had a further hour and a half's preparation between tea and evening prayers. On most Sundays there were three compulsory services in chapel (the first before break-fast), a scripture lesson and even more preparation. The routine was as gruelling for the masters as it was for the boys. Chapel was compulsory for them too and there were no free periods as there would be today. Percival always kept as much of an eagle-eye on his staff as he did on his boys and would come into a lesson and question the pupils himself: any ignorance or confusion on their part was imputed to the master.

Fletcher admits to his lack of training and gives credit to Percival and his colleagues for the guidance he received. More than once in his memoirs he mentions instances when a more senior master advised or corrected him. There is much still to be said for learning the art of teaching in this practical way and, in any case, in Fletcher's time there was not much alternative. The prevailing assumption at Oxford at the turn of the twentieth century was that secondary teacher training was misplaced and inappropriate, and that not much more was needed than a decent degree. In the year Fletcher started at Rugby the President of Magdalen expressed his opinion that 'Greats men already studied the principles of education and psychology in their philosophy reading, while the typical classical scholar, who had been a prefect at an English public school "under the Arnoldian or similar systems", would have acquired practical experience of keeping order.'[12] Cambridge took a more progressive view and had started lectures in education as early as 1870 and a certificate examination in 1880. However, it was not until after 1902, and the government's creation of a teachers' register, that Oxford became concerned that its graduates might be at a disadvantage. A postgraduate education diploma was started in the same year and George Smith (Fletcher's predecessor as master of the upper bench) ended his career as director of the Oxford teachers' training department.

Those taking the new diplomas and certificates after 1901 were presented by the Board of Education with the new one-volume edition of A. P. Stanley's *Life and Correspondence of Thomas Arnold*. This would have been an especially appropriate and useful book for Fletcher to read. Although over half a century had passed since Arnold had died suddenly after fourteen years as headmaster, his influence at Rugby was still palpable. Stanley's words in 1844 proved as true when Fletcher joined the staff exactly fifty years later: 'Throughout the whole, whether in the school itself, or in its after effects, the one image that we have before us is not Rugby, but ARNOLD.'[13]

One of Fletcher's closest colleagues and his mentor at Rugby was G. F. Bradby, author of *The Lanchester Tradition*. Bradby's father had been a pupil under Arnold, and after Balliol he had returned to teach at Rugby and later Harrow before becoming Master of Haileybury. He sent his three sons to Rugby and two joined the staff. In 1900 the younger, H. C. Bradby, wrote about Rugby for the Handbooks to the Great Public Schools series: Arnold, he says, is 'perhaps the most famous of schoolmasters; everyone has heard of him; at Rugby his name is still on all lips.'[14] Thirteen years later *The Lanchester Tradition* was published, a witty and satirical novel about the staff of Chiltern School and the trials and tribulations which beset a new and reforming headmaster. Despite the writer's protestations that 'the masters and boys who figure in the following pages have never existed outside the author's brain',[15] Chiltern is evidently Rugby and Dr Abraham Lanchester is Dr Thomas Arnold. In the minds of at least some of the masters, his writ (or at any rate their version of it) still runs:

> In spite of its ancient schoolrooms, noble grounds, and salubrious climate, Chiltern would probably never have become one of *the* public schools of England if it had not been for Dr. Lanchester ... Chiltern has lived ever since on (his) memory ... The Lanchester tradition permeates the place like an atmosphere, invisible but stimulating ... Any change in the hour of a lesson or the colour of a ribbon is regarded as an outrage on the Lanchester tradition, and is popularly supposed to make the dead hero turn in his grave.[16]

But the masters of Chiltern caricature Lanchester, just as Arnold himself has been caricatured. William Golding, in his review of T. W. Bamford's biography, describes how 'Arnold, famous in his life as a reformer, has become a totem of the Victorian public school system'.[17] Totems are magnets for both reverence and resentment, and it is not easy to get beneath the many layers of bias to find the man himself and his true impact on Rugby and other schools. So Lytton Strachey's sneering vignette in *Eminent Victorians* (1918) is full of that fashionable anti-public school prejudice which followed the First World War. 'Arnold and Arnold's Rugby were easy targets for the anti-Victorian sniper' and Strachey's Arnold is 'a high-minded but blundering and conventional prig'.[18] Reverence, on the other hand, is found in plenty in Thomas Hughes's *Tom Brown's Schooldays* (1857) but the book is just as distorting. A hugely popular and entertaining school story, it has an improving evangelical purpose, namely to win admiration for and devotion to the great Christian Doctor and, through him, to Christ, 'the King, and Lord of heroes'.[19] Although as a boy Hughes had spent eight years at Rugby under Arnold he was never close to him and the picture he paints of the school and of Arnold's influence is anachronistic. Later trends are read back into Hughes's own time at Rugby, so the Christianity is muscular and the games important and organised in a way they never were when Arnold was headmaster.

Hughes's portrayal of the Doctor is notably different from Stanley's which is certainly the more accurate and trustworthy. Stanley was Jowett's Balliol contemporary and closest friend, and he conveyed to him Arnold's thinking on every matter. In many respects, not least in his emphasis on character, Jowett did for Balliol what Arnold had done for Rugby. Stanley idolised Arnold and Arnold regarded Stanley as his star pupil, 'the almost perfect example of the kind of boy he hoped the school would produce'.[20] He was precociously intelligent and bookish and was taught by Arnold for over three years in the sixth form, putting him in daily touch with Arnold's thinking, vision and ideals. Stanley wrote in his Preface of 'the almost filial relationship in which I stood towards him',[21] and although his judgement was biased, such mutual sympathy and respect gave his biography unique insights and understanding. Stanley's Arnold is first and foremost a prophetic figure, profoundly and enthusiastically Christian, and it is this religious influence above all that he brings to Rugby. 'No account of Arnold will do him justice which fails to recognise the depth and intensity of his religious convictions; his life was indeed, as a disciple said, "rooted in God". Earnestness, zest, and "moral thoughtfulness" were the leading traits of his character, and he had an extraordinary power of communicating these qualities to others.'[22] 'His great object', wrote Stanley, was 'the hope of making the school a place of really Christian education.'[23]

When Arnold arrived at Rugby in 1828 the school, like others, was ripe for reform. Unruly behaviour, poor conditions, severe punishments and a narrow classical curriculum marred the reputation of all public schools in the early nineteenth century. The new and rising middle class aspired to send their sons to schools renowned for educating the aristocracy and gentry but they demanded change for the better. 'The two main complaints were that the rod was used too much and too little was done to foster the Christian religion.'[24] Here was Arnold's chance. 'My love for any place, or person, or institution, is exactly the measure of my desire to reform them,' Arnold wrote to Stanley.[25] And reform to Arnold meant, above all, what he called 'Christianizing'. 'God had called him to make Rugby a Christian school. This was fundamental in all that he did and tried to do.'[26]

To Arnold what a Christian believed, and what doctrines he assented to, were inevitably divisive – what mattered more was how he behaved and what moral standards he upheld. So Arnold proved a stern disciplinarian at Rugby and an awesome scourge of sin and wickedness. 'He saw himself as constantly at war with the devil, checking the vices of individual boys and, more particularly, trying to create an atmosphere in which evil was abhorred by the school as a whole.'[27] The chapel became the heart and focus of his mission and Arnold was the first to combine the offices of chaplain and headmaster. He preached to the school every Sunday afternoon and his sermons (published in five volumes) were among Queen Victoria's favourite reading. 'It was of course in their direct practical application to the boys', wrote Stanley, 'that the chief novelty and excellence of his sermons consisted … It was the man himself, there more than in any other place … combating face to face the evil, with which directly or indirectly he was elsewhere perpetually struggling.'[28]

Everything that Arnold achieved at Rugby was directed towards creating and nurturing a Christian school. His stated order of priorities was first, religious and moral principles; second, gentlemanly conduct; and third, intellectual ability. 'The moral and spiritual aspects of education mattered to Arnold far more than the intellectual and cultural.'[29] With these priorities in mind Arnold reformed the prefectorial system. All thirty members of the sixth form were prefects (præposters): these were mostly the oldest and certainly the cleverest boys, and since Arnold taught the sixth they spent much of their time in his presence. He made them 'the keystone of his whole government' and 'he endeavoured also to make them feel that they were actually fellow-workers with him for the highest good of the school, that they had, with him, a moral responsibility and a deep interest in the real welfare of the place.'[30] Other aspects of school life Arnold left much as they were. He seems to have taught with unusual breadth and vigour, he made his pupils feel that it was their duty to study hard, and he rejoiced when they won university scholarships and prizes, especially at Balliol. But he left the curriculum almost as dominated by the classics as he had found it and he took very little interest in sport and never regarded it as of any consequence.

Arnold's signal and enduring achievement was to make Rugby a school where Christian belief, worship and above all conduct were taken with the utmost seriousness. Some boys were made priggish as a result, many more were left indifferent or defiant, but none could escape his summons to follow the Christian way. This was the most profound and lasting change he brought to Rugby and through devoted disciples to so many other public schools.[a] John Percival was one such disciple. He had been appointed to the Rugby staff in 1860 by another enthusiastic Arnoldian, Frederick Temple, and was subsequently the first Headmaster of Clifton before he returned to Rugby as headmaster in 1887. 'The dominating ideal of (Arnold's) Rugby life', he wrote, 'was that a headmaster is called of God to make his school a Christian school, an idea which has no doubt been enthroned in the hearts of multitudes of other schoolmasters, both before and since; but he was determined to make it a new power in the world through the intensity with which he nursed it as a prophetic inspiration, and preached it in all his words and works with a prophetic fervour.'[31]

Fletcher was present with all 30 masters and 500 boys on a February afternoon in 1897 when a marble bust of Arnold[32] was unveiled in New Big School by the Archbishop of Canterbury, Frederick Temple. Temple had been headmaster from 1858 to 1869 before becoming Bishop of Exeter and then of London. He was the third successive Rugby head-master or master to have sat on the throne of St Augustine.[b] The inten-tion had been for C. J. Vaughan, then Dean of Llandaff, to unveil the bust but he was not well enough to attend and was about to retire from the deanery. The Dean of Westminster, G. G. Bradley, and the Dean of Durham, W. C. Lake, absented themselves for the same reason. All

---

[a] Arnold's influence was conveyed to over twenty public schools by headmasters who had been his masters or pupils at Rugby.
[b] Before Temple, Archibald Campbell Tait (headmaster, 1842–50) had been succeeded in 1883 by Edward White Benson who had taught at Rugby from 1852 until 1859 when he was appointed Master of Wellington.

three had been Arnold's pupils. Vaughan and Lake (both by then in their eighties) had been close friends and contemporaries of Stanley whom Bradley had succeeded as Dean of Westminster. The white marble bust by the distinguished sculptor Alfred Gilbert weighed three-quarters of a ton and took seven men an entire day to move it from the Temple Reading Room to New Big School. It had been designed for Westminster Abbey where it was to be positioned alongside Arnold's friends John Keble and William Wordsworth, but it was too big and came instead to Rugby. The headmaster spoke first and described 'that splendid work of art, representing the great Headmaster that had made Rugby so famous, and who did so much for English education'. Temple followed, and praised the ambition which Arnold encouraged in all who were called to educate the young: 'Never again shall we forget, I am sure, the great aim of forming the character upon Christian lines, and making the boys, to the best of our ability, true and generous, and noble, and in earnest, determined to do their duty to the very utmost of their power.'[33]

In a testimonial on Temple's behalf Matthew Arnold wrote that 'Mr. Temple, more than any other man whom I have ever known, resembles, to the best of my observation and judgment, my late father.'[34] Temple's headmastership certainly bears comparison with Arnold's and his reign is viewed with much the same regard. His personality has been described as 'granite on fire': rugged, vigorous and forthright. He was a moving preacher and an exciting teacher, and seems to have been revered by pupils and masters alike. In his eleven years the school was reorganised and the masters' conditions improved. There were new buildings, the introduction of modern languages, and the encouragement of science, and such an increase in numbers that by 1862 there were three applicants for every place.

The appointment of Temple's successor, Henry Hayman, plunged Rugby into four years of public rancour and scandal. The field of candidates had been strong and included John Percival and Theodore Walrond who had been head boy at Rugby under Arnold and was Temple's personal recommendation. But it seems that Hayman was preferred for two reasons: unlike Temple and Percival, he was a conservative in theology and politics; and Walrond, in the end Hayman's closest rival, was not in holy orders. Hayman, however, was fatally flawed. He had taken only a second at Oxford (making the majority of his staff at Rugby better qualified), his manners were coarse, and his career so far was not outstanding. 'If a Headmaster can't teach and can't preach and can't organise, he ought to be either a scholar or a gentleman,' jibed the masters.[35] It was discovered that most of his testimonials (there were thirty-seven) had been obtained for use in earlier applications for lesser headmasterships and were not necessarily appropriate for Rugby.[c] Masters and pupils were soon up in arms, slogans were daubed on the walls, and firecrackers were dropped down the headmaster's chimney. The local and national press regaled their readers with every detail of Hayman's faults, failings and unpopularity. Finally another act of dishonesty caused his dismissal in December 1873, and Disraeli offered him instead a lucrative country living.

It is customary for school governors to choose headmasters who are entirely different from their predecessors. Autocrats are often followed by democrats, liberals by conservatives, leaders by managers, academics by sportsmen, classicists or historians by scientists. Even successful, creative, reforming headmasters are likely to be succeeded by dull, consensus-minded consolidators. After Hayman the Rugby governors wanted a safe and reliable gentleman of intellect who would restore confidence in the school without noise, fuss or controversy. They chose T. W. Jex-Blake. As a boy he had been destined for Eton until his father read Stanley's *Life of Arnold* and discovered that at least one public school 'attempted to act on the Xan ideal'.[36] So he changed his mind and put his son's name down at the last minute for George Cotton's house at Rugby. Jex-Blake won firsts in mods and greats at Oxford and was elected a fellow of Queen's. Cotton invited him to teach at Marlborough where he was by then headmaster, and in 1858 Temple asked him to return to Rugby to take over G. G. Bradley's house (Bradley was moving to Marlborough to succeed Cotton). Ten years later, he was appointed Principal of Cheltenham College. Jex-Blake's only serious contender for the Rugby headmastership was Percival who was applying for the second time. On this occasion Temple supported Percival whose claims were at least as strong as Jex-Blake's. He had a double first in mathematics and classics, had also taught at Rugby, and had already established a formidable reputation after twelve pioneering

[c] It was then the custom for candidates for headmasterships to provide governing bodies with a vast collection of printed testimonials: on this occasion Percival had submitted 45 and Walrond 28, each one referring specifically to their fitness for the Rugby post. When Jex-Blake applied to succeed Hayman he offered no less than 94 testimonials in a printed booklet of 86 pages. By 1895, when James was appointed, the advertisement for the post stipulated that the names of five referees be supplied and that 'no testimonials would be required or received'.

years at Clifton. But Temple wrote to him with the disappointing news
that 'it was felt that to select a man now instead of Hayman, to whom
Hayman had been preferred some years ago, was a kind of slap to the
Trustees. This I had not at all foreseen.'[37] Jex-Blake was largely successful in restoring public confidence and reversing the decline in numbers.
New building works by Butterfield were undertaken, including the
Temple Reading Room, Art Museum and New Big School. But Jex-
Blake 'was a mild and benevolent man, very popular with the boys, and
he hated rows'[38] – three characteristics no successful headmaster can
afford. Inevitably the school became too relaxed and easy-going, both
morally and academically, and at last in 1887 Percival's strengths
would have their chance.

When Jex-Blake resigned, the governing body invited Percival to
succeed him. This time 'they asked for no other application; they interviewed no other candidates. He was the one man in England who, they
were convinced, could restore the School to its former greatness, and
they simply wrote and asked him to come; and, by return of post, he
accepted.'[39] After two years teaching at Rugby, Percival had created the
new Clifton College and in 1878 had moved to Oxford as President of
Trinity. Here he won the admiration of and had some influence on
Charles Gore, then a fellow of the college.[40] Percival was fifty-nine
when Fletcher arrived in the summer of 1894. Although they overlapped for only three terms, his influence on Fletcher and the respect he
commanded were considerable. 'Percival', wrote Fletcher, 'was a great
man; I am glad to think that I realized this from the first. His work at
Rugby did not end when he left; his ideas and ideals lived on, kept alive
by masters who had worked under him, and by them passed on as an
inspiration to others who came afterwards.'[41]

  Percival was much in the mould of Arnold and Temple, both of
whom he idealised and whose aspirations he shared. He was shocked
and disappointed to discover the extent to which the school's moral
tone and academic standards had declined since he had left a quarter of
a century before. Immediately, and with a great sense of urgency, he set
about reforming both. As a disciplinarian he was stern, puritanical, at
times ferocious, reluctant neither to flog nor to expel. 'His power lay in
the fact that he really did hate evil and never believed that it was
inevitable. He lashed vice itself with white-hot scorn and disgust; and
then with slow, deliberate strokes he beat "the moral cowardice" of the
majority who disliked the thing but were responsible for it by their

cowardice.'[42] Here William Temple depicts an occasion early in Perci-val's time when he had expelled five boys at the end of term. William, the son of Frederick Temple, had two terms at Rugby under Percival. Temple was his godson and he regarded his godfather with 'an affec-tionate veneration (which he expressed in the biography he wrote of him)'.[43] His *Life of Bishop Percival* was published in 1921, just three years after Percival's death and soon after Temple had become Bishop of Manchester. He describes how Percival directed the same righteous indignation towards improving the intellectual as well as the moral life of the school. 'He gradually introduced "that bugbear alike of the educational idealist and of the idle boy – test questions on paper at the beginning of a lesson". He created quite a sensation by treating persis-tent idleness as a moral fault and flogging a boy who had got a very bad half-term report.'[44] Percival took a keen interest in games and 'was constantly walking about the Close in his top hat, with uplifted chin, watching football or cricket'.[45] But he reduced the sportsmen's privi-leges and ensured that games were organised as thoroughly as work.

Mention has been made of Percival's skill in appointing masters, and of the unrivalled staff he created. He kept them up to the mark by examining their forms and by what Temple calls 'pinpricks'. 'Any one who has sent him a letter or a batch of papers to which the scent of tobacco clung, would receive "a little note" by return containing such phrases as "low undergraduate tone".'[46] Fletcher may have been the recipient of just such a note: he was certainly a heavy cigarette smoker in later life. Percival was supportive of his masters but he was demand-ing and uncompromising (and mean with salaries), and though he was profoundly respected, he was often criticised and never popular. Fletcher though learnt much from the last of Rugby's Victorian head-masters and he remained indebted to him for his example of moral courage, strenuous work, and insistence on the highest standards. Fletcher was not unlike him in temperament too. Temple describes in Percival a similar 'kind of shyness that made it impossible for him to be intimate ... Even where relations were closest, they seldom got beyond official intimacy–free exchange of ideas about school problems. He was not a man who could sit in an arm-chair in front of the fire and let himself go.'[47] But Fletcher was also critical of Percival and deliberately rejected certain aspects of his style:

Percival's unpopularity with some masters was partly due to the uncompromising demands he made upon them. The school was everything, the individual nothing, in his scheme ... He was, I think, too masterful and arbitrary, but, like Kent with Lear, we 'saw in his face that which we would fain call master' ... Percival no doubt had the defects of his qualities ... his system of school government was too rigid; it was based on anxiety and suspicion; he believed in preventing mischief by keeping every moment of a boy's time occupied. There was not enough spontaneity about the Rugby virtue ...[48]

Percival left in 1895 to become Bishop of Hereford. His was a hard act to follow and by chance the man the Rugby staff wanted to succeed was H. A. James, Fletcher's first headmaster at Rossall. 'It was hoped that the prestige of Rugby and the knowledge that he would be welcomed by us would induce him to stand. As an old pupil of his I ventured to write to him to tell him of the general desire, and was glad to hear in reply that he had sent his name.'[49] Remembering his school-days, and the enormous impact James had made on Rossall, Fletcher had high hopes. But when James arrived at Rugby the contrast with Percival was too great. 'For me his first years were to some extent years of disappointment: the headmaster whom I had hero-worshipped as a boy proved less heroic in stature when seen with the eyes of a master and in comparison with his great predecessor. He did not stand head and shoulders above his assistant masters, as Percival had seemed to stand.'[50] G. F. Bradby confided more frankly that 'when one has served under a great man, a little man does seem so deplorably little'.[51] In a letter written in 1900 to A. A. David (then a fellow of Queen's College, Oxford and to be James's successor as headmaster), Bradby is still cruelly comparing James with Percival: 'John Percival was a man and the boys knew it ... Jimmy is a jellyfish and the boys know it. They aren't afraid of him: they don't mind his threats ... and he can't even hurt them with a birch.'[52]

James did not possess Percival's dominant personality, but his reign was not without distinction: Rugby flourished under his more tolerant and creative regime. 'Rugby under Percival had deserved success, under James she achieved it,' wrote Fletcher.[53] James trusted his masters and was reluctant to interfere, allowing them a freedom that was in part responsible for outstanding academic success. 'The intellectual standard of the VIth form in James's time has possibly never been surpassed.'[54] He had inherited 520 boys and within five years numbers had risen to 586. As at Rossall, the boys regarded him with affection (his nicknames were Jimmy and The Bodger) and they admired his sporting prowess and his magnificent speaking voice. Despite Percival's continuing influence on Fletcher and his contemporaries, eight of Fletcher's nine years at Rugby were spent with James and they shared the teaching of the upper bench.

Fletcher taught divinity to the sixth and to his form. He enjoyed the subject and regarded it as extremely important. 'As I look back on those Rugby days, I remember great keenness in the teaching of Scripture, especially of the Gospels, and frequent discussion among us of the meaning of passages and the methods of presentation.'[55] Fletcher was in favour of the Rugby practice of entrusting divinity to form-masters rather than to chaplains, not least because it was good for the masters themselves. 'The law which holds for all subjects, that a man learns by teaching and teaches by learning, is especially true of religious instruction. I owe personally more than I can say to having had to teach the subject ever since I became a schoolmaster.'[56] And it was good too for the boys to be taught scripture by a layman and 'to realize that the Bible is everybody's book, and not just the parson's'.[57] But Fletcher also found the teaching frustrating because of the pressure, not least from James, to teach only what was considered acceptable. 'We taught and thought with a constant fear of being unorthodox. Biblical criticism was still regarded with suspicion, and people talked about the events in the Gospels as though they were remote and unreal … we were hampered by the timidity of religious authorities, who feared the light instead of following it. James himself was old-fashioned and reactionary in this matter; he prescribed textbooks which were narrow and uncritical, and vetoed others which have long since been accepted.'[58]

Tancock's teaching at Rossall, and more especially the influence of Balliol, had given Fletcher a very different and more modern approach. He believed emphatically in an interpretation of the Bible which took account of both personal insight and contemporary historical and scientific understanding. To Fletcher scripture should be taught with complete honesty and understanding. 'Choose your teachers carefully,' he later advised, 'submit them to no tests, demand no pledges; give them the freest possible hand, *and trust them*. The man who is troubled by religious doubts – and who is not? – will not desire to impart them to his pupils; he will teach with a deep sense of humility and responsibility and be all the better teacher because he is himself a searcher after truth.'[59] Fletcher was against external examinations in divinity because they hampered the freedom the subject deserves. He remembered his anger when an Oxford don examined his sixth form on one of the epistles he had been teaching and complained in his report that 'the boys do not seem to have been taught *the right* meaning of this passage'.[60]

Fletcher was reluctant to teach doctrine and preferred the gospels and epistles for the opportunity they gave to glimpse the lives of Jesus and Paul, and the context and meaning of their words and actions. Divinity prizes were awarded to the younger boys, and for these all forms had to be taught the same chapters and on the same lines. The paper was set by the headmaster and contained the kind of question which asks for an explanation of, say, the incarnation or atonement. 'Would you believe it, Page,' said James to a friend whom he met in his London club, 'I have just been looking over a collection of divinity papers, and not one of the boys could explain the meaning of the Atonement!' [61] The average age of the boys in question (adds Fletcher) was fifteen and a half.

Fletcher's instincts were right: times had changed and forty years had passed since the publication of *On the Origin of Species* and *Essays and Reviews*. J. H. Simpson complained that 'we were left with too little protection on the intellectual side against the criticism and misrepresentation of Christianity which we were bound to hear after we left school ... Our masters seemed to be quite indifferent to the rough seas of religious controversy in which many of their pupils would soon find themselves immersed.'[62] Simpson had not had the advantage of Fletcher's teaching.

Fletcher was fortunate to have been able to start his career at Rugby and to have been part of such a talented common room. He found himself (thanks to Percival) in 'a school with strong discipline and a high tone, with a number of keen young masters ... and a body of senior masters of whom several were men of high distinction'.[63] Many masters were bachelors and the communal life they shared provided companionship and distraction, as well as the opportunity to discuss ideas and problems, and to benefit from each other's experience. Single masters shared accommodation with three or four others. Fletcher lived in Crescent House, the same name, coincidentally, as his boarding house at Rossall. G. F. Bradby had rooms there which he made 'a gathering centre for all the younger and many of the senior members of the staff'.[64] William Temple was to praise Bradby as 'poet, historian, idealist, satirist, the unfailing source of mental stimulus to many generations of boys and masters to whom he is linked in ties of the most delightful friendship'.[65] He had been a pupil at Rugby under Jex-Blake and had been appointed to the staff by Percival in 1887. He was critical of James, remaining (as is usually the case) loyal to the headmaster who had appointed him. In Fletcher's time Bradby was very much the leader and counsellor of the younger masters, many of whom went on to become headmasters, so (like Arnold) extending his influence beyond Rugby. Among these were George Smith, from whom Fletcher inherited the upper bench when Smith left Rugby for Merchiston; J. L. Paton who became Headmaster of University College School and then Manchester Grammar; A. K. Watson, afterwards Headmaster of Ipswich; R. Waterfield who went on to become Headmaster of Cheltenham; A. A. David, afterwards Headmaster of Clifton and James's successor at Rugby; and Basil Wynne Willson, later Master of Haileybury and Fletcher's successor as Master of Marlborough. Another visitor to Crescent House was H. C. 'Kit' Bradby, G. F.'s younger brother, a brilliant sportsman who shared his brother's wit and gift for humorous verse. 'Each one of us', wrote Fletcher, 'felt that he held a watching brief for the good name of Rugby. It was a fine society for the training of a schoolmaster.'[66]

The older masters had been appointed by Jex-Blake or Temple. They were of a generation which did not have to retire and several were well over sixty-five. The most outstanding of these was Robert Whitelaw, a distinguished classical scholar and a fine teacher. His character was forceful and dogmatic and fools were not suffered. 'To differ from him on the interpretation of a text', Fletcher recalled, 'whether of the classics or the Bible, or even on a point of grammar, was to incur the suspicion of moral depravity. But it was worthwhile to differ in order to draw from him the scholarly and incisive utterances with which he denounced an opponent.'[67] Regrettably Whitelaw had got into the habit of opposing and criticising the headmaster, no matter who he was. He had been appointed by Temple (to whom he did remain loyal) and had played his part in the masters' resistance to Hayman. He was fiercely critical of Jex-Blake, Percival, and then James. He is closest to Mr Chowdler in *The Lanchester Tradition* – the traditionalist housemaster who opposes Mr Flaggon (Percival), the radical new headmaster who has succeeded the feckless Dr Gussy (Hayman and Jex-Blake combined).

Throughout his nine years at Rugby, Fletcher was the house tutor in

Donkin's[d] on the Barby Road. The housemaster, A. E. Donkin, nick-named 'the Moke', had been appointed by Jex-Blake in 1875 to teach mathematics. He had taken over the house in 1884, remained there for twenty-six years, and retired ten years later in 1920, the last master to have also served as bursar. Donkin's was one of nine boarding houses including School House which was the headmaster's. School House had over eighty pupils but it also had three tutors to assist; the others had fifty or more boys and one tutor. All houses were arranged on much the same pattern with a hall for meals which was also used for reading and evening preparation. Every boy had a study which (if large enough) he shared with another. The boys slept in dormitories of various sizes. The role of house tutor was an essential one, providing assistance for the housemaster, training and experience in running a house for the tutor, and an opportunity for tutor and boys to develop a closer relationship than the form-room allowed. In his handbook on Rugby, H. C. Bradby explains: 'To each of the boarding-houses a junior master is attached as tutor; his nominal duties are limited to the taking of evening prepara-tion twice a week, and in some cases the instruction twice a week of a "Tutor Set", consisting of those boys in the house who are in the Clas-sical Upper School, excluding the Sixth; but his real *raison d'être* is that he may get to know the boys in the house, to the mutual advantage of them and of him.'[68]

Fletcher much enjoyed and valued this part of his work. He recog-nised that 'it was good for the boys to have, in addition to a housemas-ter who was necessarily an older man and in those days, before there was an age-limit and time-limit for houses, was often very senior, a younger master who took a personal interest in them out of school and, with no responsibility for discipline, could do a great deal informally and unofficially to help and encourage individuals.'[69] Fletcher took his duties seriously and was able to put to good effect in the house his instinctive wish to be on easier terms with the boys. When he left in 1903 he was succeeded by the Revd Harold Costley-White, another Balliol classicist who had just joined the school, and who later became Headmaster of Bradfield and Westminster. It seems that he adopted a more old-fashioned approach because 'members of the house to which I had been tutor wrote and asked me to explain to my successor that he was not doing what they expected because he was leaving the house

---

[d] The Rugby houses were known (as they are still at Eton) by the housemaster's name. This changed in the 1930s when Donkin's became Bradley House.

immediately after preparation instead of visiting them in their studies. The contrast is symptomatic of a change which, before I became a schoolmaster, had come over the relation between masters and boys. The old aloofness and mutual suspicion had given way to something more human and natural.'[70] Fletcher describes his various official duties but adds the more significant contributions a good tutor could make:

> ... entertaining the boys in his own rooms, sharing in their games, taking them out on occasional expeditions, advising in difficulties, helping the backward, encouraging the unsuccessful, stimulating the lazy, encouraging and sympathising with those who were in any way out of the ordinary. It was both a happiness and a benefit to me to have this tutorial position all my time at Rugby; it brought me into touch with boys of all ages and every part of the school, and taught me the possibilities and limitations of intimacy between boy and master. I like to think that when I became a headmaster my relations with my sixth-form boys at any rate were not essentially different from those between me and my pupils at Rugby.[71]

Fletcher's cousin Philip Cawthorne Fletcher (known as 'P. C.') started at Rugby in January 1897. He was twelve years younger than Frank but much the same age as his youngest brothers and sister. He lived nearby in Howe Bridge and when Frank's mother died in 1900, Philip's mother, Aunt Phyllis, provided another home for him. P. C. was rather as Frank had been, a bright and industrious boy with considerable ability in the classics. Fletcher encouraged his aunt and uncle to send him to Rugby and to Donkin's. After a year Fletcher persuaded the housemaster to put P. C. and a clergyman's son named John Stocks in the same study. Fletcher took the view that they would be good for one another: Stocks was a scholar whose brilliance would stimulate P. C., while P. C.'s conscientiousness would encourage Stocks to work. The mixture was wise: they became the best of friends, were both academic and sporting successes, and ended their time at Rugby sharing responsibility for the house and winning scholarships to Oxford. Eight years after leaving school, Stocks brought his sister Katherine to P. C.'s house to play in a family tennis tournament. There she met Frank's brother Leonard; they fell in love and were married the following summer.

In 1908 P. C. joined the staff at Charterhouse after teaching for a term each at Rugby, Marlborough and Winchester. He was a formmaster and taught modern languages until his retirement in 1945. John

Stocks was a close friend of William Temple at Rugby and Oxford, and their lives overlapped again in the 1920s in Manchester where Temple was bishop and Stocks professor of philosophy at the university. Leonard Fletcher stayed behind during the First World War to help his father run the mines but both died in 1916. Leonard was only forty-four, his life cut short by the strains and stresses of wartime industry. The east window in Rossall's chapel was presented by the Fletcher family in memory of father and son. A brass plaque in the porch explains:

THE STAINED GLASS IN THE EAST WINDOW OF
THIS CHAPEL WAS GIVEN IN 1925 BY SIX
ROSSALLIANS, THEIR SISTER, AND THEIR BROTHER'S
WIDOW, IN MEMORY OF THEIR FATHER AND THEIR
BROTHER, FAITHFUL SONS OF ROSSALL, AND
FOLLOWERS OF CHRIST THEIR MASTER WHO
AS EMPLOYERS OF LABOUR IN LANCASHIRE
SERVED THEIR COUNTRY AND THEIR FELLOW-
MEN, DOING JUSTICE AND LOVING MERCY AND
WALKING HUMBLY WITH THEIR GOD.

Leonard's widow, Katherine, brought up three children, became chairman of education for the Lancashire council and helped to start the Royal Northern College of Music. Their son, Ralph, born six months after his father's death, was Fletcher's godson. He was always very fond and proud of Ralph and took him under his wing. He had been reluctant to have members of his family as pupils in the schools where he was headmaster, but he allowed Ralph to come to Charter-house on condition that he won a scholarship. This, he felt, would allow him to stand on his own. Ralph won the eighth foundation scholarship of his year and was later taught classics by his uncle. There is a photograph of Fletcher teaching the sixth in 1935, his last year: Ralph is sitting before him in the centre of the front row.[72] He won an exhibition to Balliol and firsts in mods and greats, and spent a long and distinguished career in the Ministry of Education. He died in 1974 and his obituary describes characteristics remarkably reminiscent of his godfather: 'His mind worked with extraordinary speed and incisiveness. He had no fancy ideas; he detested humbug and killed shallow or pretentious arguments stone-dead. He was superb at this job because of his sheer intelligence, his mammoth common sense, his passion for seeing things done properly and his anger at shoddy work and wasted effort. He was not arrogant, just impatient and bitingly honest.'

Schools, and boarding schools especially, are notoriously insular and self-regarding, and global, national or even local events can seem remote and irrelevant. Such introspection needs challenging but it can also have advantages when coupled with a society that is predominantly youthful. The nostalgia, pessimism, and fear of change that can afflict the adult spirit in the face of novelty and progress are still to come: for the moment, whatever is gleaned of the future is most likely to be greeted with excitement and enthusiasm. So at Rugby the general mood of exhaustion and gloom which seems to have held sway at the turn of the twentieth century was largely obscured. The combination of *fin de siècle* weariness ('England has grown old, her national vitality is exhausted. She has arrived at the state of senile decay …')[73] and the death of Queen Victoria in January 1901 after sixty-four years on the throne had little impact except as signals of new hope and opportunity. Only the Boer War had any real effect on the school, as wars always do. Donkin's house annals for 1899 record that 'a very successful house supper was held on Monday December 18th in spite of a certain amount of gloom cast over it by the war in South Africa'.[74] 268 Old Rugbeians fought in the war: of these an impressive 105 were mentioned in despatches but 26 lost their lives either in the field or in hospital. Most of the dead and wounded were scarcely older than the sixth form and many would have been remembered by pupils and certainly by masters. Reports of their fate struck deep chords and it is a relief to read in the same house records for 2 June 1902 that 'The School was given a Half-Holiday in honour of the Declaration of Peace ending the South African War'.

Fletcher's years at Rugby included a number of significant and memorable school events. During his first term he returned to Rossall to celebrate the school's golden jubilee. As far as Rossall was concerned, Fletcher had already covered himself in glory with his brilliant achievements at Balliol and now a position at Rugby. He exhibited his classical skills with a tribute to Rossall in Latin verse; he composed it during the celebrations and contributed it to *The Rossallian* the following year.[75] The festivities began on Thursday 21 June with a commemoration sermon delivered by H. A. James who was soon to move from Cheltenham to Rugby. On the Sunday a sermon was given by the Revd T. W. Sharpe, the first captain of the school who in

1847 had presented Queen Victoria with a loyal address.[76] In a nice twist of providence Her Majesty had recently honoured him as a Companion of the Bath for his life's work as an inspector of schools. 250 Old Rossallians and former masters attended the celebrations and over 180 appear in the photograph taken on the first day of the cricket. Fletcher played for the old boys' third XI alongside some distinguished Old Rossallians considerably older than himself. 'What the young Frank Fletcher was doing in such exalted company only he could have explained!'[77] The jubilee concert was the crowning glory with musicians from the Hallé Orchestra and a fifteen-year-old pupil named Thomas Beecham playing the bass drum and cymbals.

On 11 October 1896 the Archbishop of Canterbury, Edward White Benson, died suddenly from a heart attack while staying with the Gladstones at Hawarden. He had taught at Rugby during the 1850s and was now to be succeeded as archbishop by the seventy-five-year-old Frederick Temple. The Donkin's annals expressed the feelings of the school as well as the house: 'It is with deep regret that we record the death of the Most Rev. Edward White Benson, Archbishop of Canterbury, sometime assistant master of Rugby School. At the same time we congratulate ourselves on the appointment of Dr. Temple to the vacant see. Dr. Temple was for some years headmaster of Rugby, and is the third successor Archbishop who has been on our staff.' Temple's devotion to Rugby was not to be diminished by his elevation and he continued as chairman of the governing body. He returned to the school in October 1898 to re-dedicate the chapel after it had been extensively enlarged at the west end. This was the third alteration to the original chapel which had been consecrated in 1820 and much of whose stained glass had been donated by Arnold. Between 1848 and 1855 the ceiling was raised and the transepts added. To mark the school's tercentenary in 1867, William Butterfield was commissioned to extend the building eastwards with a new chancel and to fill the chapel with his characteristic colours, decorations and patterns. Butterfield's work was completed in 1872 but the effect was far from satisfactory. He had been instructed to leave the nave of the first chapel untouched and the contrast in style, colour and height was too extreme. So in 1896, and with Butterfield's blessing, Thomas Jackson was appointed to rebuild the west end by constructing two side aisles and raising the roof of the nave to the height of Butterfield's.

During the Lent term of 1899 there was a gathering of governors, guests, masters, and pupils (past and present) for the fixing on the

'Doctor's Wall' of a tablet commemorating the famous exploit of William Webb Ellis, who in 1823 had disregarded the rules of football, picked up the ball and run with it. His action was an immediate strategic success, the school adopted the method, and rugby football was born. It was never a game in which Fletcher involved himself except on the touchline: he was the wrong build and what sporting talents he had lay in hockey, rackets and fives. But Ellis's ingenuity had brought further fame to the school and Fletcher, with the rest of the company, was proud to acknowledge him.

Archbishop Temple was back for speeches in the summer of that year. He had been invited to unveil a statue of Thomas Hughes, author of *Tom Brown's Schooldays*, and a Rugbeian as popular and celebrated as Ellis. Hughes had died in 1896 after a distinguished legal and political career and a long involvement with F. D. Maurice and Charles Kingsley in the Christian Socialist movement. *The Meteor* (the school journal) reported that:

> Old Rugbeians were honouring one of their number who, perhaps, more than any other had been a worthy disciple of the great teacher – Dr. Arnold – at whose feet he sat. Judge Hughes, more familiarly known as Tom Hughes, gained a world-wide reputation as the author of 'Tom Brown's Schooldays', and certainly his contemporaries could not have chosen a better way of perpetuating his memory than by the erection of his statue overlooking the ground where he learned to play cricket and football and imbibed those qualities which go towards making a man noble and brave.[78]

Fletcher was there with the rest of the staff, the pupils, members of the governing body, Old Rugbeians, and guests who included Jex-Blake, now Dean of Wells; Percival, now Bishop of Hereford; the Dean of Westminster, G. G. Bradley; and the First Lord of the Admiralty, G. J. Goschen. The day was hot and sunny and 'the scene around the enclosure was a brilliant one, the tiers of seats occupied by the ladies in their vari-coloured summer costumes lending enchantment to the proceedings and contrasting strongly with the academic costumes of the School staff.'[79] After the unveiling Temple paid tribute to Arnold in another pious eulogy: 'It is good that his statue should stand here amongst us ... to remind us, and to remind the whole School, of what the School that Arnold taught was really like; to remind us of that wonderful past when, under Arnold's inspiration, this School became ... a model for the future of English education.'[80] The unveiling was followed by a luncheon in the town hall and afterwards a garden party in the head-master's grounds. In the afternoon an organ recital was given in the chapel and the day closed with a military display by the rifle corps.

Speeches were abandoned in 1901 to mark the death of Queen Victoria and so Speech Day the following year was of more than ordi-nary interest. It included the dedication, by Temple again, of a new west window in the chapel, made in the William Morris workshops. Temple also unveiled two marble medallions in the south transept commemo-rating the Rugby poets Matthew Arnold and Arthur Hugh Clough.[e] Temple was by then over eighty years of age, his sight was failing, and it was all too clear that the ceremony and the address he gave were caus-ing him considerable difficulty and discomfort. A long life of labour for education and the Church had taken its toll, and this was to prove Temple's final visit to his beloved Rugby. A month later he was at West-minster Abbey to conduct the coronation of King Edward VII, assisted by Bradley, the dean, his friend and exact contemporary. Each of the questions the archbishop addressed to the king had to be printed in large letters (on scrolls backed with crimson silk) and when, after plac-ing the crown on the king's head back to front, the archbishop knelt to pay homage he was unable to stand up again without the king's assis-tance. Temple died in office (as Benson had) on 22 December 1902. The debt to Temple and the devotion Rugby felt for him were considerable and news of his death was greeted with sadness and regret. After some dispute it was decided to build a speech room as Temple's memorial; Thomas Jackson was employed again and the building was opened by the king in July 1909.

Fletcher took a predictably enthusiastic interest in Rugby's debating society. Like almost every activity outside the classroom (games included) the debating society was run by the boys themselves, with masters as president and vice-president. All members of the upper school were eligible to join though they had to be proposed and seconded by members and elected by ballot. Debates took place on alternate Saturday evenings during the Advent and Lent terms and there was a joint debate with Cheltenham every December. Fletcher was voted vice-president in September 1896 and president in January 1899. Motions were mostly on school issues or Britain's domestic and foreign

---

[e] A third medallion was added later in memory of Walter Savage Landor (who had been expelled).

policies. In October 1896, soon after Fletcher's election as vice-president, the franchise was extended to the whole school for a debate on the abolition of fagging. 200 boys attended and the overwhelming majority voted for its continuation. 'In modern times', wrote H. C. Bradby, 'the duties of a fag are not very arduous: he has to sweep out and dust the study of a Sixth Form boy now and then ... a duty which he normally performs in a manner which would shock any housemaid.'[81]

John Stocks and P. C. Fletcher were both members of the debating society, as was William Temple. All three were also members of a small upper bench literary society named 'Eranos'.[f] It was a new society started in 1891 and Fletcher succeeded George Smith as president in 1898. Other members ('Eranistae') during his time included R. H. Tawney, who was to become the most influential political economist of his generation; H. H. Hardy, later headmaster of Shrewsbury; Lionel Smith, who became Rector of Edinburgh Academy; Ernest Gowers, who went on to become perhaps the most distinguished public servant of his time; Will Spens, later vice-chancellor of Cambridge; and Arthur Steel, afterwards the politician and economist Sir Arthur Steel-Maitland. This was an extraordinarily clever group of boys and testimony to the strength of the sixth form under James. Steel won a Balliol scholarship (albeit after a second attempt), took a double first in classics and law and a fellowship at All Souls, and still managed to win a rowing blue and become president of the Union. 'But', recalled Fletcher, 'in spite of this remarkable academic record I cannot put him in the same class for scholarship and intellectual ability with boys like R. H. Tawney and Lionel Smith ... who got Balliol scholarships in the same year, or William Temple ... who by his own admission used to devote to the reading of English the time that he could spare from the neglect of his classical compositions.'[82] The Eranos met several times a term at Crescent House to hear papers on literary subjects. Discussion was erudite and demanding though meetings were not without humour. The last entry in the first record book records that 'The meeting broke up in a confusion of refractory ginger beer bottles, & a paucity of glasses. The weather was sultry.'[83]

Favouritism is a hazard for any schoolmaster but enjoying the conversation and company of some pupils more than others is natural and inevitable. Fletcher certainly warmed to the cleverest of his sixth

[f] Ἔρανος in Homer was a feast to which each contributed his share.

form, encouraging, challenging, and advising them, taking pride in their achievements and, in some cases, maintaining a lifetime's friendship. He was close to his cousin P. C. Fletcher, of course, and fond of John Stocks, and he was very attached to Tawney and Temple.[g] Tawney he rated the cleverest of any of his pupils, whether at Balliol, Rugby, Marlborough or Charterhouse. He ranked him alongside R. L. Nettleship, his Balliol tutor, as 'the two finest minds I have encountered as pupil and teacher'.[84] Interestingly, both were awarded seconds at Oxford by what Fletcher calls 'undiscerning examiners'.[85]

Temple and Tawney started at Rugby in September 1894 (a term after Fletcher) and though they shared many of the same opinions and interests, both at school and in later life, and remained the best of friends, they were very different. Tawney was always an outsider, on the edge of the establishment and critical of it; Temple, on the other hand, was to the manner born, comfortable with the order of things (though critical and reforming too), and deeply secure. Although Tawney's father had been at Rugby he had spent much of his career in India and never really found a firm footing at home; Temple, by contrast, was the son of Frederick Temple, the doyen of Rugby and, at the time, chairman of the governing body and Bishop of London. The headmaster, John Percival, was Temple's godfather. Apart from his sister, Tawney did not get on with his family and was critical of his father's imperial service; Temple was devoted to his parents, especially his father. 'Father will never tell me his views', Temple once wrote from Balliol, 'because he knows how much I am tempted to accept them without thinking.'[86] At school Tawney was thin, angular and anxious while Temple was confident, exuberant, articulate and overweight. Temple was placed in School House where the headmaster was housemaster; Tawney's housemaster was Whitelaw, the scourge of headmasters. Like his father, Temple adored Rugby and 'in no Rugbeian persisted a deeper filial piety than that which began with William's first term and ended only with his death'.[87] Tawney, though successful, was never comfortable at Rugby and was soon to become a trenchant critic of the public school system; Temple became Headmaster of Repton.

[g] R. H. Tawney, fellow of Balliol (1918–21) and Professor of Economic History at the London School of Economics (1931–49); William Temple, fellow of Queen's College, Oxford (1907–10), Headmaster of Repton (1910–14), a canon of Westminster (1919–21), Bishop of Manchester (1921–29), and Archbishop of York (1929–42) and Canterbury (1942–44). They worked closely together in support of the Workers' Educational Assocation.

Tawney's mind was of the very highest order, winning the top classics scholarship at Balliol. Temple's Balliol papers, on the other hand, 'displayed the worst scholarship work the College had ever decorated, he was elected (on promise rather than performance) to an exhibition'.[88] But the promise was fulfilled and (unlike Tawney) Temple won firsts in mods and greats.

Temple's academic strengths lay in extraordinary powers of concentration and a near-perfect photographic memory,[89] both inherited from his father. In a letter to his wife in 1916 explaining 'why some Rugbeians are so intolerably conceited about their school', Temple described it as probably 'the most strenuous of Schools. There is very little free time, except for boys who by working quick can make it – e.g. I had two hours' preparation on end for two consecutive hours in School; I could nearly always do this in ¼ an hour and so got an hour and a ½ free. It was in time so made that I read the whole of 7 English poets before I left School.'[90] Fletcher was fascinated by Temple and proud to have taught him. He wrote the following in 1937 when Temple was Archbishop of York:

> I can certify that he showed as a boy the same remarkable powers of verbal memory and fluent writing and capacity for speaking ... which enable him now to address an infinitely wider audience.
>
> It is interesting in the case of a man who has become so well known, to look back to my estimate of him as a boy. As a pure scholar he was not in the first rank; and he was never head either of the school or of the School House ... But he was a marked personality among the members of the sixth, and in the debating society and small literary society ('Eranos') of both of which I was president. For Eranos he produced more papers than any other boy. One, I remember, on Shelley, gave rise to a fierce argument between us as to the meaning of the last line of *Alastor*; he called in his father to support his interpretation, but I remained unconvinced even by archiepiscopal authority ...
>
> All the while I was asking myself how much in him was memory and how much independent thinking. Since then I have gratefully read his books and listened to his utterances and metaphorically sat at his feet, and appreciate not only his marvellous power of lucid interpretation, but also the depth and vitality of his thought.[91]

Fletcher displays the best schoolmasterly humility in this passage but it is clear that both Tawney and Temple owed much to him. Tawney absorbed the same kind of humility, notwithstanding a similar 'stubborn integrity and a prickly intolerance of cant'.[92] He learnt too an ability to write stylish and ironic prose and it may well have been Fletcher who inspired his strong desire to teach. Furthermore, 'there are echoes in Tawney ... of Frank Fletcher's saturation in English verse, and penchant for oblique allusions in Latin, Greek, and other available tongues.'[93] Temple has left his own record of his indebtedness, describing Fletcher as a 'supreme teacher'.[94] In a speech at a dinner given in Fletcher's honour in 1935, soon after he retired from Charterhouse, Temple said this:

> At Rugby I had the great privilege of seeing a great deal of Mr. Fletcher ... I became acquainted with him and we formed a friendship which both of us have treasured from that day to this, and which we find among our most abiding delights ... We were members of the Upper Sixth. He was still a somewhat junior Master until the potentates of the Upper Bench thought it was their duty, as well as their privilege, in courtesy to make the somewhat timid newcomer feel at home and we did our best to encourage him by sniggering when he translated the joke from Aristophanes into a joke in English, and so forth. I have often wondered whether it remains in his mind as it remains in mine – whether truly or not – that an epoch was made by our start upon the Third Book of Lucretius. It seemed to me that that was the point at which he took hold of us and became the most inspiring classical teacher under whom it was my privilege to work ...

From Fletcher, Temple derived an ability to write and speak with confidence and unaffected clarity (Temple was president of the Oxford Union in his final year); an approach to the Bible and the creeds which was informed, critical and questioning (his doubts about the virgin birth and the bodily resurrection of Christ nearly prevented his ordination); and a love for English poetry, Browning especially, whom he described as 'the greatest product of the nineteenth century'.[95] 'I believe', wrote Fletcher, 'he credits me with three contributions to his education, with causing him to read Browning, inspiring him with an admiration for Lucretius, and on one occasion, by a casual remark about St. Paul's Epistles, giving him a salutary theological shock which set him thinking. I may add that he has told me what the remark was, and I have tried it from time to time on later generations of boys, in the hope of producing more Archbishops and brilliant theologians. But it has always failed to shock them.'[96]

Though Rugby and Fletcher left enduring marks on both Temple and Tawney, Balliol influenced them more. Fletcher cannot claim much credit for their choosing his college: there was no other place for someone as brilliant as Tawney, and Temple's father (who had been a Balliol scholar, tutor and fellow) urged his son to 'Take anything you can get at Balliol. Better at Balliol with nothing than at Trinity with an Exhibition.'[97] Fletcher was delighted and was able to commend them to the Master, Edward Caird. He also put them in touch with Charles Gore, now superior of a community of celibate priests he had founded at Mirfield in Yorkshire. Gore and Caird were to have a decisive and fundamental effect on them both, shaping and inspiring in them a practical and (in their hands) hugely influential social, political and economic idealism.[h] Fletcher remained close to these pupils but he never sympathised much with their socialist views. He was only ten years older, yet he belonged to a different generation. His Balliol had been Jowett's not Caird's, and, furthermore, he came from determined (if enlightened) capitalist stock. His family was still busy running the collieries (as he would have been too had he not been so determined to teach) and the Fletchers expressed their social conscience through a proud and practical paternalism, not through any radical desire to transform society.

Fletcher valued the long holidays that come with teaching and made good use of them to read, travel, and keep in touch with friends. The summer break was especially enjoyable as it had been when he was a boy. Holidays from Rossall were spent in the Lake District, walking, climbing, swimming, fishing and sailing. His father owned a second home and farm there, Crow How, half a mile from Ambleside. It was a large grey and red stone Victorian farmhouse (now a hotel) with two acres of garden and spectacular views across the beautiful Rydal valley. These were carefree *Swallows and Amazons* holidays, and so enjoyed by Fletcher's third brother, Bernard, that he chose to escape the collieries by farming in the area. The family's association with the Lakes was long-established. Frank's great-uncle John had owned a mansion at the head of Lake Windermere, close to Ambleside, and here Frank's father

---

[h] Temple dedicated his *Studies in the Spirit and Truth of Christianity* (1914) to Gore; Tawney did the same with his famous *Religion and the Rise of Capitalism* (1926).

and his brothers had spent their Rossall holidays.[i] In Victorian times the Lakes were a favourite escape and inspiration for the chattering classes of clerics, writers, dons and schoolmasters, and it is arguable 'that the whole course of English thought and letters in the nineteenth century would have been different if this island had not contained the mountain paradise of Westmorland and Cumberland'.[98] The Temples, father and son, were devoted to the Lake District, and Percival grew up on a farm in Westmorland. Arnold built his holiday home, Fox How, in the Rydal valley, close to Rydal Mount, his friend William Wordsworth's house. From Crow How the Fletchers could see Fox How across the River Rothay on the opposite side of the valley. The children were told stories about England's most famous headmaster and his family who would once have been their neighbours.

Despite years studying the classics it was not until he was teaching at Rugby that Fletcher first visited Italy and Greece. He went to Italy with a housemaster, W. G. Michell, and two boys in the Eranos, Arthur Steel and Henry Hardy. 'It was on this tour that I first saw Italian pictures as they should be seen, in their original setting. Leonardo da Vinci's *Last Supper* at Milan, faded though it was, made a lasting impression on me; so did Fra Angelico's frescoes in San Marco and Michael Angelo's in the Sistine Chapel ... In the Vatican Galleries I first realized the possibility of liking sculpture, which previously had been a sealed book to me.'[99]

Much of Fletcher's Rugby holidays were spent climbing in the Alps. The Lakes had given him a love for England's mountains green and an early confidence in reaching their heights. Balliol reading parties at Urquhart's chalet near Saint-Gervais had introduced him to alpine beauty and given him a taste for climbing. His tutor, Nettleship, was an established mountaineer and must have shared his enthusiasm with Fletcher. Not even Nettleship's death on Mont Blanc in the summer vacation before Fletcher's last year seriously deflected him. Most important, his uncle Philip Fletcher (P. C.'s father) gave Frank every help and encouragement, and the sport soon became a passion, first in the Engadine and later in the southern Alps. Philip had started mountaineering late in life and at sixty he climbed Mont Blanc and made his third ascent of the Matterhorn. By 1892 Fletcher had eleven expeditions to his credit, some with Philip, others with his close Balliol colleague Cyril Bailey

---

[i] John Fletcher's daughter, Edith, married Canon Rawnsley, one of the founders of the Wordsworth Trust and the National Trust.

(whose life he saved on one occasion). 'Frank Fletcher', Bailey wrote after his death, 'was a mountaineer of the old school, essentially an amateur; climbing was a joy and a recreation to him in his youth and a happy recollection in his later years. He never made a record time or discovered a new route; he never climbed seriously without guides. But he set himself to master the technique of rock, snow and ice and made himself proficient. He looked to his guides for knowledge of the weather and route, not for practical assistance: his climbs were to be his own.'[100]

Climbing in the Alps became as fashionable with those members of the Victorian intelligentsia who could afford it as the Lakes had been. Sir Leslie Stephen, for instance, was an intrepid, pioneering mountaineer and was among the earliest members of the Alpine Club and its president from 1866 to 1869. The club started in 1857 and soon acquired a reputation as exclusive and conservative. Like any London club new members had to be proposed, seconded and elected (blackballs were frequent), and for this club they had to be relatively accomplished climbers. It was 'a unique society of educated men who are yet aware of reality, who have broken their shins against rocks in the dark and know danger, fatigue, hunger and thirst at first hand. Quibbles, shams and make-believes do not get past them.'[101] Philip Fletcher was a keen member and proposed his nephew in October 1896. He was elected in December and remained proud of his membership, a regular attender at the meetings, lectures and dinners held in the club's rooms at the end of Savile Row.

The Alps proved a most providential place for Fletcher. It was when staying in the Engadine that he received the letter from Strachan Davidson offering him the Rugby post, and it was at Le Pont in the Jura he was engaged to be married. It was the Christmas holiday 1901 and Fletcher's party were almost the only English people, the rest were Swiss and French. In his memoirs he describes a young Frenchman who was there:

> He knew very little English but had tried to read some and he particularly wanted to understand Browning's *Abt Vogler*. He got me to read it aloud, while one of the younger members of our party translated it at intervals into French. I thought it then, and think it still, a remarkable piece of work. To interpret Browning is commonly thought difficult. To translate him extempore into French – that most lucid of languages in which nothing can be left

obscure – implies a quick understanding of the original and a facile command of French.[102]

The skilful translator of Fletcher's favourite poet was Dorothy Pope who became Fletcher's fiancée on the same expedition. Fletcher was shy and reserved by nature and had not mixed much with the opposite sex. He had six brothers and his only sister was fifteen years younger. Rossall was a very monastic institution – isolated, all boys, and with the vast majority of the masters unmarried, including the headmaster, H. A. James. Rugby under James was much the same; and Oxford had been almost as much of a male preserve with fewer than 200 women students in Fletcher's time: they were also independent of the university and had to be strictly chaperoned. But Fletcher had fallen in love and was entirely certain that this was the young woman he wanted to marry. He waited until the last day of the holiday, however, before asking her, for fear that she would refuse him. Dorothy was seven years younger, the daughter of a wealthy and cultivated solicitor in Crediton, Devon. She was strikingly attractive, cultured, artistic and sociable.

They were married on 2 August 1902, seven months after their engagement; Cyril Bailey was the best man. It was the start of a long and very happy marriage. 'They were so essentially, from the time of their marriage, both one and at the same time each the complement of the other.'[103] Dorothy was later to prove an invaluable helpmate as a headmaster's wife, showing in two schools 'how much can be done in that position to brighten and humanize the life of the community and to win the gratitude and affection of many generations of boys'.[104]

As an old mountaineer I am glad to remember how our marriage is trebly associated with mountains. It was in the Engadine that my father and mother first became acquainted with [Dorothy] and her parents; it was among the Lake hills, when she and her mother were my father's guests after my mother's death that I first met her; it was among the mountains of the Jura ... that we became engaged. Every year since has increased our debt to those three mountain centres. I lift up my eyes unto the hills, for from thence came my happiness.[105]

5
Marlborough
1903–1911

By the end of his eighth year at Rugby Fletcher was feeling restless and ready to take on the work of a headmaster. He was married now, and though Dorothy might have helped his chances, a headmaster's wife was not yet the prerequisite she was to become. H. A. James, for instance, never married and would not have felt out of place at the Headmasters' Conference. Fletcher's marriage would, however, have encouraged James to offer him a boarding house, where a wife was needed to supervise the domestic arrangements, but James knew of his higher ambition and no invitation came. Fletcher was not disappointed – much as he enjoyed house tutoring, there was never in his mind any contest between housemastering and headmastering, despite the fact that a housemaster at Rugby could have found himself better paid than a headmaster, and certainly the headmaster of a new and poorly endowed school like Marlborough.[a] Fletcher earned a modest £150 a term as an assistant master but this sum would have increased very considerably if he had taken on a house. He would have been allowed to run it independently and at a profit, as well as being entitled to an additional capitation fee for every boy in the school. Furthermore, the work of a housemaster could (and still can) be so much more fulfilling than that of a headmaster, and Fletcher's contribution to Donkin's suggests that he would have been good at it.

The housemaster and the house loomed over every boy. A great headmaster could always make his influence felt in the school, but once the numbers in the school had grown he had to work directly on the staff rather than on the boys, most of whom had little to do with him until their last year. The housemaster on the other

---

[a] F. W. Farrar's son wrote of his father who was Master of Marlborough, 1871–76: 'The headmastership of Marlborough [sc. £2,000] was far less lucrative than the command of a large house at Harrow and the position involved a large expenditure in hospitality.' Fletcher was paid the same as Farrar.

hand became the most important single master in the school for the boys in his house. He was the symbol of moral authority and watched the development of the personalities of the forty or so boys in his charge.[1]

If James had offered a house, Fletcher would have declined it, just as he had some flattering offers from Balliol. 'Three times during my first seven years at Rugby I was invited to return to Balliol as a tutorial Fellow ... After many searchings of heart I decided that boys rather than undergraduates were my proper field of labour. I was not really enough of a student and academic scholar for college life, and I wanted to become a headmaster some day ... I have never regretted the decision.'[2]

Fletcher was determined to achieve his ambition but there were obstacles to surmount. Still in his early thirties he was young for such a post, even allowing for a time and a profession in which youthful promotion was common (Thomas Arnold was thirty-three and Frederick Temple thirty-six when they were appointed to Rugby). Furthermore, Fletcher looked much younger than his years, and there are stories of the surprise he caused once he had been appointed Master of Marlborough. At his first Rugby v. Marlborough match at Lord's he was asked which house he was in, and Fletcher recounts how 'in the January before I became Master I had found myself in a carriage returning from Switzerland with two Marlborough boys, and in conversation with them mentioned that I was at Rugby, whereupon one of them asked "Are you in the eleven?"'[3] And it cannot be said that Fletcher's physique proved much of a compensation. He was slender and at five feet six he lacked the authority that height and build can bring. His voice did not help much either, with its curious blend of high pitch and Lancashire burr. However, the most serious impediment was the fact that he had chosen not to be ordained.

Though schoolmasters were by now mostly laymen, headmasters, at least of the most famous and prestigious schools, remained in holy orders. Arnold was largely responsible for this enduring Victorian preference for clerical headmasters, certainly at Rugby but at other schools too. The next eight headmasters who followed him at Rugby were clergymen, and Tait and Temple went on to become Archbishops of Canterbury.[b] The reason why the unfortunate Hayman was appointed,

[b] Of the eight Archbishops of Canterbury from 1862 to 1961 six had been public school headmasters and four of these had Rugby connections.

despite all objections and shortcomings, was because his nearest rival was not in orders. All the great Victorian headmasters were ordained: Hawtrey and Warre at Eton, Vaughan at Harrow, Moberly at Winchester, Kennedy at Shrewsbury, Benson at Wellington, Haig Brown at Charterhouse, Bradley at Marlborough, Thring at Uppingham. Even by the time Fletcher was looking to be appointed, a cleric was still regarded by parents and governors 'as an essential safeguard for the religious and moral content of education in a boarding school'.[4] But Balliol had discouraged Fletcher from any serious thoughts of ordination and it is a tribute to his integrity that he put his ambition at risk by refusing to join what the *Pall Mall Gazette* had called '*clergymen de convenance*'.[5] He was confident that he could preach, teach divinity and prepare boys for confirmation as well as any cleric, and Rugby had already provided opportunities for him to practise. In a revealing passage in his memoirs of 1937, Fletcher reflects on the new willingness to appoint lay headmasters pioneered by his own appointment to Marlborough in 1903:[c]

> It is a real relief to a man who feels a vocation to schoolmastering to be no longer forced to ask himself whether he has also a call to ordination, knowing that, if he has not, the chances of the best work will be denied him. It removes the temptation of the ambitious man, to mistake his personal ambitions for a 'call,' and the converse reluctance of the over-conscientious who may refuse ordination for which they are really inclined because it carries professional advantages with it.[6]

Fletcher was not to be discouraged and was indeed, as he described himself, 'a young man in a hurry'.[7] He had put in for Tonbridge in 1898 when he had been at Rugby for just four years and was still only twenty-eight. He admits that this was 'an absurd venture'[8] and the governors appointed C. C. Tancock, Fletcher's headmaster at Rossall. Two years later in 1900 Sedbergh fell vacant when H. G. Hart resigned. The fact that Hart was a layman and the thought that Fletcher's grandfather had been a boy there encouraged him to apply. Mrs Hart, however, had been very involved in the school and had contributed so much to its improvement that bachelor applicants were excluded without interview. Charles Lowry was appointed and seven years later he succeeded Tancock at Tonbridge. In 1903 Fletcher tried for Bedford,

[c] Such is the change that 100 years later the author is one of only eight ordained members of the Headmasters' and Headmistresses' Conference of over 250 heads.

predominantly a day school where a clerical headmaster was less important. This time he was interviewed but 'the governors showed anxiety, reasonably enough, as to how so young-looking a man would tackle parents'.[9]

When Fletcher consulted H. A. James about his future he 'prophesied that none of the great boarding schools would accept a layman in my lifetime'.[10] It was remarkable therefore that when, three months later, the council of Marlborough advertised for a new Master they specifically invited applications from laymen: 'Candidates must be graduates of the university of Oxford or of the university of Cambridge, but are not required to be in Holy Orders, and applications from laymen are invited.'[11] This was surprising and progressive for a school that had been founded primarily for the sons of the clergy just sixty years before. 'The advertisement', wrote Fletcher, 'attracted a good deal of notice, and I was strongly advised to stand. But it was not expected that a layman would really have a chance, and Percival, among others, regarded the advertisement as only a gesture.'[12] Nonetheless, Fletcher was supported by Strachan Davidson and by James, despite 'his prejudices in favour of parsons, for which at other times he was prepared to die in the last ditch'.[13] The testimonials of twelve candidates were considered and five were selected for interview by the council at the Westminster Palace Hotel on 17 June 1903. In addition to Fletcher, the chosen four were two laymen (Sir Arthur Hort, sixth form master at Harrow, and J. H. Rawlins, the Lower Master at Eton) and two clergymen (A. A. David, who had been a colleague of Fletcher at Rugby and was now a fellow of Queen's College, Oxford, and F. B. Westcott, Headmaster of Sherborne and son of the saintly and learned Bishop of Durham). Fletcher was by far the youngest and the only married candidate apart from Hort, who happened to have married one of the retiring Master's daughters. Fletcher generously described them as 'as handsome a pair as I ever saw; it was a pleasure to see them together.'[14] Hort had the additional advantage of being an Old Marlburian.

The interview was chaired by the Bishop of Salisbury, John Wordsworth, great-nephew of the poet, who as bishop of the diocese had presided over the Marlborough council since 1885, and continued to do so until his death in 1911 just as Fletcher was leaving. Half the council members were clergymen, including the Bishops of Winchester and Rochester and the Master of University College, Oxford. Fletcher's interview started before lunch and continued into the afternoon when he was recalled to hear the chairman choose his words carefully: '"Mr.

Fletcher, the choice of the council has fallen upon you." It was in truth, as I guessed then, their choice, and not his. He believed in clerical head-masterships, and was statesman enough to foresee that if a school like Marlborough elected a layman the cause was lost.'[15] What's more, Westcott was his godson.

In the council's judgement Fletcher had three attributes in his favour. First, he was a marked contrast to George Bell who had been Master since 1876. Bell was over seventy and had been in post for twenty-seven years. He looked every inch the Victorian headmaster – stern, patriar-chal, bushy-bearded, always robed in cap and gown; the youthful, fresh-faced Fletcher (he was the youngest headmaster of his day) could not have been more different. Second, Fletcher was a scholar and a clas-sicist, and the council included several Old Marlburians 'who looked back to Bradley's teaching of the classics as the central feature of a golden age for the school'.[16] In J. R. Honey's view, 'Fletcher's appoint-ment to Marlborough in 1903 was largely due to the reputation for scholarship successes he had built up with the Rugby Sixth.'[17] There was still an expectation that headmasters would teach the classical sixth, just as Arnold and his successors had done, and ability and distinction in this field were of paramount importance. Fletcher's appointment as the first lay headmaster of a great school occasioned a leader in *The Times* which went on to generalise about the headmas-ter's role: 'We must confess that a great headmaster who is not also an inspiring intellectual force, stimulating as by electric shocks the minds of the ablest boys and through them the intellectual atmosphere of the school in general, seems almost a contradiction in terms.'[18] And third, what better stable for the Marlborough council to turn to than Rugby? Fletcher was the sixth Master since the school's foundation in 1843 and the fourth with Rugby credentials. George Cotton, the second Master who rescued and reformed the school along Arnoldian lines, had taught at Rugby under Arnold. His successor, G. G. Bradley, under whom the school had flourished, had been a boy at Rugby in Arnold's and Cotton's time and had returned to become a housemaster. F. W. Farrar, who followed him as Master, had arrived at Marlborough with Cotton and had witnessed and absorbed Cotton's Arnoldian revolution. The revival of the Rugby tradition was extremely attractive.

The Times approved of Fletcher's appointment:

The appointment of a layman to the headmastership of a great public school is a departure which, though long foreseen, has been slow in coming ... It has been reserved for a governing body half of whom are clergymen – among them several Bishops – and who administer a public school that has special connexion with the clergy, to select not the best available clerical candidate, as they might well have done, but a candidate who in their opinion was the best man for the post and for the special circumstances of the school.[19]

The Times's view that the appointment of lay headmasters (which they hoped Fletcher's appointment would herald) would not necessarily diminish a school's religious influence was not shared by Bishop Wordsworth. Fletcher grudgingly records that

he was dilatory in giving his consent to my preaching in chapel, and when, after satisfying himself that I had the requisite knowledge, he gave me formal leave in a legal-looking document, for which I had to pay a fee, he made three conditions, that I should not preach from the pulpit, or in a surplice, or at the Service of Holy Communion. The last I recognized as important and highly reasonable; the others were trivial and seemed to have no rational basis. Neither a surplice nor a pulpit has any special sanctity. However, I welcomed anything which made it clear that I was not speaking with the official utterance of a clergyman, but as a headmaster to his boys; for this purpose gown and hood were a suitable dress, and the lectern a central and easy place to speak from. The dry comment of the Archbishop of Canterbury, that 'our brother of Salisbury has given the new Master of Marlborough leave to preach in chapel provided he does it from a place where no one can hear him,' was happily inaccurate.[20]

Fletcher was determined to take his religious responsibilities as seriously as any ordained headmaster. Indeed not being in holy orders allowed him to express some of his personal religious convictions and uncertainties, and Fletcher found this a positive advantage, just as he had in his divinity classes at Rugby. He was free not only to proclaim his faith but also to identify with his pupils' scepticism in a way that would have been difficult, if not impossible, for an Edwardian cleric. And boys could more readily identify themselves with Fletcher's religious beliefs and practices since he was not obliged by his calling to hold and do them. He may be headmaster but at least in this area he could speak to his pupils *homo homini*.

News of Fletcher's appointment was greeted with sadness at Rugby. The editor of *The Meteor* dwelt on the forthcoming Rugby-Marlborough match at Lord's: 'Our immediate hopes are for a victory against Marlborough, and this turns our thoughts to our rivals' new headmaster. They can afford to be beaten by us in view of the great loss which they are inflicting on us. Sorrow, however, at Mr. Fletcher's departure is tempered with pride, when we reflect that there is one more name added to the illustrious roll of Headmasters which Rugby has sent out with never-failing honour to itself.'[21] The Donkin's house annals describe similar sentiments: 'The House while sharing in the general pleasure at his appointment could not help feeling what a loss his departure would be to them. No one could have taken greater interest in the doings of the House than he did all the time he was with us, nor could any one have possibly had a better influence.' Just a year before, Donkin's had presented Fletcher with a silver salver and candle sticks as wedding presents and now they gave him a handsome leather-bound album containing photographs of every member of the house.

Marlborough observed its centenary in 1943 (celebrations were judged inappropriate in the fourth year of the war) and Fletcher contributed to a commemorative anthology of essays published by the Cambridge University Press.[d] He was writing forty years on from his appointment as Master and he chose for his title '*Genius Loci*', recalling Percival's taking leave of Rugby fifty years before when he had 'prayed that "the *genius loci*" might "lay year by year a stronger and more compelling hand on all who come to it".'[22] 'Marlborough, more perhaps than most schools, can boast her *genius loci*, in virtue of which she acquired from the beginning a personality and individuality of her own and took rank in a very few years beside the older and more historic institutions.'[23]

Fletcher rightly regarded the site of the school as an important factor in Marlborough's characteristic spirit. The setting today is still as strikingly beautiful and quintessentially English as it was in 1843. The school sits on the Bath Road at the west end of the town with a side of the valley rising sharply above its red roofs and chimneys. On a hill half a mile away is Savernake Forest and flowing just south of the school is the River Kennet. The surroundings are distinctly rural and shaped the country pursuits of Marlborough's earliest pupils. Later, when games

---

[d] *Marlborough College 1843–1943*, ed. H. C. Brentnall and E. G. H. Kempson: Fletcher brought Harold Brentnall with him to Marlborough from Rugby where he had been his pupil and colleague.

were organised, 'sweats', or runs across the Marlborough downs, were often a welcome source of relief and pleasure, as they were to the poet Charles Hamilton Sorley who joined the school in Fletcher's fifth year. 'The endless stretch of downs/Clad in green and silver gowns'[24] inspired his earliest poetry. Louis MacNeice, another Marlborough poet, describes in his unfinished autobiography how 'The town and the school of Marlborough are set down in a hollow and on all sides the downs rise in curves, bevel and grey and serene as perching doves ... On days too wet for games we were sent running over these downs with a time limit out and back; if you were late either way you were caned but, once you got used to the strenuous effort these runs were exhilarating. I liked it even when it hailed ...'[25] Sorley's 'little red-capped town'[26] boasts Britain's widest high street with ancient churches at either end. Traffic apart, the main street, with its red and white houses, Georgian bow windows and colonnades, tea-shops and hotels, is not so different from Fletcher's time. 'The personality of Marlborough today', he wrote, 'comes partly from her wonderful situation, between the bracing downs and the delightful forest, and from the romance and beauty of the old house which the founders had the imagination to secure.'[27] C House, as it became, was the heart of the school which grew up around it. A Queen Anne mansion, it had been turned into the Castle Inn in the mid-eighteenth century but a hundred years later, with the extension of the Great Western Railway, the Bath Road was no longer a busy coach route and the inn was acquired by the founders of the school.

In 1838 a vicar in Kent named Charles Plater had the idea of starting a school where the sons and orphans of the clergy might receive an excellent education at low cost. He managed to procure the interest of a number of country gentlemen, lawyers and clergymen, not to mention the blessings of the Archbishop of Canterbury and W. E. Gladstone. Funds were raised from those who were attracted by the prospect of having rights of nomination as governors. In 1841 a lease of the Castle Inn and its ten acres of land was secured, and by the autumn of the following year work was underway to prepare the house to receive 200 boys. At least two thirds would be clergy sons who were to pay thirty guineas a year, while the sons of laymen were to be charged fifty guineas – both modest (and unrealistic) sums. The Revd Matthew Wilkinson was persuaded to leave the Kensington Proprietary School to become Marlborough's first headmaster and the first pupils (some as young as eight) arrived on 23 August 1843. Though struck by the beauty of the place, the boys soon discovered that their surroundings concealed a brutal and barbarous school. 'There were no organised games: walking, poaching, rat-catching and occasional raids on poultry yards, varied by fighting, seemed to have been the chief amusements for hours of leisure. It was a rough and rigorous life: public floggings were a regular feature of daily life, for Wilkinson was a conscientious disciplinarian.'[28] Despite the miseries and discomforts numbers continued to rise and in five years had reached 500, making Marlborough second in size only to Eton. New buildings were added[e] but could scarcely be afforded, and a financial crisis ensued. At the same time hunger and resentment provoked insubordination, and by the end of 1851 'there was more or less constant and violent war between the boys and the school authorities: this was the famous rebellion, during which one side smashed windows and furniture, set fire to rooms and assaulted officials, while the other side flogged and expelled with desperate diligence. It finished Wilkinson who resigned early in 1852 and retired to a country living.'[29]

To save the school from notoriety and closure the council looked to Rugby, and in Cotton and then Bradley they found two devoted Arnoldians. Both appear in *Tom Brown's Schooldays*, Cotton as the kind young master who explains the Doctor to Tom and extols his virtues, and Bradley as Tom's friend, 'little Hall, commonly called Tadpole, from his great black head and thin legs'.[30] Cotton was engaged to Arnold's eldest and favourite child, Jane, but he broke off the engagement the month before the wedding, causing both Jane and her father to collapse in distress and disappointment. Arnold never recovered and died on the eve of his forty-seventh birthday. Bradley was influenced as a boy by Arnold, as a boy and master by Cotton, and as an undergraduate at Oxford by Arnold's biographer, A. P. Stanley, who was his tutor.

Cotton had considered applying for the Mastership in 1842 but thought better of it. The summons ten years later was not to be ignored and 'in the course of only six years as headmaster, he raised Marlborough from near bankruptcy and virtual anarchy to the position of a flourishing and important school'.[31] To achieve this Cotton employed three main methods, each indebted to Rugby. First, and despite the fact

[e] Most were designed by Edward Blore, a pioneer of gothic revival, and chosen not least for his reputation for being cheap.

that Marlborough could only offer meagre salaries, Cotton managed to attract excellent young masters, several from Rugby, including Jex-Blake whose enthusiasm and dedication matched his own. Second, he immediately introduced the prefect system which Arnold had developed and made his chief means of restoring order to an unruly school. When this innovation was resisted, Cotton addressed the boys in words that both appealed to their pride and affirmed his authority:

> The Council informed me on my appointment that the School was in a bad state of discipline, and they hoped I would allow no boys to go out except in pairs with a master. I told them that I could not accept office on such terms, that the School I hoped to govern was a public school, not a private one, and I would try and make it govern itself by means of prefects. The School knows now how matters stand. They must either submit to the prefects, or be reduced to the level of a private school, and have their freedom ignominiously curtailed. The prefects are and shall be, as long as I am head, the governors of this School. As soon as I see this impractical I will resign.[32]

And third, Cotton put a stop to the boys' carefree rambles across the countryside and the trespassing and wanton destruction that accompanied them. 'He was the first at Marlborough in the fifties to realise that games could be organised to eliminate the pastimes and idleness that got boys into trouble.'[33] This was very much a post-Arnold development, and it must be remembered that Cotton had remained at Rugby for ten years after Arnold's death. Cotton wrote a circular letter to parents towards the end of his first year as Master in which he set out his plans to promote the general welfare and discipline of the boys: 'The mass of the School are not trained up to cricket and foot-ball at all, which, as healthy and manly games, are certainly deserving of general encouragement ... Many do not spend their half-holidays in the playground, but in wandering about the country – some in birds' nesting, or in damaging the property of the neighbours, or other undesirable occupations.'[34] E. A. Scott was another of the masters who accompanied Cotton from Rugby (he returned in 1859) and he played a major part in the development at Marlborough of rugby football, rackets and fives, and in the introduction of house matches and colours.

Cotton's had been missionary work, and his appointment as Bishop of Calcutta in 1858 was not inappropriate. In his farewell speech he set Marlborough three goals for the future: the improvement of the chapel, a Balliol scholarship, and a victory over Rugby at Lord's. Cotton was drowned in the Hooghly eight years later (there is no evidence to support the rumour that he was devoured by an alligator!).

Cotton wanted only Bradley to succeed him and he ensured that he did so without competition. Cotton had known him as man and boy and Bradley had often visited Cotton at Marlborough. Benjamin Jowett described Bradley in a letter to his friend Florence Nightingale as 'the best of schoolmasters'[35] and his twelve years at Marlborough were full of success. Building on Cotton's foundations, Bradley 'speedily raised Marlborough to a place in the very front rank of public schools'.[36] He was a brilliant classicist and an outstanding teacher, and under him Marlborough surpassed even Rugby's record for university scholarships. Indeed he fulfilled Cotton's aim as soon as 1859 by winning both open scholarships to Balliol. Two more were won in 1862, the year the cricket XI defeated Rugby for the first time.

Bradley's most enduring contribution to Marlborough was his modification of the school's original, centralised (and cheaper) hostel system. Wilkinson had added A and B Houses close to the original C House (the letters were those on the architects' plans). Cotton had turned A House into a junior house where the youngest boys lived apart from their seniors. But these 'in-college' houses were not the independent, self-sufficient houses they were at Rugby and other schools. Instead their inhabitants all ate together in a central dining-hall, and studied and socialised in other rooms and buildings, according to age. Bradley added two Rugby-type houses, the Hermitage and Preshute, and in 1872 Cotton House and Littlefield were opened. These houses eased overcrowding, reduced the threat of disorder and epidemics (outbreaks of scarlet fever were common), and allowed boys an altogether more comfortable, domesticated and civilised existence, with a housemaster to keep a close and watchful eye.

Francis Heywood, Marlborough's tenth Master, described Bradley's tenure of office as 'all glory'[37] and certainly he must rank second only to Cotton. The Bradleys used to holiday at Freshwater on the Isle of Wight where their neighbour was Alfred Tennyson who sent his son Hallam to Marlborough. When asked why, he is said to have replied, somewhat testily, 'I sent him not to Marlborough, but to Bradley'![38] In 1870 Bradley was invited to return to University College, Oxford as Master. He had been a scholar and fellow there and the offer was not to be refused. Ten years later Queen Victoria commanded him to succeed Stanley as Dean of Westminster.

Bradley was replaced by Frederic William Farrar who proved a curious mixture. On the one hand, he was still very much in the Arnold mould. Cotton had brought him to Marlborough and, after two years, he moved to Harrow to serve under Charles Vaughan, a friend of Stanley at Rugby and a fellow-worshipper of Arnold. Farrar was proposed by Bradley for the Mastership of Marlborough and seconded by Stanley. He shared their moral earnestness, and his sermons in chapel had a similar effect to Arnold's, winning the admiration of Queen Victoria who appointed him her chaplain. Farrar dedicated his popular school story, *Eric; or, Little by Little* (1858), to Cotton and it certainly looked back a generation to the battles Arnold and Cotton once had to face. The mawkish *Eric,* with its sexual obsession, has been described as 'the kind of book Dr Arnold might have written had he taken to drink'![39] However, in many of his attitudes Farrar was modern and forward-looking. He was a friend of Darwin and Huxley (as he was of Browning, Ruskin and Matthew Arnold) and, as a fellow of the Royal Society, he championed science against classics in the curriculum. As soon as he arrived at Marlborough he set up a science committee which advised that boys in their first two years should have at least one hour a week of science and that, on the modern side, science should become a regular part of the work. He poached the distinguished George Rodwell from Clifton to be the science master and built him a laboratory. Farrar managed to write a 900–page *Life of Christ* (1874) while he was Master: it proved another best-seller and won much admiration in the Church. After just five and a half years, Farrar was invited to become Rector of St Margaret's and a canon of Westminster; he was appointed Dean of Canterbury in 1895.

For all the trials and tribulations of Wilkinson's reign, Fletcher was certain that, if Cotton had been appointed instead, Marlborough would not have fared so well. Those difficult first ten years laid unique and distinctive foundations which could not then be demolished by the introduction of Arnoldian principles and practices by Cotton, Bradley and Farrar, essential though they were. Fletcher argues that it is in the mixture of these two layers that a part of Marlborough's individual style and spirit, her *genius loci*, is to be found:

> The history of Marlborough is the history of a Victorian school which took its place early in the ranks of so-called public schools, not by slavish imitation of the older institutions, but in virtue of an independent and individual personality which it developed. Its

story begins with ten years of anarchy under an inadequate Master, culminating in a rebellion which lends romance to those early years ... But chaotic as those years were, I have always held that they were of great value in the development of the school. When the great headmasters came, first Cotton and then Bradley, both from Rugby, they found a school which had already an individuality of its own, waiting for organisation and discipline, but too far developed for the imposition of any ready-made system from another school.[40]

So, though regulated sport replaced rough and ready raids through the neighbouring countryside, Marlborough retained its rural character, and country pursuits have survived. And though out-college boarding houses were added by Bradley and Farrar, something of the corporate, collegiate arrangements of the earliest school persists, and the perplexing combination of the two systems remains part of Marlborough's singular charm.

Fletcher felt a certain rapport with Marlborough from the start. James's two short stints there under Bradley and Farrar had imbued him with the Arnoldian spirit and pointed the way for his reforms at Rossall. 'He brought many Marlborough ideas to his administration and more than one Marlburian to Common Room. Thus I was familiar with many details of the Marlborough system long before I went there: and the knowledge helped me considerably when the time came.'[41] George Bell too was helpful, despite his sorrow that his son-in-law was not succeeding him. 'No sign of this disappointment appeared in his relations with me. He helped me with carefully recorded information, remembering how he himself had suffered from lack of such records when he succeeded Farrar. He never thrust advice upon me, but always gave it generously when asked. He was, after the Marlborough custom, made a member of council when he ceased to be Master; and his successor never had cause to regret his presence there.'[42] The Marlborough Fletcher inherited was Bell's. He had been a safe and steady pair of hands, autocratic but essentially a consolidator. It is understandable that the council should have chosen such a man after Cotton, Bradley and Farrar, but nearly thirty years of treading water had left Marlborough weaker and complacent.

Bell's legacy is to be seen most in the buildings, especially the chapel. Edward Blore's original was too small now for a school of 600 boys and 30 masters and the building was not inspiring. An appeal raised £31,000 and the famous architectural firm of Bodley and Garner was employed to design a new chapel in late decorated gothic style.[f] The exterior is certainly imposing but perhaps too hybrid to be entirely satisfactory. The interior, however, with its soaring height, pre-Raphaelite decorations, and early arts and crafts furnishings 'is one of the finest creations of nineteenth century church architecture'.[43] Seven years later in 1893 the same firm built eight classrooms known as North Block, and between 1897 and 1899 the Memorial Reading Room with three more classrooms beneath. Museum Block with its distinctive white oriel windows had been added to the centre of the court in 1883 to house the natural history society, the first public school society of its kind.

The Fletchers moved into the Master's lodge during the summer of 1903 and immediately the presence of such a youthful Master and his wife signalled a new and radical departure for the school. Bell had left at last after a generation as Master, and Bradley and Farrar had both died earlier in the same year.

> I am amazed, looking back, to remember how lightheartedly I assumed so great a responsibility. Not that I did not take the work seriously. I was eager and determined to do it well. But I do not think that I was at all conscious of the difficulties, or of the anxiety with which I was watched by all concerned, by the colleagues at Rugby who had known me, the council who had elected me, and above all the Common Room at Marlborough, who found their fate and the future of the school in the hands of a man not only young in years but still younger in looks.[44]

Like any good headmaster's wife Dorothy made an enormous differ-ence, not least to the way Fletcher was at first perceived. She entered immediately into the life of the community, entertaining boys and masters in the lodge, visiting wives and encouraging the servants: her beauty and charm attracted them all. In Fletcher's obituary in *The Marlburian* George Turner, one of his senior prefects and later a succes-sor at both Marlborough and Charterhouse, described how

> His years at Marlborough were the apprenticeship of a great headmaster. In a still Victorian society the young Balliol scholar from Lancashire was received with some reserve, and his direct

---

[f] The same firm had previously been employed to decorate the interior of Blore's chapel.

and confident approach was not always reciprocated. He was immensely helped by Mrs. Fletcher, who won all hearts from the first. ('They hate Frank but they love his wife,' wrote a friend from the Lodge in 1904.) She made the Lodge an enchanting place for all who knew it. We first entered it as new boys for Sunday tea-parties, and later it became almost a second home for many of us.[45]

Fletcher too appreciated the importance of Dorothy's help. In a letter to the Archbishop of Canterbury, Cosmo Lang, in 1935, in which he offered advice about his successor at Charterhouse, Fletcher urged the governing body to appoint a man with a wife like his, recalling that 'I should have been quite lost at Marlborough without my wife.'[46] In his memoirs published two years later Fletcher praises Dorothy for her help in encouraging and cultivating the sixth:

> Nothing contributed more to the achievement of my object than the way in which my wife threw herself wholeheartedly into the task of making the Lodge a place to which intelligent boys liked to come and where they felt that they were welcome. Thanks to her it gradually became what a headmaster's house should be, an intellectual and humanizing centre for the school. Thus when difficulties arose I had a nucleus of boys partially prepared to understand what I was aiming at, or at any rate to give me credit for having a purpose behind what were superficially unpopular acts. And the friendly relationship of the Lodge made the boys I taught more receptive in the classroom, thereby contributing to successes which the sixth afterwards achieved.[47]

After tea on Sundays Dorothy would read to the junior boys, a ghost story by M. R. James perhaps, or some Kipling or Kenneth Grahame. And with the sixth she would sing or play the piano or read Shakespeare (she was remembered half a century later for 'her voice in the parts of Viola and Rosalind. For she had always an artist's unerring taste and sharp instinctive view, so that the combination of her sensibility with the Master's intellect made talk with them a stimulus and a challenge and was, I think, uniquely educative for boys approaching manhood').[48]

Improving the sixth by making greater academic demands and putting them more in charge of the school (as at Rugby) was Fletcher's priority and central strategy. Bell's tolerant regime had allowed the games that Cotton had introduced to become dominant; the school's heroes were those who excelled in sport and not the scholars. This is invariably the case unless headmasters exert a determined and consistent counter-force. Most boys enjoy vigorous physical exercise and competition and, given a choice between translating French prose, practising the violin or kicking a ball, it is an unusual boy who does not choose the latter. Although Bell, particularly towards the end of his time, expressed some concern about the school's athleticism he did very little to resist it, and it was not until after he had retired that he dared donate the Bell Trophy for academic performance. Cricket, rugby, hockey (pioneered at Marlborough), swimming, shooting, fives, rackets and athletics – all these were played with enthusiasm and a fierce determination to triumph over other schools:

> ... one athletic rage,
> Has seized Marlburians of every age,
> Now, filled with frenzy, cricket all will play,
> Now, all-absorbing football rules the day,
> Where'er you go, the topic is the same,
> And all our talk at tables is 'the game' ...[49]

In Bradley's son's *History of Marlborough College* (1893), more than a quarter of the pages are devoted to games.

Athleticism can have a number of unwelcome consequences. First and foremost, as Fletcher was painfully aware when he started at Marlborough, the sportsmen not the intellectuals are promoted to positions of authority in the school. This athletocracy is contrary to Arnold's concept of prefects which Fletcher had experienced at Rossall and Rugby, and at Marlborough it was different from the way things had been under Cotton and Bradley. So important was this matter to Fletcher that he sets out his views at some length:

> Self-government is an essential characteristic of the 'public' school ... The traditional constitution is aristocratic, in the proper and literal sense of the word; it is government by those who are, or are supposed to be, the 'best'. Originally these were the sixth, and the sixth only ... a uniform body, taught as one form, mainly by the headmaster, and easily addressed by him whenever occasion arose ...
>
> With the development and organization of school games in the later half of last century masters began to turn to the athletes as

well as, sometimes instead of, the sixth for their rulers; in the witty phrase of E. E. Bowen, they 'called in the barbarians for the defence of the Empire.' The extent to which this was done varied in different schools. It increased with the extra importance attached to games, and it tended to increase that importance, going far to justify the charge brought against English schools that games counted for too much in the eyes of all concerned, masters and parents as well as boys. With the boys this is natural enough; physical distinction is more immediately impressive and attractive than intellectual ... It is the business of schoolmasters to emphasize the other side, to get a better sense of realities and the true proportion of things into boys' minds ...[50]

Second, an athletocracy can make a school a rough and brutal place where physical force is used to intimidate and suppress those who are younger or less physical. At Marlborough the miseries of Upper School survived Fletcher's time as Master and continued until it was demolished by Turner in 1936. It was a vast, bleak, ugly building, inhabited during the day by over 200 boys of all ages, and ruled over by the captains who were the leading sportsmen. At either end were coal fires – Big Fire, as it was called, was for the use of the captains and their cronies, and Little Fire was supposed to provide heat for the rest. Louis MacNeice's ironically dispassionate description conveys the misery and dread of those like him who had to endure the cruelties and privations of the place:

I have never been anywhere like Samoa, but I fancy that the rites of Upper School should interest professional connoisseurs. Our last meal in the great dining-hall was at 6.30 p.m. and an hour's preparation of work began in Upper School at 7.15. Those of us who belonged to Little Fire were expected to be sitting at our desks by 7.00 at the latest ...

The Captains entered at 7.15 but that did not mean that we could all start working. The Captains marched up and down the alley-ways slapping the desks with their canes and inspecting the lids to see if they were flush; if the lid of any desk were even a quarter of an inch raised its owner was booked to be caned. Meanwhile the junior boys had to go round the hall 'scavenging', gathering up in their hands the fruit-peel, match-ends, fluff, muck and paper which had been lavishly thrown on the floor during the day, and carrying these nasty little handfuls to an enormous

wastepaper-basket. The Captains would keep an eye on the scav-
engers and flick at their ankles with their canes if they scavenged
too slackly.

The wastepaper-basket had another purpose. Once in a while
... Big Fire decided that someone was undesirable and should
therefore provide a Roman holiday. They would seize him, tear off
most of his clothes and cover him with house-paint, then put him
in the basket and push him round and round the hall. Meanwhile
Little Fire, dutifully sitting at their desks, would howl with delight
– a perfect exhibition of mass sadism.[51]

John Betjeman's autobiographical poem, *Summoned by Bells*,
records a more terrifying memory of this torture:

> What chance had Angus? They surrounded him,
> Pulled off his coat and trousers, socks and shoes
> And, wretched in his shirt, they hoisted him
> Into the huge waste-paper basket; then
> Poured ink and treacle on his head. With ropes
> They strung the basket up among the beams,
> And as he soared I only saw his eyes
> Look through the slats at us who watched below.

A third regrettable result of the games cult is the atmosphere of insti-
tutionalised philistinism which it breeds. 'It is surprising how much
athletes were exalted and school work despised,' wrote Sir Douglas
Savory who arrived at Marlborough in 1891.[52] Charles Sorley wrote
to his form-master after leaving school: '... we were always encouraged
to despise and reject such as knew the first line of the *Odyssey* ... and to
love, honour, and obey such as were better than us at hockey.'[53] Intelligent and sensitive boys like the poets Sassoon and Sorley at Marlborough, and later Betjeman and MacNeice, can be easily wounded and
embittered under an athletocracy, which turns them into rebels in the
guise of precious and snobbish aesthetes. Anthony Blunt is an interesting case. He was a contemporary and friend of MacNeice and Betjeman
in the twenties, a flamboyant aesthete at school, and in later life the
distinguished art historian and traitor. Julian Mitchell's play, *Another
Country*, explores this link between ostracism and humiliation at
public school, and subversion and revenge exacted on one's country.
Blunt and Betjeman produced *The Heretick*, a controversial school
magazine. It aimed, Blunt wrote later, 'to express our disapproval of the

Establishment generally, of the more out-of-date and pedantic masters, of all forms of organized sport, of the Officers' Training Corps and of all the other features that we hated in school life, not so much the physical discomforts – they were almost taken for granted – but, you might say, the intellectual discomforts of school.'[54] 'The abler boys', wrote Fletcher, 'who might have been used for leadership may, if shoved aside, turn into dissatisfied "high-brows" – a type of school failure which is particularly to be regretted, because it represents good material gone wrong.'[55]

Fletcher took his time before introducing improvements. 'My first two years were a time of vague disappointment and dissatisfaction, of what Herodotus calls "that most hateful form of trouble, to have many ideas and realize none".'[56] On the other hand, he was wise to recognise that 'a new headmaster must necessarily spend the beginning of his time in getting a firm seat in the saddle and getting the reins into his hands. He must establish his control over the many-headed creature under him before he can direct its course.'[57] Discipline came first when it was time to act, and in his second year Fletcher moved against a vicious group of bullies. 'Severity was necessary; a bad patch in college had to be cleared; and a few boys (only a few) had to be dismissed or withdrawn. The school accepted the severity and responded to the demand I made upon them. But they resented the dismissals and there was, I believe, more discontent than I was aware of.'[58] The chance for a headmaster to show his steel early in his time is an opportunity not to be missed and the benefit can be felt for years to come. The boys' reaction as Fletcher describes it is predictable: respect for justice mixed with sympathy for those who have to be punished. 'I did not expect popularity, but I did desire to carry the school with me in the suppression of actual evil. In spite of their resentment, which was not without its creditable elements of chivalry and sympathy for the unfortunate ... I believe that they did come down on the right side; though there was sympathy for those who suffered there was no disposition to encourage or condone moral offences. The "row", as is often the case, cleared the air.'[59]

Nonetheless, Fletcher was isolated. The masters Fletcher inherited, all but four of whom had worked only under Bell's more easy-going regime, also had to be convinced. More important, Fletcher needed the right boys working hard on his side at the top of the school. In the Arnold fashion he made sure that he taught the classical sixth and influenced their ideas and attitudes. These boys made up the majority of the school prefects and Fletcher encouraged them to be more active and confident in exercising responsibility. But unfortunately the captains (who were subordinate officers, 'often appointed for athletics only'[60]) still held sway in the eyes of boys and masters, with the result that 'there were too many elements of athleticism in the system and the atmosphere'.[61] It was not uncommon throughout Fletcher's time for the captain of cricket or rugby to be considered more important than the senior prefect, and indeed for the prefects' authority to be blatantly ignored in favour of that of the captains.

Fletcher's error was to leave the captains' power intact while nurturing and encouraging the prefects, thus unwittingly sowing seeds of often bitter rivalry between aesthetes and 'hearties' which was typical of the time, and afflicted Marlborough for the next thirty years.[62] Fletcher should have abolished the position of captain if he was really to do away with the athletocracy he had inherited. He admits that when he tried to persuade a quiet and talented member of the sixth that he might be a school prefect he refused because of what he had seen happen to a boy Fletcher calls 'B-'. 'Now B- had been the head of his house, an able scholar who might, if the tradition of government by athletes had not been so strong, have carried the weight which his ability deserved instead of leaving the school with a sense of frustration. Later in life he became a schoolmaster, and as a public school housemaster exercised a remarkable influence over his boys. But his school experiences left him with a touch of bitterness and a prejudice against athletics which warped his judgement and diminished his ultimate success.'[63] However, Fletcher goes on to say that within a few years boys of even less athletic prowess than B- 'were wielding, in virtue of their brains and character and the changed attitude of boys towards intellectual gifts, an unquestioned authority, which was of the greatest value to the school. This was the aim for which I was working; I like to think that it was attained, and that the tradition established in that period has lasted.'[64] Certainly there were improvements and a fairer balance between brain and brawn. Sorley, who overlapped with Fletcher's last three years, observed that 'One can rise to a big position and have all one's words taken as gold, without knowing anything more of the world than in one case dead phrases from a dead language, in another how to hold a bat straight.'[65] But Fletcher was mistaken in concluding that his reforms were either radical or permanent. If they had been, the miseries and bullying suffered by subsequent generations of Marlburians would not have occurred.

Fletcher was certainly fortunate in many of the senior prefects he appointed, though even here he tended to choose clever boys who were also good at games. Geoffrey Fisher, the future Archbishop of Canterbury, was the first to understand what Fletcher was aiming at and he put to good use his own precocious moral standards and considerable organisational skills. After failing to win a scholarship to Rugby he had started at Marlborough two years before Fletcher and became senior prefect in September 1905. He introduced regular prefects' meetings and it is clear from his minutes that he exercised a leadership which was confident and assertive, if at times a touch pompous and priggish:

> Prefects – at any rate at the present time – are liable to forget that they have any duties, and the school are also liable to forget that Prefects serve any useful purpose. Prefects' meetings are essential to remind Prefects they are a corporate body with practically unlimited powers if they act together, and to remind the school that Prefects are awake to their duties. Meetings should therefore be called on secular matters of public importance … on matters of public conduct, & when necessary on matters concerning the moral conduct of the school.[66]

Fletcher records that the rules and traditions of prefects' meetings 'were the outcome of a summer [Fisher] spent with us in Cornwall, during which I outlined to him my conception of what prefect government should mean, and suggested means of organizing it.'[67] The ideas may have been Fletcher's but the administration and determination were Fisher's, and show in the boy talents he put to good use in later life as headmaster, bishop and archbishop. He remained in close touch with Fletcher until the latter's death in 1954. Fisher was a star pupil and protégé, like William Temple whom he succeeded both as Headmaster of Repton and thirty years later as Archbishop of Canterbury.[g] Fisher loved his time at Marlborough, winning a scholarship to Exeter College, Oxford where he achieved a triple first in mods, greats and theology. Fletcher invited him back to Marlborough where he taught for two years before moving to Repton. Four years before, Fletcher had

---

[g] Temple and Fisher make an interesting comparison. Both were intellectually brilliant but in different ways: Temple's mind was speculative and idealistic, Fisher's practical and analytical. Temple was ill-at-ease as a headmaster and left Repton after four years; Fisher relished it all and stayed for eighteen. As bishop and archbishop Temple threw himself into social and political reform, while Fisher was content to bring order and discipline to the Church, as he had to Repton. Fisher was much more in Fletcher's mould than Temple.

tried to dissuade Temple, recognising correctly that he was not cut out to be a headmaster; this time he recommended Fisher with enthusiasm, though he also pointed out that he was only twenty-seven.

Four years later, toward the end of Fletcher's time, George Turner was appointed senior prefect and proved another of Fletcher's 'most cherished pupils'.[68] He was a clergyman's son like Fisher and he shared Fletcher's vision of clever and cultivated leadership. He too was a talented classicist who returned to Marlborough to teach but not until after the First World War. He was unusual in showing sympathy to aesthetes like Blunt, Betjeman and MacNeice. As an assistant master Turner agreed to be president of Blunt's art society and, when appointed headmaster three years later, he made Blunt a prefect which MacNeice saw as a triumph for the aesthetes. Turner continued the struggle for intelligent leadership that Fletcher had started and exerted a persuasive liberalising and civilising influence. 'I am sure,' Fletcher had written to him from Ambleside soon after Turner left school, 'whatever you find for your life's work, that you will look back on this last year as among the most valuable bits of preparation for it. I am working still on experience gained in a similar position at Rossall.'[69] Turner remained devoted to him and to Dorothy.

Fletcher worked hard to get to know the boys he taught in the sixth and to win their trust and confidence. He had done the same at Rugby, but now it had greater effect on the school as a whole. 'The respect for work and intelligence produced a higher standard of general industry and, what was more important, a less Philistine attitude towards general culture. And the sixth benefited by the knowledge that they counted for something, by the extra responsibility put upon them, and by the stimulus to mind as well as to character which such responsibility gives.'[70] Fletcher's teaching was rigorous and exacting but exciting too, with excursions into his favourite authors. He expected work to be accurate and thoroughly prepared but was not slavish or unimaginative in his teaching. Though he knew a red herring when it was launched his way and was quick to deflect it, he was willing to digress into matters of philosophy, theology and English literature. Fletcher relished his teaching and there was nothing 'more pleasant than to read with appreciative boys some of the great works of English or Greek or Latin literature, to introduce them to Hamlet or Lear or the Agamemnon or either Œdipus or the Epistles to the Corinthians or the second or fourth or sixth Æneid. It was as delightful a task at sixty-five as at

thirty-three.'[71] There is no doubt that Fletcher's pupils caught his enthusiasm and enjoyed being taught by him. Fisher remembered Fletcher's
arrival:

> Frank Fletcher was thirty-two at the time, slim, not impressive to
> look at, with rather a strange voice. He did not make a good
> impression. I remember the first time that he came into the Sixth
> to greet us all, shaking hands with each one. He had no ready
> conversation; he was a little awkward; we were all a little
> awkward and thought: 'This won't take us very far.' How wrong
> we were! He very soon established himself amongst us by his char-
> acter and by the brilliance of his mind, and it was not long before
> some of us learned that we had only to observe what he was doing
> and how he did it to benefit from him immensely. He made
> changes, and I, by nature rather a conservative person except
> when I saw that changes were necessary, had not yet learned from
> him the art of changing effectively when change is needed. I did
> learn it from him; as I learned very many other things from him.
> He was a brilliant teacher, especially of the things that he loved.
> Like William Temple, his passion was for Plato, Browning, St.
> John, and St. Paul's Epistles. When he preached from them, boys
> didn't much take to his sermons. But they were very good, if you
> would give your mind to what he was trying to say in his rather
> strained and ineffective voice. I learned from him the one great art
> of saying to myself what he said openly to any statement – 'Why?
> Why is this? Why does this person say that? What does he, or it,
> mean?' And thus he taught us all, or those of us who learned it,
> never to be content with a superficial impression, never to take a
> thing at second-hand, but to work through it until we found the
> underlying and satisfying reason, so far as there was one to be
> found … Those who were taught by him learned never to be
> content with the second-rate, the ambiguous or the obscure.[72]

Once again, scholarships were won at the best colleges. In 1908,
when Fletcher's first boys were in the upper sixth, three Balliol awards
went to Marlburians: the first classical scholarship, a major exhibition
for classics, and a history exhibition. 'It was not merely the number of
scholarships won that was satisfactory. Marlborough has always been
successful in that respect; it was the quality of the distinctions that gratified us.'[73]

Although Fletcher taught only the classical sixth, he did his best to

promote and expand the modern side which was unusually well established at Marlborough, and had been since Cotton created a modern
class as early as 1854. In the letter to parents at the end of his first
year he had explained that 'so many boys are now not intended for an
academical career, that the feeling is becoming general, that it would
be well if in our large School classes were instituted by the side of the
present course of preparation for the Universities, in which modern
languages and science should form the principal subjects, and where
boys should be prepared for military, naval, engineering or other
pursuits.'[74] In addition to French, German and science, the modern
school was taught mathematics, history, geography and English literature. English composition was compulsory, on the grounds that a boy
who was not studying classics would not be able to write his own
language properly. Music, drawing, bookkeeping and shorthand were
all optional extras. Since boys on the modern side were generally less
intelligent, and were aiming for a career rather than a university, the
classicists regarded them with contempt. Their own staple diet was
primarily Latin and Greek, plus ancient history, divinity and English
literature, with options in French, German, mathematics, geography,
science, music and drawing. Indeed these subjects were so entirely
optional that from the moment MacNeice entered a classical form he
'was taught no more modern languages, modern history, science or
mathematics'.[75]

The advantages and disadvantages of Marlborough's hostel system
probably struck a balance when it came to arrangements for the sixth
form. After three or four years, first in Lower and then in the dreaded
Upper School, the sixth had studies and a common room in another
block of their own. At last there was privacy after a very public existence, as well as enough corporate life to engender companionship,
discussion and debate. Certainly boys like Betjeman and Blunt, who
had hated school lower down, came into their own in the sixth.

> Under such conditions the common life of the Marlborough sixth,
> living as they do together, and not cut off in their separate houses
> as they would be in the older schools, may be very pleasant and
> very stimulating. The arrangement has all the advantages of the
> system which exists at Winchester and Eton and Westminster,
> whereby the scholars live together in college and form a house of
> their own, while it avoids the serious defects of that system, which

deprives the rest of the school of a valuable intellectual leaven and tends to a hot-house development of the scholars themselves.[76]

Fletcher recognised too the dangers of the Marlborough system, namely the infectious nature of idleness as well as industry, but was confident that it was up to 'those who watch over the school to see that it does not happen'.[77] Certainly, if university scholarships are anything to go by, the sixth form arrangements were made to work to advantage.

Less successful though was the provision for the rest of the school, about which Fletcher is disconcertingly sanguine. The strict economies of Marlborough's early years and the centralised design of the buildings continued in and beyond Fletcher's time, and do not appear to have concerned him. Lack of privacy, poor food eaten together in what MacNeice calls 'a great bleak hall',[78] bullying, fagging, infrequent and freezing baths – all these were the order of the day and were taken for granted, not only by the Master but also by his assistants. Only the boys objected but were mostly ignored. Lewis Upcott, who shared the sixth form teaching with Fletcher and left with him in 1911, wrote: '... even at the end of my career a Royal Engineers Colonel, bringing his boy to the College, after a round of inspection, said to me bluntly: "I should not pass your domestic arrangements for Army barracks."'[79] T. C. Worsley, a contemporary of Betjeman, remembered a school that 'prided itself on its toughness. Amenities of life were non-existent: life was lived on the barest of bare boards, at the smallest and hardest of desks, in the coldest of cold classrooms, in a total absence of any possible privacy. One was always cold, usually hungry.'[80] Nonetheless, Fletcher seems to have actually approved of these conditions, and even of Upper School:

> Upper School is a peculiarly Marlburian institution. It is a strange experiment to put about 200 boys of fifteen to seventeen to live together in one large room. Many people on hearing of it for the first time would consider the arrangement disastrous. I must confess that this was my own first reaction to it. Subsequent experience and reflection have made me regard it as one of the essential elements in Marlborough education. No doubt there have been periods when the life there was unduly rough for its inhabitants. But normally a boy who has spent a year or more in that centre of common life has had a valuable and enjoyable educational experience. He has learnt how to live in a crowd. If he is by nature gregarious, he will enjoy the life from the start. If not, he may take

some time to learn the ropes and to adapt himself. But all his life afterwards he will be the better for the experience, unless he is of the over-sensitive type which is too essentially retiring to face a life lived so constantly in public.[81]

The special pleading here is clear, and even allowing for a revolution in attitudes to children and their welfare during the last hundred years, it does seem extraordinary that Fletcher tolerated what he must have known to be a place of misery and abuse. But Fletcher was tough, and his plain if comfortable Lancashire childhood, followed by Rossall and the high-mindedly spartan Balliol and Rugby, had left him largely indifferent to the advantages of less frugal conditions. Certainly very little improvement was made during Fletcher's time as Master. At least these arrangements might be said to have helped those many Marlburians who had soon to endure the brutally public life of barrack-room and battlefield!

Fletcher did contribute though to the addition of boarding houses which had started under Bradley and Farrar. There were over 625 boys in Fletcher's time, and with 400 in-college the school was still overcrowded. A severe epidemic of measles had erupted in the year before Fletcher arrived, causing the deaths of two boys, followed by two more who contracted pneumonia. This was a particularly bad year with a fifth boy dying suddenly from what the council minutes intriguingly describe as 'long standing though latent brain mischief'.[82] From the start Fletcher pressed the council to build accommodation for a hundred boys to relieve pressure in the in-college houses but it took five years to convince its members that the expenditure was justifiable.[h] A number of possible solutions were discussed and in the end the council decided to build what was named Field House across the Bath Road and opposite the school gates. A bridge over the road was to connect it to the library, and from there to the centre of the school. The architect, Sir Aston Webb, was invited to submit plans which were approved by the council in March 1909. His design was in an austere neo-Georgian style in red brick to match the rest of the buildings. Ten builders submitted tenders and (as before) the cheapest was chosen, namely Jacob Long & Sons of Bath who had recently built the new chapel at Hertford College, Oxford. The new house was not ready for occupation until September 1911, just after Fletcher had left,

---

[h] Fletcher's other building at Marlborough was the new gymnasium (1908), which incorporated part of the old town gaol.

and was filled with boys from C2 and B3 (the C and B buildings by then contained three houses each). Fletcher had hoped that Field House would provide quarters for two married housemasters but this was rejected by the council. Since lack of space meant that all in-college housemasters had to be bachelors, Fletcher had been severely restricted in the number of married housemasters he could appoint, and the opportunities he could offer at Marlborough for a more lucrative career.

Fletcher had at his disposal what was called The Red Book. It stayed in the common room and was used by the Master to communicate a variety of notices to his staff. Messages concerning the timetable, accounts, syllabuses and disciplinary matters were all included. It is reported, for example, that Easter in 1907 was to be spent at school. In 1905 the one term appointment of Fletcher's cousin, 'P. C.', is announced. In March 1906 Fletcher reminds the masters of their duty to attend chapel: 'It necessarily rests with each master individually to decide what is an adequate reason for absence: but without such adequate reason we are all of us, equally with the boys, bound by our membership of the school to be present at the regular daily and Sunday services.'[83] Tactfully put, for the obligation was as considerable as it had been at Rugby with chapel in the morning and evening on weekdays and three services on Sundays. Ten days before this notice, Fletcher has a reminder about the perils of cribbing and copying, and in October 1909 he includes an instruction about beating:

> a. There is a danger of too frequent use of corporal punishment: & we need to watch against this.
> b. It is most undesirable (apart from exceptional reasons) that corporal punishment should be inflicted on Sundays.[84]

Most of the book is used to describe 'reviews', or examinations of a form by the Master, a practice which Bradley employed to help raise standards. Fletcher was ruthless right from the start in using this very public means to expose any underachievement, and in the masters more than in the boys. Fletcher reviewed seven forms during his first month and was evidently unimpressed. Of the Revd P. W. Taylor's remove he wrote: 'The form generally gave me the impression of being depressed & rendered rather hopeless by the difficulty of the work expected of them.'[85] A year later Fletcher wrote the following exasperated comments about another man's form:

One or two general observations ...
1) it was difficult to get boys to listen carefully to the questions asked ...
2) I don't think the boys had realized that it 'paid' to think.
3) ... the boys' minds needed more testing for elementary mis-understandings than the form-master had perhaps realised. It seems worthwhile to record these somewhat obvious observations in view of the warfare which we have to wage against indolence of mind & unwillingness to think, which seems to be the besetting danger of our boys.[86]

The Marlborough culture was very different from Rugby's, and Fletcher was determined from the beginning to change it for the better. Inspiring the sixth by his own teaching was one method, goading and stimulating the staff he had inherited from Bell was another, and recruiting new, young and very able masters was a third. In 1908 Fletcher persuaded A. C. B. Brown, a brilliant classics fellow of St John's College, Oxford, to leave the university and teach at Marlborough. The letters Fletcher wrote to him express his priorities, as well as his wise and practical approach to the schoolmaster's task: 'The absence of athletic qualifications is of no importance, provided that a man is prepared to throw himself with interest & sympathy into the general life of the school. But it is important to get masters who have an intellectual ideal & the power of imparting it to the boys among whom they live as well as those whom they teach.'[87] Three days later Fletcher wrote again to offer Brown a post which included teaching the lowest classical form:

I think you will find the personal interest a great compensation for the elementary character of the subjects, & will perhaps come to regard the intellectual problem of how to get into touch with underdeveloped minds as no less interesting than the study of more advanced work ... As I think you understand, the more you can get into personal relations with the boys out of school the better. When I took a form of small boys at Rugby I found the out-of-school relations with them very pleasant & very help-ful to the actual work ... They will want a lot of discipline in some matters, punctuality, attentiveness etc. In these ways it is best to begin with rigidness & relax (so far as relaxation is desir-able) later. I tried the opposite process myself, & can't recom-mend it.[88]

Brown, along with nearly half of Fletcher's twenty appointments, was still teaching at Marlborough when Louis MacNeice arrived in 1921. The 'parade of masters' in his autobiography exudes all the cruelly penetrating insights of a boy's perception of his teachers:

> A young master comes up fresh from Oxford or Cambridge, full of ideas and charm; after a few years the ideas shrivel away, the charm becomes a convention. In order to do their job well they have to become more or less mechanical. The nicest masters are the eccentrics, but these are eccentric before their time in a way which belongs to the old, have little tricks and crotchets dipped in a petrifying stream, spinsters and proud of it too.
> There were fifty masters at Marlborough, half of whom were insignificant, pleasant enough but incurably trivial, fawning on their seniors, saving up money for a sports car, backbiting each other in the Common Room. Of those who were academically brilliant the majority had stuck at a point. And the great athletes were getting stiff in the bones and short in the wind, still changed into flannels, exposed their thinning hair to the weather, but their souls lingered in ancient *Wisden's Almanacs*, in framed and crested photos of forgotten teams.[89]

Fletcher had to make his first appointment before he arrived. Since he was not ordained the school needed a chaplain and the Revd R. C. Abbott, who had been teaching mathematics at Marlborough since 1892, was given this additional responsibility and the £50 per annum which would otherwise have gone to the Master. He had been a boy and a master under Bell and, after four years as chaplain, was appointed by Bishop Wordsworth to be principal of the clergy training college at Salisbury. He and Fletcher complemented each other well, and while Fletcher supported his work as chaplain, Abbott welcomed Fletcher's regular presence and preaching in chapel.

M. H. Gould was one of MacNeice's eccentrics. He had been a boy at Marlborough under Bradley, returned to teach in 1875 and stayed for thirty-five years. Sorley remembered him fondly, as did Siegfried Sassoon who was in his house and left school early in 1904. Gould nurtured political ambitions (he had been president of the Oxford Union) and 'as a schoolmaster he brought a whiff of the outside world into a somewhat narrow community ... he was in touch with able men outside, who sent their sons to his house, to the advantage of the school.'[90] However, he was too fond of food and drink and the clubs of

St James's, and had problems keeping order in class, making matters worse for himself by playing to the gallery. Fletcher recalls that 'his colleagues were shocked by the studied buffooneries and gross puns by which he enlivened his teaching, and by the shouts of apparently disorderly laughter which came from his classroom'.[91] The effect was more serious in the house where the boys were allowed to do entirely as they pleased.

The Irishman John 'Pat' O'Regan, who had been appointed to teach history in 1894, had been a contemporary of Fletcher at Balliol, and had played hockey with him in both college and university teams. He was an outstanding master at Marlborough; 'an affectionate and enthusiastic character, he proved himself an ingenious form-master of lower boys, a successful teacher of history specialists, and for a while a stimulating and warm-hearted, if eccentric, housemaster. He was essentially out of the ordinary, and it is good for boys to have masters among them who are out of the ordinary.'[92] George Turner recalled the 'splendid teas in his room, where he kept a chameleon fed on flies and a mongoose fed on eggs'.[93] O'Regan read poetry to his pupils and encouraged them to write some themselves, offering a prize of half a crown. Sassoon looked back on him with gratitude and devotion: 'You were the only person at Marlborough who ever asked me to write poetry.'[94] He had Siegfried's first poem framed and hung on his form room wall:

> My life at school is fraught with care,
> Replete with many a sorrow.
> When evening shadows fall I dare
> Not think about to-morrow.

But despite (or rather because of) their friendship at Oxford, relations between O'Regan and Fletcher were strained. 'It was naturally not easy for him to believe that one whom he had known intimately as a callow undergraduate could have developed the qualities required for the Mastership. Nothing could have exceeded the loyalty of his co-operation; but his sensitive Irish conscience made him alternately reproach himself for being jealous of an old friend and hold aloof from me lest he should seem to be presuming on the previous intimacy.'[95]

Sorley too was inspired by O'Regan though it was another master, John Bain, who had the same powerful influence on him that O'Regan had on Sassoon. Bain was known at the school as the 'Marlborough Laureate' and Sorley rated him among the greatest living poets. He too was something of an eccentric: 'oddly informal for the period', as his son put it.[96] Although well qualified to take the classical sixth he preferred to teach a limited modern syllabus to the lowest of the low in the army class. He was critical of public schools in general (though he loved Marlborough) and while good at games, he disapproved of athleticism.

F. A. H. Atkey, G. L. Bickersteth and A. R. Gidney were three of the masters Fletcher appointed. All were first-rate classicists but determined too to share with their pupils their love of English literature. Fletcher had introduced the subject into the syllabus and was anxious to find new masters who could teach it alongside their other disciplines. Atkey started at Marlborough with Sorley in 1908 and became his form-master. Sorley much admired his independent thinking and opinions and they stayed in touch after Sorley left in 1913. Sorley was killed at Loos in 1915 and Atkey on the Somme the following year. Alongside Bain and Atkey, Sorley counted George Bickersteth among the three best masters at Marlborough. He was an enthusiastic member of the new senior and junior literary societies, the latter of which he started mainly for Sorley's benefit. Sorley respected the breadth of his knowledge and his readiness to question received truths. He converted Sorley from Browning to Meredith, arguing that there was a 'lack of *earth*' in Browning, whereas Meredith's poetry was closer to nature.[97] A. R. Gidney founded the senior literary society in 1910. His approach to literature was rigorous, rational and demanding and lacked the popular appeal of Bickersteth and Atkey. For him English literature was a branch of classics and not (as for the others) an exciting escape into a freer and more imaginative world. Betjeman loathed him and maintained a bitter vendetta against him for over fifty years.

Fletcher boasts of a visit from the headmaster of an aristocratic school in Vienna. He stayed for several days and sat in on classes, watched games, and attended chapel. 'But what seemed to impress him most was the social standing of the masters. "These men who came to dinner last night, were they your masters? But they were gentlemen! I could not ask my masters to dinner." The remark was made during a walk, and shortly afterwards we met one of my colleagues riding, who stopped to speak to me. "That man you spoke to, was he one of your masters? What did I tell you? He was a gentleman!"'[98] The Austrian headmaster had noticed an abiding characteristic of English public schoolmasters who 'make an assumption which they greatly value: that although they have chosen to follow a calling which will not make them rich, they talk on equal terms with the parents of the boys they teach – and secretly believe themselves with good cause to be superior to many of them.'[99]

Fletcher was proud and appreciative of his common room and was skilful in balancing a demand for hard work and excellence with sympathy and encouragement. He won the confidence of the many older masters who had been appointed by Farrar or Bell, while at the same time directing and integrating his new and youthful recruits. Fletcher does not seem to have suffered much from a head's easy temptation to be autocratic. He understood that a school can only work well when a headmaster delegates, allowing as much scope and freedom as possible, while insisting that high standards are met and cohesion observed.

> A headmaster must in his time play many parts. In every department of school life, teaching, discipline, organization, he must be the ultimate authority. For everything that happens in the school he is responsible to the parents, the governing body, the general public and his own conscience...
>
> But the greater the responsibility the more the need for delegation of the details of the work. If he wants a particular job doing well he will as a rule *not* do it himself, but find the man best capable of doing it and entrust it to him, while at the same time retaining in his own hands such parts of the school work as may best keep him in touch with the various sides of the life of the school...
>
> At Marlborough I had no boarding-house. I did the main part of the upper sixth classical teaching. I drew up the time-table and decided the curriculum. Correspondence about individual boys I left in ordinary cases to housemasters; finance and domestic administration and the register of entries and admission and distribution of new boys were managed by the bursar and his staff, who would only refer to me when questions of policy or emergencies arose.[100]

When Fletcher started at Marlborough in 1903 he had 'found a community full of patriotism, with a strong belief in itself, a bit stiff in the joints, slow to move and suspicious of change, but with a strong vitality under the surface ready to burst forth, and with as yet unrealized potentialities of intellectual life'.[101] Eight years later much of that vitality and potential had been realised and the school's reputation was riding as high as it had under Bradley. Discipline and what Percival would have called moral tone were strong and there had certainly been no disadvantage in having a lay headmaster; indeed, Fletcher's unpompous and practical sermons had made chapel more popular. Academic standards had been raised, scholarships to Oxford and Cambridge were second to none, and the school was less philistine in its tastes. Parents were grateful to Fletcher, and the masters took pride in playing their part in a school that was evidently succeeding. The council too was satisfied with the risk it had taken in appointing him.

Inevitably, Fletcher's reputation was spreading beyond the confines of Marlborough and in 1909, when James was about to retire, Fletcher was asked to apply to Rugby but he refused. It was a flattering and tempting invitation but Fletcher had left only six years before and he was not confident that he could command enough authority with those who had been his colleagues. Two years later he was approached by the Archbishop of Canterbury, Randall Davidson, who was chairman of the governing body of Charterhouse. Charterhouse was in trouble after thirteen years of weak leadership and Fletcher was the man to revive it:

> The invitation came entirely unsought. The inducement held out was not the attractiveness of the place or the historic distinction of the school, but the difficulty of the task which it presented. The masters, a fine body of keen men, were, I knew, very anxious about the tone and the discipline of the school, and it was notified to me unofficially that they would welcome my appointment. I refused to apply, or to commit myself beforehand to acceptance of the post if it was offered me: but when in spite of this refusal I received a letter from the Archbishop of Canterbury ... inviting me to go there, backed by a strong letter from the vice-chairman urging it, I regarded this as a call and regretfully, but unhesitatingly, accepted.[102]

Though Fletcher was convinced it was right to accept the offer, there is no doubt about the sense of sacrifice involved. In his account of his schooldays, A. R. Pelly records how 'He withstood approaches from Charterhouse and other offers until the Archbishop of Canterbury told him that Charterhouse was in such low water that he must look upon it as his duty to go there. He was very upset and broke down telling us the news, but he felt that he must give way and go.'[103] Fletcher confides:

When the call to Charterhouse came, things were running smoothly at Marlborough. The work of headmastering, so difficult at first, had by the co-operation of boys and masters been made easy, perhaps too easy ... there were no urgent problems calling for solution ... It was the stage at which a man becomes conscious of the temptation, which he must at all costs resist, to rest on his oars and let the boat move along at its own pace without effort on his part ... Is there any happier life than that of a headmaster who sees the ideas he has worked for beginning to bear fruit in his school?[104]

Fletcher's father, then nearly seventy and still involved in Church schools, was staying at the time at Bishopthorpe Palace with Cosmo Lang, then Archbishop of York. He wrote to his son a letter which contains a proud and charming description of the archbishop's table-talk:

At dinner there was some conversation about Charterhouse, and I asked Claude Letham (father of the Charterhouse rackets champion) who was to be the new headmaster. His reply was 'the Master of Marlborough was expected.' I said that I thought not, as I knew he had not applied. Letham had not yet realized that you were my son. Later on I heard the Archbishop talking to his neighbour at table about you, and he afterwards turned round and asked me what I thought of your 'latest achievement' (or some words like that). When I replied, 'What?' he said, 'Oh! evidently you haven't yet heard. I'll tell you privately after dinner.' After dinner he waited in the dining-room and said that the Charterhouse Governors had been putting great pressure on you to accept their headmastership, as the school needed working up, and you were the right person to tackle it – and you had 'reluctantly consented' to accept the offer. He quite understood that you had only done so because someone (I don't know if it was the Archbishop of Canterbury) had told you it was a 'call of duty'. He was very nice and his whole tone was complimentary and considerate to you.[105]

Three months before he died, the Bishop of Salisbury, John Wordsworth, wrote Fletcher a letter that showed how the reluctance he had felt on appointing him to Marlborough was by then forgotten. 'I trust – and this is saying much – that you may do as well there as you have done at Marlboro'. You will be greatly missed by us all and I am

not at all happy at the prospect of having to help to choose your successor.'[106] G. F. Bradby wrote from Rugby: 'Congratulations and condo-
lences! You will have a hell of a time for a bit, and a corresponding
triumph at the end of it, I hope. There must be a great work to be done
there, and undoubtedly you are the man to undertake it. 'More power
to your elbow!' It will be a bad wrench leaving Marlborough, and
worse for Mrs. Fletcher even than for you.'[107] Fletcher's two star senior
prefects, Fisher and Turner, wrote from Oxford. Fisher's letter is typical
in both its sadness and sense of service: 'The blow has fallen. We have
been waiting in dumb suspense up here since the beginning of term ...
The worst part of all was that in our inmost hearts we had an uncomfortable feeling that you ought to go, and therefore would go. Judging
from the accounts of Carthusians up here, they need you, and so I
suppose that Marlborough must regard itself as doing its Christian
duty, in giving what it can ill spare itself to others whose need is greater.
But our hearts are torn.'[108] Almost by return of post Fletcher offered
Fisher a position at Marlborough which he accepted 'without hesita-
tion'[109] but with considerable regret that Fletcher would no longer be
there as Master.

The council placed on record 'their deep regret at losing a Master
who for eight years has presided over the College with brilliant
success',[110] elected him a member, and set about finding his successor.
The terms and conditions were identical to those in 1903 and the inter-
views were again held at the Westminster Palace Hotel. Six candidates
were chosen: a tutor at Christ Church, Oxford and five headmasters,
three of whom were in orders. The story of how the Revd St John Basil
Wynne Willson was selected is remarkable, and indicative of both
Fletcher's role in the choice and, given that Wynne Willson was an
unmarried cleric, of school governors' usual predilection for appointing heads who are decidedly different from their predecessors. Fletcher
recommended Wynne Willson: they had been colleagues at Rugby for
four years before he was appointed Master of Haileybury in 1905.
Here he had raised academic standards and showing a determined
intolerance of poor performance and conditions which pampered. The
council minutes record that the interview was optional: each candidate
was 'offered an opportunity of appearing before the Council at their
meeting if he should wish':[111]

The first five had expressed a desire to do so and were interviewed
by the Council ... Mr. Wynne Willson had not proposed to be

present, but as some members of the Council wished to see him a message was sent asking him to come. After some discussion in the Council an adjournment till the afternoon was proposed to allow time for Mr. Wynne Willson's arrival, but as several members of the Council had other engagements it was decided to proceed at once to a vote. On this being taken it was found that there was a clear majority in favour of Mr. Wynne Willson. The newly elected Master arrived just in time to receive the congratulations from the chairman and other Members of Council.[112]

Wynne Willson's five years at Marlborough were not a success and the old athletocracy soon revived. He was subsequently appointed Dean of Bristol and then Bishop of Bath and Wells. He married the heiress to the Wills tobacco company and was wittily referred to as the Bishop of Bath and Wills. His obituary in *The Times* suggested that his appointment to the episcopate was due perhaps to the fact that only a wealthy man could have afforded to run the bishop's moated palace with its twenty-seven bedrooms!

It is not until a headmaster relinquishes his post that his importance and achievements are fully realised and appreciated. A few years before, Fletcher had been far from popular; now the boy editor of *The Marlburian* was full of praise: 'In eight all too brief years, Mr Fletcher did the work of a century. Anything Marlburian seemed a real pleasure to him: and whether it was in our games or in our work, we know we could always rely on his whole-hearted support and encouragement. Lucky Charterhouse!'[113] The council commissioned George Harcourt to paint a full-length portrait in oils which hangs today with those of other Masters in the Norwood (dining) Hall. It shows Fletcher in benign and cheerful mood but Fletcher disliked it. As a parting gift Fletcher had the sixth form room repanelled in oak, with the inscription *Sextae Marlburiensi Francus Fletcher Magister Discedens Desiderans Multarum Amicitiarum Memor* ('To the Marlborough sixth form (from) Frank Fletcher, the departing Master, in fond memory of many friendships').

It was indeed the sixth whom Fletcher missed and remembered most. Geoffrey Fisher wrote round to all ninety-six of Fletcher's prefects to invite donations for a leaving present. They gave two silver dishes, a drawing-room clock, and a seventeen-volume edition of Robert Browning. 'My dear Fisher,' wrote Fletcher, 'It is to associate my greatest teacher with my dearest pupils to give me a set of Browning in their name.' He goes on to admit that 'we are both wishing and wishing that it was all a dream, and that we cd. wake and find Marlborough was still to be ours. I cannot tell you the gloom that comes over us at times at realizing (as I never did before) what we are cutting outselves loose from … However – except in my worst moments – I still believe that it had to be done, though if the choice came again I don't think I shd. have the strength to make it.'[114]

Turner never forgot 'a week of July in 1911, when about ten of us were there to spend with Mr. and Mrs. Fletcher their last week at Marlborough. Lovely weather and incomparable friendship made it an unforgettable time.'[115] The Fletchers had invited every one of their senior prefects to stay. George Turner and Arthur Jenkins had spent all their entire Marlborough years under Fletcher; Jenkins had just left school with a scholarship to Balliol and Fletcher was especially proud of him. Three years later he joined the Royal Flying Corps and in 1917 was killed while night-flying over Yorkshire. Turner, on the other hand, had what was called a good war: he was promoted to captain, won the MC, was mentioned twice in dispatches and was appointed to the general staff. Leslie Woodroffe, Fletcher's second senior prefect, was teaching classics at Shrewsbury when war broke out. He joined the 8th Rifle Brigade and was a captain by the end of 1914. He too won the MC but in 1916 he died of wounds received at Ypres. His two brothers, Kenneth and Sidney, both Marlburians, had been killed the year before. So many of Fletcher's pupils were to suffer a similar fate. One page taken at random from the *Marlborough College Register* lists seventeen boys who joined the school in September 1909: of these eight sacrificed their lives – 'killed in aerial combat at Beaulencort on the Somme', 'killed in action, Hohenzollern Redoubt', 'killed in action at Hooge, Flanders', 'killed in action on the Somme', 'killed in action near Lens', 'killed in action in Gallipoli' … Nearly a quarter of the boys who entered the school during Fletcher's time as Master died in the war.[i]

In Dorothy's obituary Turner again recalled that treasured week staying at the Master's Lodge nearly fifty years before:

It was a radiant summer, and I look back on that week as an enchanted time, the climax and the end for us and for our friends in the school who were leaving, of companionship in that lovely

[i] 733 Marlburians were killed in the First World War and their names are inscribed in the War Memorial Hall (1925).

setting. It was near the end of an epoch too, for within very few years several of that party and many other Marlburian friends had fallen in the war. But those of us who came through found just the same welcome and joyful friendship in the homes which Lady Fletcher made beautiful at Charterhouse and in her native Devon. No change of circumstance or new attachment affected that at all.

It was, I know, a deep disappointment to her and to Sir Frank that they had no children of their own; but perhaps their parental instinct found some outlet in the affectionate care they had for other people's children. Certainly what many Marlburians and Carthusians have owed them can never be told.[116]

Those of Fletcher's Marlborough pupils who survived were certainly very precious to the Fletchers and though, as Fletcher admitted to Turner, 'it's hard to keep up with everyone, & I'm a lazy correspondent',[117] he stayed in touch as best he could with what he called his 'constantly increasing family',[118] and there was always a welcome for them when they visited. The Fletchers were childless but, like the widowed Mr Chips, they felt as though they had '"thousands of 'em ... and all boys ..."'[119]

6
Charterhouse 1
1911–1918

Frank Fisher, Archbishop Geoffrey Fisher's son, was heard to say that a man's first headmastership is like a love affair and his second like a marriage. Fisher was appointed Warden of St Edward's, Oxford in 1954 and Master of Wellington twelve years later. His achievements at both schools were considerable, but while he found St Edward's an exciting and testing school, it was at Wellington that he settled and made his more mature and measured contribution, and not only to Wellington but to the independent sector as a whole. Much the same can be said of Fletcher at Marlborough and Charterhouse (though he would not have used the same metaphor!). In *After Many Days* he remembers the task he and Dorothy faced at Charterhouse as similar to that at Marlborough – 'but there was this difference among others, that we started our Charterhouse work with eight years' experience behind us, to give confidence both to ourselves and to those who worked with us. The difficulties to be faced were far greater than those we had found at Marlborough; but we were better equipped for tackling them, and the task was made easier by the fact that we came to a school dissatisfied with itself and conscious of the need for improvement.'[1] All but one of the twenty headmasters since the school's foundation had been in orders and so Fletcher had to deal again with the novelty of being a lay headmaster. And at Charterhouse the headmaster was also a housemaster, adding to his workload and burden of responsibility.

As H. A. James had managed to convey something of the spirit of Marlborough to Fletcher when he was a boy at Rossall, so Tancock, his second headmaster, did the same with Charterhouse. He certainly seems to have given Fletcher an idea of the natural beauty of the Surrey site with its foxes and deer and acres of woodland and turf. And James as well, soon after he had left Rossall, wrote to Fletcher from Charterhouse where he was staying with T. E. Page, the brilliant classical scholar and sixth form master. Charterhouse, he wrote, is 'like an Italian valley: Tancock must find Rossall a great contrast.'[2] The buildings, with their combination of Victorian gothic and yellow bargate stone, are imposing and impressive, and were just forty years old when Fletcher arrived. He had also absorbed from Tancock a picture of Charterhouse's rich, colourful and what Fletcher called romantic history. Founded in London in 1611 on the site of what was once a Carthusian priory, Charterhouse had followed its own course and developed a very distinctive character.[a]

The school traces its deepest roots to the Black Death of 1348. Almost beneath its foundations lies a plot of land near Smithfield where tens of thousands of plague victims were buried. When the pestilence abated a Carthusian cloister for twenty-four monks was built close by. Thomas More lodged there as a young man and was profoundly influenced by the order's discipline, devotion and learning which set it apart from the worldly monasteries of the time. But despite the Charterhouse's exemplary condition, the prior was hanged, drawn and quartered in 1535 for joining More in resisting Henry's marriage to Anne Boleyn. Other monks shared the same fate or fled to Bruges. After the dissolution the monastery remained empty and unoccupied until 1545 when it was granted to Sir Edward North who converted the buildings into a Tudor mansion. It was here that Queen Elizabeth first held court and from there she journeyed to her coronation at Westminster Abbey. The house passed to the Duke of Norfolk and became a grand ducal residence. Four years later he was arrested there, found guilty of complicity in the Ridolfi Plot (hatched at the Charterhouse) to put Mary Queen of Scots on the throne, and was executed in the Tower. Norfolk's son, Thomas Howard, the first Earl of Suffolk, held possession at the end of Elizabeth's reign and received James I who was declared king in the great chamber. In order to raise money for the building of Audley End Howard sold the Charterhouse to Thomas Sutton who turned the buildings into a school and almshouse. Sutton paid the enormous sum of £13,000 for what the disapproving Sir Francis Bacon called a building 'as fit for a hospital as a rich embroidered cloak to a beggar'.[3] Daniel Defoe, writing a century later, describes Sutton's foundation as 'the greatest and noblest gift that was ever given for charity by any one man, public or private, in this nation'.[4]

Sutton had made an immense fortune and, like Fletcher's family, much of his money came from coal. He had held the lucrative office of

---

[a] The name Charterhouse is a corruption of Chartreux, high in the French Alps, where the Carthusian order began in 1084.

General of Ordnance in the North and had married Elizabeth Dudley, a wealthy widow. He moved to London where be became a successful merchant and moneylender. Sutton's charitable motives in founding his school and hospital were undoubtedly confused with a craving for respectability and immortality. Mindful too of the bloody and tempestuous times in which he had lived, Sutton determined to appoint the great and good to govern and preserve his foundation. He provided for sixteen governors, persons distinguished by high birth or dignified position: they included the Archbishop of Canterbury and the Lord Chancellor with additional royal governors. Among Prime Ministers, Sir Robert Walpole, the Pitts, Lord Liverpool (who had been there as a boy), the Duke of Wellington, Sir Robert Peel, Gladstone and Disraeli all served as governors.

The hospital was intended to provide for eighty elderly men, and the school for forty poor scholars, or gownboys. The pensioners, or brothers, were to be gentlemen who had fallen on hard times, and the scholars, aged between ten and fifteen, were to be fed, clothed and instructed in the classics, writing and arithmetic at the sole expense of the charity. The governors had the right to nominate both brothers and gownboys, and to appoint the master, the preacher and the schoolmaster. The reputation of the school was soon established and sixty fee-paying pupils, or townboys, were accepted in addition to the forty scholars. The old men and the boys were housed together in frugal conditions, though in the most august of settings. 'In after years, whether in this tight little island or thousands of miles away, the Charterhouse boy could call up to remembrance the spacious courts, the quaint quadrangles, the oaken halls, the tapestried chambers, the trim little gardens, the echoing cloisters, the ghostly staircases, the sparsely verdured greens, and the straggling plane trees, which had been such a source of delight to him in his youth.'[5]

The fourth schoolmaster (or headmaster) is recalled today in Brooke Hall, the name of the building which houses the masters' common rooms. Robert Brooke was educated at Charterhouse and served as usher, the schoolmaster's assistant, until he took charge in 1628. He was ejected from office in 1643 because of his strong royalist sympathies and after his death his chambers in the cloisters were given over to the masters. Among Brooke's pupils were the metaphysical poets Richard Crashaw and Richard Lovelace. They were the first of a distinguished line of literary Carthusians: Joseph Addison and Sir Richard Steele, joint founders of *The Spectator*; William Thackeray, whose novel *The Newcomes* is set in the Charterhouse; Francis Palgrave, editor of *The Golden Treasury;* Max Beerbohm, Osbert Lancaster and Robert Graves. John Wesley, the preacher; Charles Manners Sutton, Archbishop of Canterbury; Henry Liddell, the Greek lexicographer and father of 'Alice'; Viscount Alverstone, the Lord Chief Justice – these had all been pupils at the London school. Robert Baden-Powell was one of the boys who started in London and migrated to Surrey in 1872.

Charterhouse's reputation and influence were at their highest during the last decade of the eighteenth century and the first half of the nineteenth, thanks to three impressive headmasters, Matthew Raine, John Russell and Augustus Saunders. When in 1820 the Duke of Wellington heard that his adoring friend Lady Shelley intended to send her son to Eton, he wrote to her to protest: 'I am astonished that you don't send your son to the Charterhouse, which I believe is the best school of them all.'[6] By then the numbers had trebled and at a time when Westminster's roll was fast declining.

Raine was a renowned classical scholar as well as a fellow of the Royal Society with a keen enthusiasm for science. He was highly regarded as a headmaster, 'dignified in manner and eloquent in the pulpit'.[7] He reformed the school, leaving it more organised and better equipped (with a separate bed for every boarder!). On his death the school register described how 'he ruled by love more than by fear and has left behind him the blessings of all who knew him, the deepest feeling of regret in all his scholars and a bright example to his successors.'[8] The first of these was his pupil, John Russell, who followed him in 1811 at the age of twenty-five, full of drive and opinions. He suggested the creation of four new scholarships, open to competition rather than patronage, but this was promptly rejected by the governors. Next he tried to replace floggings with fines but the boys thought this 'ungentle-manly' and rioted until Russell backed down. One reform which brought success and excitement at first but then dismal failure was his introduction of the Madras system of teaching. Dr Bell, chaplain to an orphanage in India, had had to train boys to instruct each other, and on returning to England he published a book about his method. Charterhouse was the only school of its kind to try the experiment and there seemed much to commend it: when it started in 1817 there were 450 boys but only 5 masters. The 350 boys of the under school were taught crammed together in one big schoolroom while the 100 in the sixth form were taught separately and single-handedly by Russell. The Madras scheme allowed him to turn praeposters into monitors, or senior boys chosen to keep order into those trained to instruct, albeit in an entirely prescribed and mechanical manner. But the monitors had neither authority nor knowledge to teach properly, the system was soon discredited, and numbers fell.

Russell resigned in 1832 and was succeeded by another Carthusian, Dr Augustus Saunders. He had tutored Gladstone at Christ Church and returned to Charterhouse to restore a school where there were now fewer than 140 pupils. He immediately discarded what remained of Russell's methods but revived his idea of competitive examination for some of the scholarships. With support from Sir Robert Peel, Saunders eventually won over those reluctant governors who resented their loss of patronage. Numbers increased again and Saunders accommodated fee-paying boarders in his house, a custom which continued under every headmaster in London and Godalming until Fletcher moved out to a private house in 1924. The school's roll peaked in the mid-1840s before Charterhouse began to lose out to new schools like Marlborough and Cheltenham, with their healthy country sites and spacious grounds. By comparison Charterhouse was cramped and confined, and surrounded by London's filth, vice and squalor.[b] It was beginning to seem that Sutton's munificent foundation had run its course.

It is rare for a school to have two enterprising headmasters in succession and three, as at Marlborough with Cotton, Bradley and Farrar, and Charterhouse with Raine, Russell and Saunders, is most unusual. Edward Elder and Richard Elwyn who followed Saunders were poor appointments and stayed only five years each. To be fair, they came to Charterhouse when the school's fortunes were low and circumstances were against them. The ensuing crisis was precipitated by the Clarendon Commission,[c] set up by Palmerston in 1861 to inspect the nine 'great' schools – Charterhouse, Eton, Harrow, Merchant Taylors', Rugby, St Paul's, Shrewsbury, Westminster and Winchester. The commission published an enlightened and searching report in 1864. It made some general recommendations but mostly applied itself to detailed improvements for each of the schools. The most important and radical recommendations for Charterhouse were that all scholarships should be open to competition and that the school should separate from the hospital and be removed from London. The governors were

[b] There were said to be 38 gin palaces, 37 stores which specialised in stolen goods and 50 pawn shops in the area.
[c] The commission took its name from the chairman, the diplomat George Villiers, the 4th Earl of Clarendon.

divided on both suggestions, and vehemently so on migrating from London. The matter was debated in parliament and *The Times* joined the lists in support of the move.

Providentially for Charterhouse, the governors appointed the Revd Dr William Haig Brown in 1863, the most illustrious and indomitable of all Headmasters of Charterhouse, before and since. He was very much in the Victorian headmasterly mould (complete with bushy beard, cassock, cap and gown) and deserves his place among the ranks of Arnold and Temple, Bradley and Benson. He is the first and, apart from Fletcher, the only headmaster to have imported the Arnold spirit to Charterhouse (he had taught for a while at Harrow under Arnold's pupil, Dr Vaughan, who had impressed him greatly). 'Haig Brown resembled those "very superior men", as the Victorian headmasters have been called. He had all the energy and confidence which distinguished the Victorians and gave the Edwardians such a feeling of inferiority, well displayed in Lytton Strachey's *Eminent Victorians*.'[9]

Haig Brown had been a boy at Christ's Hospital and had read mathematics and classics at Pembroke College, Cambridge where he became a fellow. After teaching at Harrow he was appointed Headmaster of the Kensington Proprietary School where Matthew Wilkinson, Marlborough's first Master, had been headmaster fifteen years before. With the enthusiastic support of his wife, the much loved Annie Marion (who bore him seven daughters and five sons), Haig Brown served as headmaster for thirty-five years and then for a further ten as master of the hospital where he died in office aged eighty-four. His most significant and enduring achievement was the removal of the school from London to Surrey. He had seen the necessity from the start and, sensing growing opposition to the governors' conservatism, he wrote to 400 Old Carthusians, to ask their opinion. Their reply was overwhelmingly in favour and Haig Brown persuaded the governing body to agree to the move. In 1866 Philip Hardwick,[d] the hospital's architect, advised that the sale of part of the London site would pay for the new school and in May the final decision was made.[e]

Haig Brown drew Hardwick's attention to a seventy-acre site on

[d] Hardwick also designed the entrance to Euston Station, the front of St Bartholomew's Hospital and the hall and library of Lincoln's Inn.
[e] Merchant Taylors' School, which had an even more cramped site near Cannon Street station, paid a modest £90,000 for the buildings and moved there in 1872. Today the London Charterhouse is inhabited only by the pensioners.

a hill above Godalming: it was near a station, largely self-contained and very beautiful. Beneath it lay a quarry of bargate stone with which the new school could be constructed. Hardwick was commissioned to plan the new buildings which were to duplicate those of the London school but in an entirely different style. His distinctive red and grey striped roofs, pointed towers, spires and pinnacles, courts and cloisters make a bold statement of the pride and confidence which Haig Brown had in this new venture. His confidence was soon repaid. In June 1872, 117 boys moved with him from the old school and 37 joined them as new boys: 18 months later the numbers had risen to nearly 300 and to 500 by 1876. Haig Brown also managed to convince the governors to free all scholarships from patronage, so improving the quality of the pupils while giving the headmaster complete and proper control over their selection. He heeded too the commission's advice that the curriculum should be expanded and, drawing on his experience at Harrow, he extended the provision for science. Haig Brown's twenty-six years as headmaster in Godalming laid permanent foundations for the future. Buildings expanded and increased; games pitches were created and the school's sporting prowess established (in 1881 the Old Carthusians won the FA Cup); art, music and theatricals flourished and academic success was considerable. Haig Brown is Charterhouse's second founder and, like Thomas Sutton, is commemorated in Godalming by a statue and small chapel where Haig Brown and his wife are buried.

1911, the year of George V's coronation and the 300th anniversary of the school's foundation, was an opportune time for Fletcher to start. The summer quarter (term) had witnessed splendid tercentenary celebrations, culminating on a very hot Old Carthusian Day in July when a service in chapel was followed after lunch by cricket, a concert given by the band of the King's Royal Rifle Corps, a production outdoors of *Love's Labour's Lost*, and the first performance of *The Masque of Charterhouse*, written and composed especially for the occasion.[f] The masque consisted of several scenes featuring incidents from the school's history, including the eviction of the monks, the founding of Sutton's school and hospital, John Wesley revisiting on his eightieth birthday,

---

[f] Masques originated in entertainment for the court and included lavish pageantry, music, songs and dance. The Charterhouse Masque was composed by Edward Rendall, cousin of the headmaster who had appointed him director of music. Another cousin, Monty, was appointed Headmaster of Winchester in 1911.

Thackeray's vision of Colonel Newcome (played by General Baden-Powell: all the main actors were Old Carthusians), and finally the migration to Godalming thirty-nine years before. The evening finished with the singing of the *Carmen Carthusianum* and a fireworks display. It all made for a proud climax to Dr Gerald Rendall's thirteen years as headmaster and in some respects the school he was bequeathing to Fletcher was still in the good order Haig Brown had established. In Rendall's final report to the governors he described an overfull school whose academic distinctions were at an average level, with eight scholarships at Cambridge, three at Oxford and four medical scholarships at London hospitals.

Although Haig Brown was a first-class mathematician and 'had been a brilliant classic, and knew all the great Latin and Greek authors thoroughly',[10] he was never an inspiring teacher, and in any case he had had to devote much of his prodigious energy to finance and administration. So, when it came to appointing his successor, the governors had looked for a scholar to strengthen the academic side and invited Dr Rendall to apply. He was born in 1851 and was a boy in his father's boarding house at Harrow.[g] He won a scholarship in classics at Trinity, Cambridge and spent the next thirty years in universities, first as a fellow of Trinity and then as Gladstone Professor of Greek and Principal of University College in Liverpool. His obituary in *The Times* described a man of 'high character, spiritual earnestness, great industry, and wide scholarship'.[11]

Rendall was very different from Haig Brown: tall and ascetic-looking where Haig Brown was short, plump and hirsute; remote and cerebral where Haig Brown had been realistic and practical; and ignorant of and ill-at-ease with boys where Haig Brown knew and cared deeply about his pupils. Adverse comparisons with any new headmaster would have been inevitable after Haig Brown's long and prosperous reign but Rendall's character and style made these invidious. The masters had little respect for him and were caustic in their criticisms, while the boys interpreted his gentleness as weakness and his aloofness as indifference.

After a very brief acquaintance with Dr. Haig Brown, I finished

---

[g] There are parallels between Rendall and his headmaster at Harrow, Montague Butler, who succeeded C. J. Vaughan in 1860. Butler's father had been Headmaster of Harrow and Rendall's a housemaster. Butler like Rendall had been head of school and had won a classics scholarship to Trinity, followed by a fellowship. Butler returned to Trinity in 1886 as Master.

my school career, and was Head of School under Dr. Rendall. I should think that there could not be a greater contrast between any two scholars than between these two Headmasters. If Dr. Haig Brown resembled Plato by his broad geniality, Dr. Rendall was a Stoic by his impassive gravity ... In his study there was over his mantelpiece a phrase quoted from his favourite author, Marcus Aurelius, '*zesen hos en orei*' (live as on a mountain). That might be a sound maxim for an esoteric philosopher, but a head-master must come down to earth, and put himself on a level with his callow pupils. I should be inclined to doubt whether he had ever taught in a junior Form in any school before being appointed to a Headmastership.[12]

This is an accurate and perceptive account: the author, the Revd Dr Leonard Patterson, had spent seven years at Charterhouse, two under Haig Brown and five under Rendall. Certainly, Rendall had never taught in a school and Stoicism was the philosophy he espoused. He spent his leisure hours translating the *Meditations* of Aurelius, the Roman emperor and Stoic philosopher, and the motto he had inscribed over the fireplace is still to be seen. Rendall's life on a mountain, a life of scholarship and inner calm, rooted in a sublime indifference to the ups and downs of life and the cruelties and malice of others, was an ideal to strive for, and indeed one he achieved with admirable self-discipline and determination. But, as Patterson observes, these qualities do not make for a good headmaster and the school suffered as a result. Rendall was too trusting of the boys, taking virtue, reasonableness and goodness for granted, where vice, selfishness and cruelty were just as likely. A contemporary of Patterson who had been in Rendall's house described how 'Haig Brown's successor, Dr Rendall, a don, had noble qualities as a scholar, a writer and a gentleman, but he knew nothing, and never at Charterhouse learnt anything about boys'.[13]

The best known account of Rendall's Charterhouse is in Robert Graves's autobiography, *Goodbye to All That*, published in 1929. Graves seems to have detested Charterhouse and he begged his parents to remove him. He wrote to his younger brother just as he was leaving at last in 1914: 'I would like to save you from Charterhouse which though better than most of the Public Schools is one of the vilest places on God's Earth.'[14] Unfortunately, Graves had every disadvantage: he was a clever and industrious scholar, he was not very good at games, his clothes 'were ready-made and not of the best-quality cloth that all the other boys wore',[15] he was prudish and puritanical and, worst of all, his full name was Robert von Ranke Graves, which, to his contemporaries, 'meant military menace, Prussianism, useless philosophy, tedious scholarship, loving music and sabre-rattling'.[16] The fact that these were all seen as handicaps which singled him out for persecution says much about the kind of school Graves had joined and he is graphic and detailed in his descriptions of the unhappiness and indignities he suffered.

Two particular aspects of Charterhouse are emphasised by Graves and, even allowing for his characteristic exaggeration, they depict what can occur in any boys' boarding school where leadership is weak or misguided. First, homosexuality seems to have been an integral part of a culture where romantic attachments to younger boys were accepted and even idealised, and where vicious, predatory sex was not uncommon:

> G. H. Rendall, the then Headmaster of Charterhouse, is reported to have innocently said at a Headmasters' Conference: 'My boys are amorous, but seldom erotic.' Few cases of eroticism, indeed, came to his notice; I remember no more than five or six big rows during my time at Charterhouse, and expulsions were rare. The housemasters knew little about what went on in their houses, their living quarters being removed from the boys'. Yet I agree with Rendall's distinction between 'amorousness' (by which he meant a sentimental falling in love with younger boys) and eroticism, or adolescent lust. The intimacy that frequently took place was very seldom between an elder boy and the object of his affection – that would have spoiled the romantic illusion – but almost always between boys of the same age who were not in love and used each other as convenient sex-instruments. So the atmosphere was always heavy with romance of a conventional early-Victorian type, complicated by cynicism and foulness.[17]

Second, Graves describes the same dominance of sport over learning, and with it the same athletocracy, brutality and philistinism that Fletcher had been confronting at Marlborough. School-work was despised and the scholars were mocked and bullied. 'Unless good at games, and able to pretend that they hated work even more than the non-scholars ... they always had a bad time.'[18] The 'bloods' (members of the football and cricket teams) ruled the school and took precedence over the monitors. 'The bloods were the ruling caste at Charterhouse;

the eleventh man in the football eleven, though he might be a member of the under-fourth form, enjoyed far more prestige than the most brilliant scholar in the sixth.'[19]

> Oh, we are the bloods of the place,
>   We shine with superior grace
> At the goal or the wicket, at footer or cricket,
>   And nothing our pride can efface.
> The worms of the Sixth we despise ...
>   We count them as dirt in our eyes.[20]

The bloods were permitted to dress distinctively and to walk about the school arm-in-arm. Graves narrates an incident when they returned to school after an away match, full of beer, and burst into a meeting of the debating society, cheering, cat-calling and slamming books on the library table. Three sixth form members of the society's committee wrote a contemptuous letter of complaint to *The Carthusian*, followed the next Sunday by 'the bravest deed ever done at Charterhouse. Chapel began at eleven in the morning ... At two minutes to eleven the bloods used to stalk up ... On this Sunday, then, when the bloods had entered with their usual swaggering assurance, an extraordinary thing happened. The three sixth-formers slowly walked up the aisle, magnificent in light-grey flannel trousers, slit jackets, butterfly collars, and each wore a pink carnation in his lapel. Astonished and horrified by this spectacle, everyone turned to gaze at the Captain of the First eleven; he had gone white.'[21] This turned out to be one of those moments when an example of courage or conviction changes things, at least for a time. The school which had both admired the bloods and envied their privileges but suffered too under their despotism, now began to regard their vanity and distinction as foolish, and 'the prestige of the bloods declined.'[22]

Fletcher was generous and discreet in his estimate of Rendall but he was firmly of the view that, though a good and well-meaning man, he had harmed the school. Fletcher's was a very different character and he was a very different headmaster; it is clear why the Archbishop of Canterbury had invited him to Charterhouse. In a sermon preached soon after the war, Fletcher remarked (and he must surely have had Rendall's maxim in mind) that 'the hard work of the world, by which alone men's evils are cured, cannot be done if we remain on the heights'.[23] Roger Eckersley remembered Fletcher's first sermon in chapel, and how he 'turned a cold, appraising eye on us ... For once, the concentrated Carthusian stare had met more than its match.'[24] His text embodied his manifesto: 'For Zion's sake will I not hold my peace, and for Jerusulem's sake I will not rest, until the righteousness thereof go forth as brightness, and the salvation thereof as a lamp that burneth.' If the sermon was soon forgotten, Fletcher's layman's dress made a lasting impression on the boys: in their eyes it invested Fletcher with greater authority than if he had been another ordained headmaster.

It was obvious that before Fletcher could achieve anything in the school he would have to enforce order and discipline. The same had been true at Marlborough and his reputation preceded him. 'The school was supposed – by us who were boys at the time – to be in a bad way: discipline lax and so on. The Governing body had specially selected a martinet: things would be radically altered, and we were not to be allowed to go on as we had.'[25]

> I was surprised to learn that school rumours at Charterhouse credited me with having in my first two years at Marlborough expelled forty boys. The rumour was, of course, as Mark Twain telegraphed about the report of his death, 'a gross exaggeration'. But the belief, though absurd, was perhaps useful: it served as a warning to evil-doers. In spite of some modern theories, I have no doubt that the fear of the headmaster has a salutary effect in a big school. It may coincide with great personal respect and even affection: but it is good for boys to feel that if necessary strong measures will be unhesitatingly taken.[26]

In his address at Fletcher's memorial service, Archbishop Fisher described him as 'no respecter of persons or of public opinion or of popular favour. He had a measuring rod of his own by which to form his judgements: and having formed them (carefully, as we came to know, and not always easily), he acted upon them with a quiet inflexibility.'[27]

Fletcher was wary of intervening without careful consideration: 'he did nothing until it had to be done: it simmered long and peacefully in his mind, and when the time came he was ready.'[28] There were one or two superficial adjustments to be made immediately though, and within the first two months he did away with the wearing of house caps, restricted permission to visit Godalming ('so often the cause of a wasted afternoon')[29] and made improvements to the conduct of chapel services. Much more difficult to tackle was what Fletcher calls 'the general lowering of tone that lax discipline brings', and which he describes as 'a far graver mischief which it takes far longer to remedy'.[30] A number of boys had to be expelled, largely *pour encourager les autres*. Though never afraid to take such drastic action, Fletcher was reluctant to do so, especially as the years went by and the school improved. 'Expulsion', he wrote, 'is only to be employed as a last resource, when either in the interest of the school or for his own sake it is expedient that a boy should leave. It is a remedial and precautionary, not a vindictive penalty.'[31]

Rugby had taught Fletcher the importance of prefects in fostering the right atmosphere in a school, and in his second year he adjusted the monitorial system which he had found working tolerably well in the houses but not in the school. When he arrived the school monitors consisted of only the top six boys in the sixth form. Their authority was nominal and their prestige limited to the right to wear the same style of collar as the bloods (a privilege secured after the protest Graves describes). In a paper circulated to the housemasters Fletcher emphasised that 'it is most desirable for good government that there should be recognised boy authorities for the whole School and not merely for each House.'[32] As a result, a large body of twenty to thirty boys was selected from the sixth and charged with the same responsibility for the school as house monitors had for their houses. The new system worked and remained intact throughout Fletcher's time. To begin with, though, its efficiency was impeded by the enduring power of the bloods, and Fletcher was faced with similar problems to those he had tried to address at Marlborough. Again he worked hard to boost the confidence of the scholars, not least this time by reducing the prestige and standing of their rivals, the athletes. In the long run this helped to produce a culture in which the more scholarly boys could flourish.

> The athletic 'bloods' – a term which I dislike but cannot avoid – were too much in evidence. They were allowed and encouraged by custom to take liberties denied to other boys ... The intellectual boys had come to suffer from what we should call to-day an inferiority complex, with results detrimental to their normal and wholesome development ...
>
> The result was bad for the athletes, who were tempted by the system to be arrogant, and did not always resist the temptation. It was bad for the intellectual boys, who either accepted their position of inferiority or asserted themselves by eccentricities and ill-timed violation of recognized conventions. This tendency came to

a head in the generation immediately before the war. The sixth at that time contained several clever boys ... But they were a warped generation, whose outlook on life was distorted by their experiences during their first two years at school. These had left some of the best of them morbid or cynical and turned others into intellectual rebels, with an exaggerated idea of their own intelligence and a prejudice against a society which seemed to have given them inadequate recognition ... I was working to make intelligence and culture an object of respect and admiration, trying to develop a healthy public opinion, for which the things of the mind should have their due importance. By their behaviour they were bringing ridicule on what I was trying to make respected ... It was no part of my purpose to replace the arrogance of an athletocracy by the conceit of an intelligentsia ...[33]

Fletcher was especially stern when it came to the obscenities Graves describes and here he spared neither the rod nor his power to expel. On the other hand, while he never suffered from Rendall's naivety, he was quite capable of recognising and allowing a relationship between boys in different years if he regarded it as innocent and positive. Graves had fallen in love with a boy three years younger and he insisted that the relationship was entirely platonic. 'I puzzled [Fletcher]', he wrote, 'by the frankness with which I confessed my love for Dick ... I refused to be ashamed, and heard afterwards that he had described this as one of the rare friendships between boys of unequal ages which, he felt, was essentially moral.'[34] Any behaviour though that Fletcher deemed indecent, brutal or offensive, however puerile, was punished severely: 'I was birched (age 16) by Frank Fletcher for obscene behaviour. The papers were full of pictures of massive bulls at the annual Agricultural Show in London. I put two tennis balls in a sponge-bag and hung it on my pyjama trouser cord & offered to 'serve' anyone for £1.'[35] Fletcher was never able (and never tried) to banish all homosexual activity from such an enclosed all-male community but he withdrew the licence, not to say encouragement, that had been there in Rendall's time. In balancing deterrence and disapproval of bad behaviour with praise and reward for good, Fletcher restored the school's moral sense and created the right kind of atmosphere where wrongdoing became an aberration not a norm.

Fletcher won Graves's immediate respect as a headmaster who would 'evidently keep the School in good order'.[36] Like most boys who have suffered under a lax regime, Graves welcomed the new discipline, and the freedom and protection it afforded him. Despite the scornful tone of much of what Graves writes about Charterhouse in *Goodbye to All That*, his life at school had begun to improve during the summer quarter before Fletcher arrived. He had a poem published in *The Carthusian*, he was invited to join the poetry society and he became friends with Raymond Rodakowski[h] who encouraged him to take up boxing. In Fletcher's first term he joined the debating society, distinguished himself at rugby and served with enthusiasm in the officers' training corps. In September 1912, at the start of his fourth year, Graves was promoted to the classical sixth and was taught by Fletcher throughout his final two years.

A more profound influence on Graves than Fletcher was the mountaineer George Mallory, whom Rendall had appointed in 1910 and who famously disappeared on Everest fourteen years later. 'The most important thing that happened in my last two years, apart from my attachment to Dick, was that I got to know George Mallory: a twenty-six or twenty-seven-year-old master, not long up from Cambridge and so youthful-looking as to be often mistaken for a member of the school. From the first, he treated me as an equal, and I used to spend my spare time reading in his room, or going for walks with him in the country.'[37] Mallory had been a scholar at Winchester where he combined cleverness with sporting prowess and discovered the thrill of climbing in the Alps. After Winchester Mallory went up to Magdalene College, Cambridge to read history. He was a charming and strikingly handsome young man who caught the attention of men as much as women: for his tutor, Arthur Benson,[i] it was love at first sight. Mallory's Cambridge friends, Rupert Brooke, James Strachey (with whom he had a brief affair) and Maynard Keynes introduced him to other luminaries of the largely bisexual Bloomsbury set: James's elder brother Lytton, Leonard Woolf, Virginia Stephen, E. M. Forster and the Stracheys' cousin, Duncan Grant. The character George in Forster's novel *A Room with a View* was based on Mallory and he was painted and photographed in the

[h] Rodakowski was the same age as Graves but started at Charterhouse a year before; like Graves he joined the army on leaving school in 1914. He was killed in action at Passchendaele in 1917.

[i] Arthur Benson was the son and biographer of Edward White Benson, Archbishop of Canterbury (1883–96) and brother of the novelist, E. F. Benson. He taught at Eton before his appointment as a history fellow at Magdalene in 1904. He was Master of Magdalene, 1915–25.

nude by Grant. Virginia Woolf described him as 'a divine undergraduate with a head like a Greek God – but alas his teeth were bad'.[38]

Mallory was ill-at-ease as a schoolmaster, finding the requirements of examinations limiting and the boys difficult to teach and control. He was modern in outlook and (like Fletcher when he started) wanted to befriend his pupils, and to teach through mutual trust and respect. Many of the masters disapproved and many of the boys took advantage but to Graves Mallory was exciting and liberating, 'the only friend to a succession of Carthusian Ugly Ducklings who but for him would have gone under altogether. I'd have burned off my hand for him ...'[39]

Fletcher held Mallory in high regard. They were fellow members of the Alpine Club and Fletcher was grateful for his inspirational teaching of English literature, and for the interest he took in his pupils and the encouragement he gave them to read and discuss. Fletcher's approval was not reciprocated though and Mallory took a strong personal dislike to him. He had been more at home under Rendall's easy-going rule and he saw Fletcher's new discipline as a return to the Victorian age, not as an essential prerequisite for a kinder and freer school. In fact Fletcher and Mallory had more in common than Mallory realised, and his own longing for trust and friendship between boys and masters, of 'aestheticism without softness, honesty without priggishness, sportsmanship without heartiness'[40] were very close to Fletcher's own ideals. But Fletcher's banning of the poetry society towards the end of his first year as headmaster was an action Mallory never understood or forgave, and it blinded him to Fletcher's qualities and good intentions.

Graves had taken immense pride and pleasure in his membership of the society. He describes it as 'a most anomalous organization for Charterhouse',[41] consisting of just seven members of various ages, with poetry readings held once a month at a master's house. The society fell victim to Rendall's legacy when the love poems of two senior members were published in *The Carthusian*. Both poems, signed with pseudonyms, were acrostics which linked the names of bloods to younger boys.

It was a foolish act of aggression in the feud between sixth form and the bloods. But nothing much would have come of it, had not another of the sixth-form members of the Poetry Society been idealistically in love with one of the smaller boys whose name appeared in the acrostics. In rage and jealousy he went to the headmaster ... and called his attention to the acrostic ...

The headmaster took a very serious view of the matter. The two poets lost their monitorial privileges; the editor of *The Carthusian* ... lost his editorship and his position as Head of School ... The Poetry Society was ignominiously dissolved by the headmaster's orders.[42]

Fletcher was actually as sorry as Mallory to see the end of the society but he was convinced that the nature of the scandal left him no choice.

In his memoirs Fletcher describes the three years before the war as full of 'difficulties and anxieties and disappointments'.[43] The stresses, strains and relentless workload began to affect his health. *The Carthusian* of February 1914 (when Robert Graves was assistant editor) reported that 'the Headmaster has most unfortunately been the victim of a slight attack of pneumonia. Consequently he will be unable to perform his duties as Headmaster for some weeks. This is a great calamity for the School. Charterhouse without Mr. Fletcher seems inconceivable. It is the business of all of us to see that things go on in his absence as he would have wished them to do if he were present.'[44] Fletcher was so weak that he was unable even to answer letters. This was to be the first of several disabling attacks of pneumonia during the next ten years. In September 1916, for instance, he was unable to return to school from a summer holiday in Devon. A chill turned to pneumonia again, he did not come back until December, and was not able to take up teaching and preaching until the following summer.

News of the assassination of the Austrian archduke Franz Ferdinand on 28 June 1914 was reported extensively in British newspapers the following day. The seriousness of what had happened and its potential consequences were soon realised, though no one guessed just how quickly another Balkan crisis was to lead to war. Charterhouse broke up for the summer holiday exactly a month after the assassination and on the same day that Austria-Hungary declared war on Serbia. The boys' first week at home was full of questions and arguments as the European powers dusted down their treaties, dug out their war plans and rehearsed their grievances. It was all fascinating to observe from the sidelines in Britain until Germany's brutal invasion of neutral Belgium on 4 August transformed British opinion, and convinced her people that it was now their moral duty to fight. The next day *The Times* published a call to arms to all unmarried men between the ages of eighteen and thirty and the appeal was repeated every day until the 11th. Robert Graves was one of thousands of boys who had just left school who pleaded with their parents to be allowed to enlist in what seemed to them a great (and short) adventure.

The attack on Belgium had certainly persuaded Fletcher that war was justified and unavoidable. Writing two years before the outbreak of the Second World War he suggested that

> some of the younger men of to-day, rightly convinced of the futility of war, appear to think that England in 1914 might have avoided it. They are influenced unconsciously by the subtle German propaganda, and accept too easily the suggestion that all countries were equally responsible at that time for the outbreak of the conflict. Most particularly they fail to realize the importance of the invasion of Belgium and the genuineness of the regret with which a large section, perhaps the majority, of the English people saw themselves forced by that event into a war which they would have given anything to avoid.[45]

In fact throughout August, as millions of men were mobilised, there was much enthusiasm and the younger generation rather rejoiced at the prospect of playing their part. Looking back on that summer Fletcher remembered feeling only gloom and foreboding; it is likely though that the ordeal of the next four and a half years had erased memories of the idealism and excitement he was bound to have shared with his pupils:

> Let no-one suppose that we who accepted the war desired it ... Unquestionably at the beginning of the Great War, if there were any in England who welcomed it, it was the younger and not the older among us. We who were older felt that the solid ground was giving way beneath our feet and the heavens falling. The younger, who could play their full manly part in the fight, might regard it more lightheartedly as a great adventure and noble opportunity ... But we could not feel like that either at the beginning, when we looked forward bewildered and anxious to an unforeseeable future, or, still less, later, when we watched our boys going out one after another to fight our battles.[46]

Of the younger masters at Charterhouse George Mallory was keenest to enlist. Most of his friends, including Rupert Brooke, joined up in September, and even the pacifist Duncan Grant was looking for a way to help. By the end of November Mallory was finding it 'increasingly impossible to remain a comfortable schoolmaster'[47] and he badgered Fletcher to grant him leave. Fletcher refused, saying first that he was needed at

Charterhouse, and second that in any case the government's position on the recruitment of schoolmasters was still undecided. Fletcher had been appointed chairman of the Headmasters' Conference in 1913 and it was now his responsibility to seek official guidance on this and other military matters. Early in August 1914 Lord Kitchener, the Secretary of State for War, had summoned Fletcher to Whitehall. While most people assumed that hostilities would be over by Christmas, Kitchener had warned that war would last three or four years and that Britain would need to raise an army of millions, and he wanted to talk to Fletcher about the contribution the public schools could make. When Fletcher arrived at the War Office he found that the king had sent for Kitchener and he had to see the under-secretary instead. After a long conversation Fletcher returned to Charterhouse to draw up a statement of the apparent wishes of the War Office which he circulated to other headmasters. Regrettably (and awkwardly for Fletcher) the War Office failed to endorse and implement most of its decisions. In the same post a few weeks later, for example, Fletcher received both a letter of confirmation that the minimum age for commission was eighteen and commission papers duly signed for a boy of just seventeen. As far as schoolmasters were concerned the War Office discouraged indiscriminate enlistment, 'arguing very reasonably that if the educated youth of one generation were to be lost to the country it was the more important that those who were growing up in their place should not be deprived of their education.'[48] The correspondence on this matter is important enough to quote in full. Fletcher wrote first on 4 December to the Prime Minister, Herbert Asquith:

Dear Sir,
    I write as Chairman of the Headmasters' Conference on behalf of all the Public Schools and as Headmaster of Charterhouse on behalf of my own Assistant Masters. I am asked to obtain from you, if possible, the views and wishes of the Government as to the duty of public school masters in regard to Military Service.
    So far every Public School has a few masters absent on active service, their places being filled by substitutes. There are still in each school a number of men qualified physically and by education to undertake military service, some of them with previous military training, most without. There must be not less than 500 such men in the 115 schools of our Conference; and they are asking anxiously for directions as to what they should do.
    They cannot leave their present work without impairing to a

greater or less degree the work of the schools which they serve; but if the need for officers and soldiers outweighs the need of the schools of the country, we are ready to spare them, and they are ready, and more than ready, to go.

Are they wanted? If so, is it possible to lay down any guiding principle, *e.g.* by distinguishing between trained and untrained men, married and unmarried, younger and older? So far the only guidance we have received has been with regard to masters serving as officers in the school O.T.C., whom the War Office has instructed not to seek active service unless they can be spared from the O.T.C. work.

It may facilitate an answer if I venture to suggest various forms which the demand might take. The Government might ask:

1. For *all* masters of military age.

2. For *those only who can be spared without seriously impairing the work of the school.* (This would throw the responsibility on Headmasters.)

3. *For a certain definite percentage,* say 10 per cent. (or more) of each staff.

4. For all under the age of 30.

I am sure that a definite lead from you as representing the Government would be warmly welcomed and loyally followed. No one who is not in a position to take a wide view of the situation, realizing both the needs of our education and the military urgency, can give us adequate advice. This must be my excuse for writing direct to you.

Yours faithfully,
FRANK FLETCHER[49]

Five days later Fletcher received this reply from Lord Kitchener:

Dear Mr. Fletcher,

The Prime Minister has submitted to me your letter of the 4th instant, in which you ask his advice as to the part which Assistant Masters should play during the present military emergency.

I have had it carefully examined, and it seems to me that the second demand which you have mentioned represents the best course to adopt – only that I would word it – 'for those, and those only, who can be spared without impairing the work of these schools and the training of the O.T.C.,' for at the present moment both are equally important.

I take this opportunity of assuring you how deeply we are indebted to our Universities and Public Schools for the whole-hearted manner in which they have assisted and still continue to assist us in providing officers for the various Armies. In a paper which I have now before me I see that it is calculated that since the war began some 10,000 ex-members of the Officers' Training Corps have been accepted for Commissions. These figures speak for themselves and show what valuable work this Corps is doing.

Yours very truly,

(Sgd.) KITCHENER[50]

Whether the government was in fact more concerned to enhance the OTC than to preserve a good education for the next generation is debatable. Certainly the OTC had been taken more seriously in the years before the war, by both the public schools and the military authorities: it was now essential to the system of national defence and had become 'an integral part, not merely a by-product, of school education, and was no longer regarded as merely playing soldiers'.[51] Throughout the war the corps was open to all ages and its drill and exercises (which occupied at least twelve hours a week) became even more important to the boys than sport. At Charterhouse the commanding officer was Major 'Fwankie' Smart, an eccentric master and the subject of all kinds of unlikely anecdotes which obscure his undoubted military efficiency and commitment. The editorial in *The Carthusian* in October 1914 adopts a sincere if portentous tone:

While history's being made on the Continent and at home, while hundreds of thousands are giving their lives to satisfy a madman's lust, we are returning to study the fall of Troy and the Peloponnesian war. But even the seclusion of our cloistered life cannot quite escape the world-wide effects of this armageddon of to-day

...

We who stay at home, who live in perfect safety when others are in peril, we must do the little we can. If we cannot join Lord Kitchener's army, Major Smart is giving us the necessary training preparatory to commanding troops. We must show our appreciation of his untiring efforts by readily acquiescing in the loss of our half-holidays.

Mallory's anger with Fletcher at not being allowed to enlist was intensified in April 1915 when Rupert Brooke died on his way to

Gallipoli and, on the very same day, a climbing friend, Jack Sanders, was killed at Ypres in the first German gas attack of the war. Mallory had little fear of death or danger and he was certain where his duty lay; it was decidedly *not* as an officer of the Charterhouse OTC. To be fair, Fletcher, like other headmasters, was finding it increasingly difficult to withhold leave from young masters like Mallory who were keen to obtain a commission. The school and its pupils had to come first, of course, but as the war dragged on and casualties multiplied, there were more pressing and important concerns to address, and headmasters were being placed in an impossible position. In a letter to *The Times* on 29 May 1915 Fletcher and the Headmasters of Clifton, Tonbridge and Haileybury urged the government to introduce conscription:

> The Archbishops, speaking for the clergy, have declared to the Government the readiness of the country to accept 'any service or sacrifice' that the Government may call for. As laymen of a kindred profession we wish to echo this declaration ...
>
> We feel strongly that the time has come when, for all classes and all ages, the decision between the conflicting claims of civil and military service, of patriotic and family duties, must be made by the Government. It is for them, as national representatives, to interpret and enforce the will of the best mind of the nation, to assign to each citizen his post and his task, to organize all of us so that everyone may do his share towards the shortening of the war and the achievement of the only possible peace.

Edward Marsh (whom Mallory knew through the Bloomsbury circle and who was then Churchill's private secretary at the admiralty) came down to Godalming to urge him to join Churchill's élite Royal Naval Air Service. Fletcher got to hear of this and allowed Mallory to make at least some preliminary enquiries 'so that in case the War Office asked us for more officers you might be ready among others': until then, he warned, 'I cannot consent to your going.'[52] In the autumn of 1915 Mallory's brother-in-law offered to get him a commission in the artillery 'if and when you manage to arrange things satisfactorily with your headmaster'.[53] Mallory encouraged him to go ahead, a commission was given, Fletcher was persuaded, a substitute master was found, and training started in January 1916.

Mallory's frustration had also been exacerbated by the fact that at the start of the war Fletcher had given permission to three other masters to enlist, including his cousin P. C. Fletcher. The government's policy had not been clear at the time but nonetheless Fletcher regretted the precedent he had set, not to mention the deaths of two of the masters; and though P. C. survived, he regretted too the anxiety he caused the family. The first master to lose his life was Harry Kemble who joined the London Regiment, became colonel of the 23rd Battalion, won the DSO and MC, and was killed in action in June 1917 at the Battle of Messines near Ypres. The second, William Gabain, was killed at Pargny-sur-Somme in March 1918. He had been a boy at Charterhouse and was the first master Fletcher appointed. He also won an MC, served with the 2nd Rifle Brigade and was promoted captain shortly before his death.

P. C. joined the 42nd East Lancashire Regiment and served in Egypt and Gallipoli (where he was wounded) and afterwards as divisional signals officer in France where he too was awarded an MC. Four of Fletcher's six brothers (Ernest, Bernard, Clement and Denis) served with the 5th Battalion of the Manchester Regiment and, like P. C., fought in Egypt and in the Gallipoli débacle. Ernest rose to the rank of colonel and Denis (who was ordained in 1906) was chaplain of the regiment. Molly, the only daughter and youngest of the family, joined the Voluntary Aid Detachment of nurses sent to assist the army's medical corps. She served in Italy and was mentioned in despatches. The fact that all six serving members of the same family survived is remarkable and there is no doubt that, though the casualties at Gallipoli were very severe, not least for the Manchesters, the brothers were very fortunate not to have been in one of the three battalions that fought on the Somme. Frank and Leonard stayed at home, Frank because he had a school to run and Leonard to help his father to keep the mines working. In 1916 he and his father died from influenza, both of them exhausted by the government's demands to increase production and to do so with a seriously depleted workforce.

Fletcher's feelings of separation and remoteness from his family were intensified during the war and his brothers regarded him as still more superior and aloof in the safety of his Surrey school. After the war Ernest resumed his legal practice near the Fletchers' home at Howe Bridge; Bernard went back to farming at Ambleside, close to where the family had spent their summer holidays; Clement rejoined the family firm as a mining engineer and became the leading figure in the management of the pits until nationalisation in 1947; and Denis returned from France to become rector of the Rossall school mission in an overcrowded suburb of Manchester. Fletcher remained at

Charterhouse, and though his distance from his family and his roots made him feel uneasy and regretful at times, he never doubted that he was where he ought to be and that there was important work for him to do. When his brother Leonard died he took particular comfort from a letter he received from a retired master whom he held in very high regard:

> Dear Fletcher,
>
> I was more than grieved to see the sad news in this morning's *Times* – the more so because Mrs. Fletcher told me that he was a brother very dear to you.
>
> About your personal loss, however, I must say nothing, but I cannot help saying how much all, who have the welfare of Charterhouse at heart, hope and pray that you may have the strength and courage to face this trial.
>
> There is big work for you yet to do, work never more needed than in these awful days, and the knowledge that you can do this work as few other men could will, I trust, help you a bit to bear your burdens and overcome them.
>
> I can only very partially express what I feel, but you will grasp the meaning of these poor words.
>
> No reply.
>
> > Yours very sincerely,
> > T.E. PAGE[54]

Throughout the war Charterhouse sent on average over a hundred boys a year straight from school to minimal training and then, as second lieutenants, to the Western Front. Life in the trenches, not least for a junior officer, was nasty, brutish and short. Robert Graves gives the statistics with clinical candour:

> At least one in three of my generation at school died; because they all took commissions as soon as they could, most of them in the infantry and Royal Flying Corps. The average life expectancy of an infantry subaltern on the Western Front was, at some stages of the war, only about three months; by which time he had either been wounded or killed. The proportions worked out at about four wounded to every one killed. Of these four, one got wounded seriously, and the remaining three more or less lightly. The three lightly wounded returned to the front after a few weeks or months of absence, and again faced the same odds. Flying casualties were

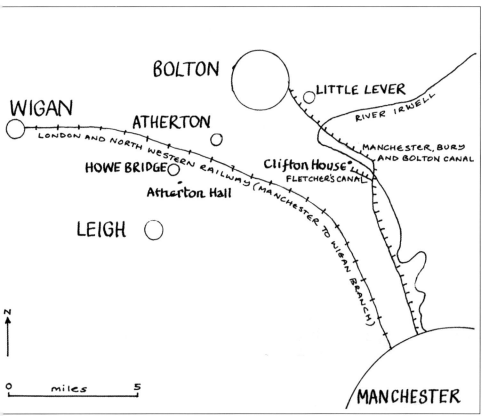

Sketch map of the area around Howe Bridge, adapted from the 1845 Ordnance Survey

Frank's boyhood home

The family's pony and trap with Frank aged fifteen standing behind his mother;
his sister Molly is in the pram

Frank (on the right) with his brothers and sister in 1895

Frank's great-grandfather, Colonel Ralph I

Frank's father, 'Young' Ralph III

A contemporary cartoon of Peterloo

H. A. James with his Rossall staff in 1886: Furneaux is sitting to the left of James and Seaman is sitting on the ground in front of Furneaux; Ogden, Fletcher's housemaster, is standing on the left

Rossall's poetry club in 1887: Furneaux is seated in the centre with Fletcher standing on the right

LEFT Alfred Gilbert's marble bust of Thomas Arnold   RIGHT Benjamin Jowett in 1893, shortly before his death

Shrimpton's caricature of *Oxford types: Balliol*

The first quadrangle at Balliol with Butterfield's chapel in the corner

Balliol's past and present hockey players: Tawney is in the back row on the right and Urquhart and Fletcher are sitting third and fourth from the left

New Big School at Rugby

Percival's Rugby staff in 1895: Fletcher is standing at the right end of the back row;
G. F. Bradby is at the end of the middle row on the left and his brother, H. C., is standing
four along to the right; A. E. Donkin is sitting second to the left with Percival in the centre

The Eranos Society in 1898: Fletcher is seated in the middle, R. H. Tawney is seated on the left and William Temple is standing on the right

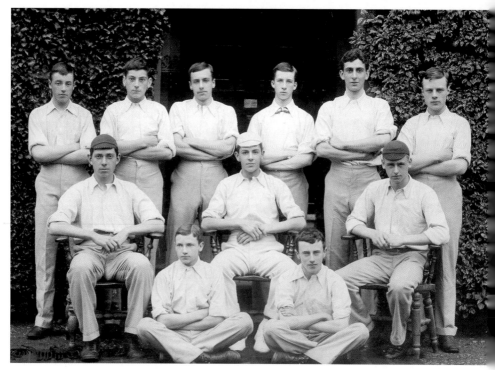

Donkin's cricket XI in 1901: John Stocks is sitting in the centre and P. C. is standing behind him on the right

even higher. Since the war lasted for four and a half years, it is easy to see why most of the survivors, if not permanently disabled, got wounded several times.[55]

Of 169 boys who left Charterhouse in 1912, 50 were killed, and out of a total 3,500 who fought in the war, 687 lost their lives. The strain on Fletcher and his colleagues was immense. Every Sunday in chapel Fletcher, like other headmasters, had to read out an ever-lengthening list of those wounded or missing, taken prisoner or killed. He had known and taught many of them, certainly the youngest, and most of the masters had known and taught them all. As their names were announced so their young faces and voices, their triumphs and misdemeanours were remembered. Worse perhaps than that, 'for more than four years, day after day, I had looked round the School Chapel, with the knowledge that of the 600 faces before me many would before long be looking upon the sordid horrors of war, silently asking myself how many, before a year was passed, might be lying dead on some battlefield.'[56] Every month *The Carthusian* published the latest War List of Carthusian casualties with their rank, name, regiment, house and school dates – Capt. J. P. Benson, East Surrey Regt. (Verites, 1891–1895); Major G. D. H. Ewart, South Lancashire Regt. (Gownboys, 1888–1890); 2nd Lieut. J. B. Harman, Royal Field Artillery (Weekites, 1906–1910) ... As well as lists there were obituaries, promotions, distinctions and letters from old boys serving at the front.

The most moving document of all in the archive is Fletcher's wartime scrapbook. It begins with his letter to Asquith and Kitchener's reply. There are sepia photographs of young men in uniform, letters informing the headmaster of their deaths, and black-edged letters from parents in reply to Fletcher's letters of sympathy. There are copies too of official communiqués describing heroic deaths, including one from George Turner about Harry Kemble. There are photographs of the OTC, Christmas cards from the trenches, poems and press-cuttings. Some of the pupils included are Marlburians and some Carthusians. A cutting announces the award of a posthumous VC to nineteen-year-old Second Lieutenant Sidney Woodroffe, the youngest brother of Leslie, one of Fletcher's senior prefects at Marlborough. This was 'for most conspicuous bravery on July 30, at Hooge', two miles from Ypres. A proud letter from Leslie boasts: 'Isn't it simply splendid dear old Boodles getting the V.C.? You can imagine our delight. My people are awfully happy & I am so especially pleased for their sake.' Fletcher adds in the margin:

'Leslie Woodroffe was killed a few months later.' The middle brother, Kenneth, had lost his life two months before.

A Carthusian, Archie McNair, was also awarded the same supreme military distinction and also at Hooge. Fletcher knew McNair well and admired him. He had been in Saunderites, the headmaster's house, and Fletcher had made him head of school. He left in 1913 after two years being taught by Fletcher in the sixth form and with a scholarship to read classics at Oxford. He enlisted after a year and served with the Royal Sussex Regiment. *The Carthusian* quotes his citation: 'When the enemy exploded a mine, Lieut. McNair and many men of two platoons were hoisted into the air, and many men were buried. But, though much shaken, he at once organised a party with a machine-gun to man the near edge of the crater and opened rapid fire on a large part of the enemy who were advancing. The enemy were driven back, leaving many dead ... His prompt and plucky action and example undoubtedly saved the situation.'[57] McNair died in hospital in Genoa three months before the end of the war. He was twenty-four.

These were difficult and trying years when, as Fletcher describes them, 'the cares and troubles and drabness of the war checked further progress and even undid some of the results obtained'.[58] The dullness was lightened at times, not least by the mixed bag of substitute masters who were drafted in, as well as by the need to adapt and innovate, and to abandon some old restrictions and customs. The temporary masters were mostly elderly but they coped well enough with a curriculum which had scarcely changed since their retirement. They had difficulty keeping order, however; a weakness predictably exploited by the boys and the cause of much fun and amusement. With some other schools Charterhouse offered hospitality to the sons of Belgian refugees who were admitted free of charge. In his report to the governors in May 1915 Fletcher records: 'We have been able to offer the tuition and hospitality of Charterhouse to 9 Belgian boys (5 boarders and 4 day boys). Masters and boys have co-operated to make them welcome; they have themselves been receptive and appreciative; and the unusual experiment is proving very successful.'[59] Feeding 600 boys became increasingly difficult, especially in a district only 30 miles from London and with military camps nearby. Fletcher pays tribute to the house-masters' wives who managed somehow to satisfy the daily hunger of their sixty-five boys plus another ten or fifteen members of staff. 'They "fed us with faithful and true hearts", at the cost of great labour to themselves, and deserve to be gratefully remembered among those who "did their bit" on those difficult days.'[60] The situation was eased when the government introduced food rationing in 1917, though food cards and limited choice only added to the irritations and drabness of life. On the sporting front, the war compelled schools to break down barriers that had dictated the very limited number of schools good enough to play each other.[j] Before the war Rugby only played cricket against Marlborough, while Marlborough only played Rugby and Cheltenham. Charterhouse played only Westminster and Wellington, and Eton, Winchester and Harrow played each other but no other schools. But the war meant that cricket clubs and Oxford and Cambridge colleges were not able to field their usual sides and matches against schools were cancelled. Charterhouse therefore started to play Eton, Harrow and Winchester, all of which have remained annual fixtures.

The drab monotony of wartime school was certainly relieved (and its difficulties greatly increased) in March 1918 when Verites, one of the three main boarding houses, was partially destroyed by fire. The blaze started at 8 a.m. in a dormitory on the top floor and a high east wind swept the fire along until it engulfed the house. Health & Safety had yet to be invented and in those days each house had its own fire brigade, manned by boys. They were quick to take action, clambering up on to the roof and struggling to prevent the fire spreading to Gownboys next door. They were joined by four Surrey engines and later by two from London. The wells ran dry and the single hydrant proved inadequate. Volunteers were busy in the house salvaging as much furniture and possessions as they could and, it seems, with mischievous relish:

> I remember very well the big fire in Verites. Everyone was on the way to morning Chapel, when Mr. Tod's House was observed to be in flames. No Chapel, and no hash, that morning! All threw down their books, and rushed to help, or hinder, as best they could. Before long I found myself in A. H. T.'s bedroom ... Here we found innumerable pairs of striped trousers, which we decided to rescue by flinging them through the window onto the lawn below. While we were engaged in this light-hearted pursuit, the Great Man himself entered the room. 'It's very good of you fellows to help', he said, looking at us rather sadly.[61]

[j] When in the nineteenth century Eton was challenged by Rugby to play a cricket match, Eton's captain replied, 'Rugby, Rugby ... well, we'll think about it if you'll tell me where it is.'

Fletcher was in bed when the fire broke out, convalescing from another attack of pneumonia. He could see the smoke from his window and was soon on the scene. Streams of blackened water were pouring out of doors and windows, piles of bedding and furniture were piling up outside, tiles were falling from the roof, and acrid smoke was aggravating the healthiest lungs. The fire was brought under control at about 1.30 p.m. and the next few days were spent clearing away the rubble and moving the contents of the house into the school hall. During the fire someone had fastened a union jack to the top window of the house and it stayed there as an emblem of wartime spirit and determination to carry on without complaining. The governors met five days later to inspect the damage and decided to rebuild, though the house was not fully insured. The boys exiled from their house were accommodated in the sanatorium and fed by Dorothy Fletcher in Saunderites. Taking stock, the housemaster concluded that things could have been much worse: 'On the whole', he wrote twenty years later, 'the house came through the ordeal very well. No one had remained asleep when upper cubicles caught fire; no one was hurt; not even tempers were lost; all escaped influenza, then prevalent; not one letter of complaint came from any parents.'[62]

What Tod would not have said is that he was the hero of the hour, which was certainly Fletcher's view. Tod had been one of the boys who migrated from London to the new school in Godalming and he returned to teach there in 1880. Despite his diminutive stature and a glass eye he was a fine footballer and had played for the Old Carthusian team which won the FA Cup in 1881. Tod was a master whose life was dedicated entirely to the school. A revered teacher of classics, he was dry and demanding but also witty and humorous. He recreated the cadet corps, making it both popular and professional. In 1906 Tod took over Verites, the house where he had been a boy. At the time of the fire he was over sixty but had agreed to Fletcher's request to stay until after the war.

Now in the eleventh hour of his occupation [writes Fletcher], he saw himself suddenly dispossessed of his house by fire and water, and his belongings and furniture, much of it valuable, scattered in confusion. But he remained cheerful and humorous and imperturbable, like Horace's 'just man', unflurried when his world was crashing upon him. He was to be seen going about amid the débris with an unlighted cigarette in his mouth. 'Me house is on fire, and I can't get a light for me cigarette.' It was the only complaint we heard from him: his coolness and good humour did much to keep everyone good-humoured and helpful.[63]

Schools, and boarding schools especially, are capable of extraordinary comradeship, co-operation and community spirit. The war certainly inspired this quality at Charterhouse and it was to be seen during and after the fire in Verites, and again eight months later when the war ended and peace was declared. It happened that Professor Gilbert Murray and his wife were staying with the Fletchers on the weekend immediately before the armistice was announced. The Murrays had a son in Saunderites, and they had chosen Charterhouse not least because of Fletcher's own reputation as a classicist. Murray himself had been Regius Professor of Greek at Oxford since 1906 and was to become one of the founders of the League of Nations, created in 1920 to preserve the peace. In 1918 the League was still just an ideal but earlier in the year Fletcher had invited Murray to address the school on the subject. His address was duly delivered to an appreciative audience at 9.30 a.m. on Monday 11 November. 'When we came back to my house after it, the telephone bell was just ringing. It was a message from a friend at the War Office to announce that an armistice was to begin at 11 o'clock.'[64] In a sermon preached a month later at the annual founder's day service in London, Fletcher spoke eloquently of 'one of the great memories of my life.'[65]

It was good to be an Englishman that day; good too, to be a Carthusian; good above all to be with the School at Charterhouse. None who were present will easily forget our service an hour after hostilities ceased, when not only boys and masters and masters' families, but the workmen on the buildings and estate, and the women working in the laundry, thronged to Chapel to sing the Te Deum and join in thanksgiving. It was a wonderful service: and hardly less inspiring was another which was held in the evening by special request of the servants of the households who could not come earlier – in which more than a hundred of them joined, helped by the boys' choir who are with us to-night. For once at least our Chapel was the centre and expression of our highest and strongest feelings, and of our common Charterhouse life. For once at least we had met together, high and low, young and old, rich and poor, one with another, to give thanks with one accord to Him Who maketh wars to cease in all the world, Who is to be praised both for the living and the dead.[66]

7

Charterhouse 2

1918–1927

How 600 boys, 50 masters and their families, not to mention the workmen and laundry ladies, all managed to squeeze into the chapel on that first armistice day is hard to imagine. Within just two years of the school's move to Godalming there had been more boys than seats, and though a gallery was added in 1903, a further increase in numbers meant that the chapel was still bursting at the seams. The chapel was never the best of Hardwick's buildings and it suffered too from the fact that funds had been exhausted before the interior was furnished. A hotchpotch of decoration and furniture was assembled during the first years of the new school: the east window was given by Queen Victoria in memory of Prince Albert, Mr G. T. Clark of Dowlais presented a reredos of Venetian mosaic, and five windows on the north side were donated by Old Saunderites, the Duke of Buccleuch, the Earl of Dalhousie, dayboys, and the Benson Fund. All these gifts were gratefully received and no attempt was made to integrate them by offering guidance to the donors. The over-all effect was of rather 'a gaunt building, not adorned or relieved by any bright colour or brilliant ornament'.[1] In his report to the governors at the end of his first year Fletcher was adamant that the school's 'most obvious need – but, unfortunately, the most difficult to satisfy – is in connection with the Chapel. Lighting, ventilation, means of entrance, seating accommodation, are alike inadequate; and in spite of great recent improvements in the woodwork and panelling, the interior, especially the East End, still falls far short of what is to be desired in the Chapel of a great School. I have no scheme for remedying this to suggest: but I am anxious that the need should not be lost sight of and that we should be on the alert for any opportunity of satisfying it.'[2] The war and its casualties provided that opportunity though its outbreak had put a stop to plans for a new chapel drawn up in 1913 and for which Viscount Alverstone,[a] the Lord Chief Justice, had promised £10,000.

[a] Alverstone had been a boy at the London school and was a member of the governing body.

The building of a new memorial chapel was supremely important to Fletcher and he regarded it as his crowning achievement. Church building was in the Fletcher blood: three generations had built or furnished parish churches and an uncle by marriage had founded a renowned architectural practice in Lancaster[b] which designed nearly 200 churches, including the Fletchers' church at Howe Bridge and the chapel at Rossall. Furthermore, Fletcher laid the greatest emphasis on the importance of school chapel. In this he was at one with Thomas Arnold, though he differed from the Doctor in valuing chapel primarily for its power to engender community spirit rather than as a place where moral lessons might be learnt. In an article for *The Architectural Review* to mark the consecration of the chapel in 1927 Fletcher challenges the common sneer 'about men who never go to church in later life because they "had enough of that at school": I suspect there are quite as many who absent themselves from their parish churches because they fail to find there something which, all unconsciously, they found in their school chapels, a sense of unity and brotherhood and membership consecrated and lifted by the daily gathering in a sacred building.'[3] Fletcher was determined from the start that any new chapel should be big enough to accommodate the entire school. He was also insistent that the seating should be inward-facing in the monastic collegiate style, allowing members of the congregation to be visible to one another. And the chapel had to be a beautiful building, making it at once a contrast to its predecessor, a worthy tribute to the fallen, and an inspiring influence on present and future generations:

> It is all the more important, if we believe with Plato that the architectural surroundings of the young, even the very furniture in the presence of which they live, have a vital effect on their development, to secure that these buildings, which represent our common life raised to its highest power, shall be as beautiful in proportion and equipment, as free from what is garish or second-rate as we can make them, as worthy as may be of what they express, and of the emotions and associations which will inevitably gather round them.[4]

By August 1917 nearly 500 Carthusians had been killed, and though no end to hostilities was in sight, the school felt that the time had come to announce its plans for a war memorial. Fletcher's conviction that

[b] Edmund Sharpe married 'Old' Ralph Fletcher's daughter, Elizabeth: the partners were Sharpe and E. G. Paley, joined later by H. J. Austin and H. A. Paley.

only a new chapel would do was not shared by those governors and masters who wanted to provide a fund for the relief of widows and orphans. In the end both schemes were adopted and Fletcher won the battle over which was to take precedence. A committee was formed with Fletcher as chairman and a printed letter was sent to all 5,000 Old Carthusians:

> All Carthusians will desire, we feel sure, not only to provide help to the families of those who have fallen, but to commemorate their names and services in some visible form at Charterhouse: and they will ask that this visible memorial shall be something notable and as far as possible worthy of the unique circumstances and sacrifices which it is to recall. We are therefore asking you to co-operate in raising a fund to meet the greatest need of Charterhouse to-day by building a new Chapel, which may commemorate the Carthusians who have fallen or shared in the sacrifices or labours of the Great War ... and further, if a sufficient sum can be raised, to supplement the War Scholarships founded by the Governing Body, and thereby enable the sons of such Carthusians to enjoy the advantage of an education at Charterhouse.[5]

The letter set a target of not less than £60,000 (nearly £2 million in today's money) and Fletcher gave the lead with a contribution of £1,000.

£60,000 in 1917 after three years of war was an ambitious sum and not without its critics. 'We were told that we were aiming far too high, that we should never raise more than half the sum, that it was the worst possible time for collecting money (it always is!), that the scheme would prove unpopular.'[6] In his Silver Jubilee speech to parliament in 1935 King George V looked back to the end of the war and described 'a world exhausted by its ordeals and impoverished by its destruction ... Everywhere a feeling of uncertainty and lack of confidence hung like a shadow over human endeavour.' This debilitating mood was itself a palpable and powerful obstacle and it was not helped by strong feelings of attachment to the old chapel, despite its many inadequacies and discomforts. School chapels in every generation cast an enduring spell over the pupils who attend them. The sense of belonging they engender, and which Fletcher valued above all; the space they give to be still and reflective in a crowded and busy life; the inspiration which music and preaching can provide – all these make chapel a valued part of school

experience, if mainly in retrospect. 'Among the affectionate associations and memories which gather around the period of school life',
wrote Fletcher, 'those of the chapel play a great part; old boys when
they come back revisit their school chapel, take part in its services, and
re-people in imagination the seats before them with the forms of the
boys who were their school fellows in the past.'[7] To many past pupils
the proposal to make the chapel redundant and to replace it with something entirely new was unthinkable and their resistance to the scheme
was vociferous, even vindictive. A letter to *The Carthusian* from one
who signed himself 'AN OLD CARTHUSIAN OF NO IMPORTANCE'
describes 'very mixed, and even antagonistic feelings' on the part of
those for whom the chapel was a place 'round which some of the pleas-
antest and most sacred memories of our school days cluster'. 'I think it
is also worth considering', he continues, aiming for the heart, 'whether
many of those Old Carthusians to whose memory the new Chapel is to
be raised would have cared to think that their memorial was to consist
in removing the Chapel which they loved ... as many of their fathers
had done before them, and in substituting a new building, strange to
them all, and lacking all the memories and traditions which hover
round the present building.'[8]

The next five years were spent reassuring critics, encouraging supporters, and debating ideas, schemes and designs. It was often an uphill
struggle and demanded all Fletcher's characteristic doggedness and
determination. 'Many a time', he remembered, 'I went up to a committee meeting full of doubts, wondering whether we were ever going to
get any further: and each time I would come back encouraged and
hopeful, realizing that in spite of disheartening appearances we were all
the while gradually moving forward.'[9] Deciding exactly where to build,
in what style and which architect to commission was itself a testing
process: getting the building exactly right was supremely important and
there was in the school a wide variety of passionate opinion. Though
Fletcher was always clear in his own mind that an entirely new building
was required, his committee began by exploring the possibility of
extending the present chapel. The architect, Herbert Baker, was
employed as an adviser. He agreed with Fletcher and recommended a
site separate from but within reach of the Victorian buildings. This was
eventually agreed.

Fletcher was keen to employ a Carthusian architect and one of the
younger and most promising was asked to submit a design. However,

the committee was advised that it was not good enough and Fletcher had to disappoint him. 'A headmaster', he wrote, 'is paid to sacrifice personal feelings, his own and other people's, for the sake of the community. This was an occasion on which I felt I was earning my pay.'[10] With some reluctance Fletcher agreed to launch a competition and the architect Ernest Newton was invited to act as an assessor. Newton was an admirer of Giles Gilbert Scott and he was adamant that he was the one and only architect who was entirely suitable. 'I should not advise you to have a competition', he wrote, 'unless you are sure that Giles Scott is willing to compete; and if he is, you need not have a competition.'[11] Newton's advice was followed and Scott was invited to submit a preliminary plan. The best qualified on the committee were immediately enthusiastic though the others were not entirely confident about the more modern and unconventional aspects of the design. Nonetheless, Scott's appointment was unanimous and, as plans developed and multiplied, the committee became increasingly convinced.

Giles Gilbert Scott was still in his thirties. He was the grandson of Sir George Gilbert Scott, famous for the Albert Memorial, St Pancras Station and the Foreign Office. Giles had won the competition to design Liverpool Cathedral in 1903 when he was only twenty-two.[c] This vast edifice, the second largest cathedral in the world, established Scott's reputation as a brilliant architect with a very distinctive style. After the chapel at Charterhouse his most important designs included Waterloo Bridge, Battersea Power Station, the first telephone kiosk and the university library at Cambridge.

Fletcher and his committee soon discovered that translating an architect's blueprint into an accurate picture of a building is far from easy. The correspondence between Fletcher and Scott was considerable and filled with suggested alternatives and requests for more detail and explanation. Right at the start Fletcher had drawn Scott's attention to Bodley and Garner's chapel at Marlborough which he admired for its dignity, the beauty of its interior, and its capacity to include the whole school. As it happens Scott had been apprenticed to Bodley who had guided him during the early stages of the cathedral at Liverpool. Bodley's own style was unashamedly Victorian gothic: this Scott had absorbed but he wanted to transform and modernise it, and to add touches of detail from different architectural styles. He agreed with Fletcher that the scale of the chapel would be similar to Marlborough's,

[c] Sharpe, Paley and Austin came second out of over 100 competitors.

and with the same central aisle, inward-facing pews, barrel vault and apse at the east end.

Scott's design was essentially gothic (and in tune with Hardwick's school buildings) but this was gothic reinterpreted in new and unfamiliar ways.[d] Fletcher warmed to this, not least because he wanted a war memorial that would be light and airy and filled with hope. However, Scott's drawings showed lancet windows that were extraordinarily high and narrow, and so deeply recessed that they would be invisible from most angles, both inside and out. Was this too innovative? Would it work? 'As regards to the lighting,' Scott replied, 'my experience in church building has given me a very clear idea of how much window will adequately light a building, and in this respect I quite agree that in a Chapel of this kind we must certainly avoid a dark interior. I have provided sufficient window area to give a good light in the building provided these windows are not blocked up with stained glass.'[12] Scott's modernised gothic was to be seen too in his plans for the west end where a Norman arch above the door sits beneath windows with pointed arches; it was apparent too in the romanesque vaulting inside the four porches. But most revolutionary and controversial were those five slit windows on both sides of the chapel which, instead of being positioned between the buttresses, are actually set inside them, leaving cliffs of masonry in the bays on either side.

Opinion was inevitably divided between those who wanted a traditional, Victorian design and those with confidence to embrace something more imaginative and forward-looking. Overall the drawings showed a building of striking restraint and simplicity: to some it looked like a Zeppelin shed; to others it was 'as if the Cenotaph had grown into a glorious temple, church, shrine'.[13] Fletcher found himself in the middle. As headmaster and chairman of the committee he was duty-bound to try to reconcile a variety of views and tastes, but personally he welcomed a design that was rooted firmly in the familiar but was not afraid to innovate. He was convinced that the grandeur and dignity, light and restraint of Scott's design promised a monument worthy of those whose names were to be commemorated inside.

Five years after the launching of the appeal Scott's designs had been agreed by the committee and progress was being made in convincing Carthusians that this was indeed a cause which merited their enthusiasm

[d] Scott's plans were inspired by the cathedral at Albi in south-west France: a massive, fortress-like edifice with the same apsidal end and similar high, narrow windows. The style is certainly gothic but less typically so than other French cathedrals.

and generosity. It had been decided that the school's own works department would build the chapel (itself an extraordinary achievement) and
that the stone would be quarried on the site, just as it had been for the
original buildings. This kept costs down to an estimated £50,000 to
complete the fabric of which £48,000 had already been raised. Though
an additional £10,000 was needed for internal fittings, there were sufficient funds to start building. Plans were made for the laying of the foundation-stone on 17 June 1922, the fiftieth anniversary of the migration
of the school from London. 'It seemed to many of us', wrote Fletcher
tactfully, 'that the memory of Dr. Haig-Brown's great achievement might
be not unfittingly associated with another act of faith by Carthusians,
involving a smaller but no less real sacrifice of old sentiments and associations for the sake of those who should come after.'[14] 2,000 visitors
came, including Baden-Powell and A. H. Tod who had both been among
the boys who had moved from London.[e] Nearly 700 Carthusians who
had fought in the war were present – by coincidence, about the same
number as those who had died. At 4 p.m. the company assembled for the
laying of the stone by the Archbishop of Canterbury, Randall Davidson.[f]
The ceremony began with the national anthem accompanied by the band
of the Royal Artillery. Fletcher spoke first and introduced General Sir
Thomas Morland who had been a boy at the school forty years before
and had commanded X Army Corps from 1915 until the end of the war.
Fletcher expressed the hope that in fifty years' time, and on the same
spot, some pupils present would be giving thanks to God for the lives
and examples of those in whose honour the chapel was to be built.
General Morland spoke next of the 3,500 Carthusians who had served
on land and sea during the war and of the 687 who had died for king
and country. Before inviting the archbishop to lay the stone, the general
read the words Fletcher had written to be engraved inside the four
porches:

> You who enter this Chapel think upon the Carthusians in memory
> of whom it was built who died for their country, and remembering
> them, quit you like men, be strong.[g]

[e] Five Carthusian bishops were present at lunch where grace had to be said by the head
monitor because the bishops could not agree on which of them should have the honour:
'You ought to ask Norwich – he was senior to me.'
[f] Randall Davidson had succeeded Frederick Temple in 1903. He was chairman of the
governing body as were all Archbishops of Canterbury from the school's foundation in
1611 until the 1960s.
[g] The inscription contains a reference to 1 Samuel 4.9.

After prayers and a hymn the head boy buried a jar containing a list of Carthusians who had served in the war. The archbishop performed the ceremony and gave the blessing. The last post and reveille by buglers of the OTC brought the ceremony to a close.

Fletcher's own Christian convictions had played a considerable part in his determination to build a memorial chapel. Though his faith was complicated and never obtrusive it was profound, disciplined and unwavering. As is invariably the case, Fletcher's faith was very much the product of his upbringing and experience. From the low church Anglicanism of his childhood he retained a devotion to the Christ of the gospels, a reverence for the Bible, a firm belief in moral accountability, and an impatience with ritual and religiosity. Jowett's Balliol and Arnold's Rugby had reinforced these same convictions but had added a critical scepticism towards the Bible and the creeds and the easy answers that Christianity often claims. The Bible remained central and fundamental to Fletcher but it had always to be interpreted rigorously and in its historical context if its true import and meaning were to be discerned.

Fletcher taught divinity at Charterhouse as he had at Rugby and Marlborough. In addition to textual analysis with the classical sixth, he held a divinity class after chapel on Sunday mornings for the entire sixth form, modern and classical. The Book of Job was a favourite of Fletcher's for these extraordinary occasions when more than a hundred boys sat in the school hall to listen to the headmaster interpreting scripture as he paced up and down the central aisle. Pupils were expected to take notes though what they absorbed in these circumstances is difficult to imagine. One remembered his neighbour writing on the first Sunday, 'Job was a very patient man', and then writing no notes at all until on the last Sunday he added 'im' before 'patient'.

The whole school had to attend chapel every morning of the week and twice on Sundays. Fletcher hardly missed a service during his twenty-four years as headmaster and by his constant presence he helped to impress on the boys the supreme importance of chapel and what it stood for. He rehearsed members of the classical sixth when it was their turn to read the lesson. Fletcher read himself on Sundays and always began with a short synopsis and explanation of the passage. He preached on three or four Sundays each term and he was spared the bishop's reluctance to permit a layman to preach that he had faced at

Marlborough. Indeed when the Bishop of Winchester, Edward Talbot,[h] came to give addresses in Holy Week in 1918 he insisted that Fletcher should give the address on Good Friday.

> It was, I think, in July of the same year that I found myself preaching to the Archbishop of Canterbury (Dr. Davidson) himself. He was staying in the neighbourhood and arrived for our evening chapel five minutes after the service had begun. It was in the old chapel, and there were no vacant places, but I turned out a modest parent who was sitting next me, and gave him his seat. It was fortunate that the second lesson that evening was not the second chapter of St. James.[i] I was told afterwards that the Archbishop's only comments on the service were that the boys behaved very reverently, and that the preacher's coat ought to have been black.[15]

A collection of Fletcher's sermons was published in 1936, the year after he retired. It includes nineteen addresses, all but four of which were given at Charterhouse. The title, *Brethren and Companions*, which he took from the psalms, expresses Fletcher's cardinal conviction that 'Christianity is essentially a social religion, a spirit which enables human beings to live together as members of a society'[16] and this is a theme common to almost every sermon. Only one other sermon survives from the two to three hundred preached at Charterhouse and it is dangerous to generalise too much from this small collection. Nonetheless, certain characteristics ring true. First, the sermons are preached with the humility of a layman who is not entirely confident that he belongs in the pulpit. In 1916 Fletcher had been the first layman to preach to undergraduates in the university church at Oxford. On the same occasion in 1930 Fletcher asked the congregation 'to think of me as in the fullest sense a layman, an amateur – one who desires to profess and call himself a Christian, a would-be follower of Christ, but does not seek to impose his own way of thinking upon others or presume to speak with authority'.[17] This is very much the tone of all the school sermons and it is this which gives them their paradoxical authority.

[h] Talbot had been a boy at Charterhouse and was the first Warden of Keble College, Oxford and later successively Bishop of Rochester, Southwark and Winchester.
[i] James 2.1–4: 'My brethren, show no partiality as you hold the faith of our Lord Jesus Christ, the Lord of glory. For if a man with gold rings and in fine clothing comes into your assembly, and a poor man in shabby clothing also comes in, and you pay attention to the one who wears the fine clothing and say, "Have a seat here, please," while you say to the poor man, "Stand there," or, "Sit at my feet," have you not made distinctions among yourselves, and become judges with evil thoughts?'

Second, the subjects of the sermons are often practical, always appropriate to schoolboys, and (like Arnold's and Jowett's) largely moral not doctrinal. His titles included – Healthymindedness, Self-Forgetfulness, Gossip, and Personal Influence. Third, the sermons are biblically based, opening with a text in the traditional manner and assuming a knowledge of the scriptures that would be impossible today. St Paul features often, as does Fletcher's desire to interpret him as a man of his age and place and not as a timeless oracle from on high. 'He is a saint, a prophet, a man of genius, as well as a hero: and we ordinary folk cannot match ourselves with such. But we may do well to remind ourselves that behind the prophet and saint and hero and genius there is Paul the man, the impulsive, enthusiastic, loving and lovable personality, full of human weaknesses and human temptations.'[18] And fourth, with St Paul, and all the other biblical characters Fletcher describes, stands always the figure of Christ. 'The Bible is indeed an inspired guide: by it we may see God through the eyes of men who in successive generations sought after Him and each in some measure found Him. But Christianity is not the religion of a book, but of a Person.'[19]

What kind of impact Fletcher's sermons had on the boys of the time is hard to tell. It is difficult to gauge their attitude to preaching nearly a century ago, though Fletcher was confident that 'it is a mistake to suppose that boys don't listen to chapel sermons or that they are not interested in religious questions'.[20] To A. L. Irvine, who shared the teaching of the classical sixth with Fletcher, it was 'hard to imagine better school sermons: not a word wasted, so steeped in the language of Bible and Prayer Book that ancient and modern become one, never long and never obscure, not beyond the comprehension of the simplest and yet the most scholarly would admire them most'.[21]

Fletcher's more devotional and poetic side found expression in writing hymns, a not uncommon occupation for headmasters, certainly of the era before Fletcher's. Fletcher had already tried his hand as a young master at Rugby where he had contributed to G. F. Bradby's parodies of H. A. James's hymns (of which there were far too many). One year they challenged each other to write an even worse hymn for the confirmation service than the one usually sung: Fletcher won. *The Clarendon Hymn Book,* published by Oxford University Press in 1936 (and which superseded *The Public School Hymn Book* of 1903), contained six of Fletcher's serious compositions. The verses are competent but the content and tone are sentimental, a touch cloying, and certainly Victorian. Two hymns are simply adaptations of others and of the four originals a carol is the best and most typical of Fletcher's central beliefs: there is no escaping the trials of life but it is within them that Christ is to be found:

> Let joy your carols fill;
>   Away with sin and sadness!
> To men of gentle will
>   Be peace on earth and gladness!
>
> *O men with sorrow worn,*
>   *Your chains the Lord hath riven;*
> *To you a Child is born,*
>   *To you a Son is given.*
>
> Mid cares and toil and stress
>   And worldly hearts unheeding,
> In paths of humbleness
>   A little Child is leading:
>
> All ye that labours bear,
>   Take now his yoke upon you.
> Your toil he comes to share,
>   Light burden lays he on you:

Two years after the laying of the chapel's foundation-stone Fletcher was able to secure another important change and improvement. Like his predecessors Fletcher was a housemaster as well as headmaster. He had seen the same arrangement at Rugby but not at Marlborough and was not convinced that it was right, either for the school or the headmaster:

> Housemastering is a full-time job as far as a master's out-of-school activities is concerned. To do justice to the forty or fifty or sixty individuals who are assigned to a housemaster's special care requires more time and thought than a headmaster can possibly devote. The prestige of his authority may make his task of main-taining order and discipline easier; but he cannot, without neglect-ing his other duties, give that individual care and attention which is of the essence of good housemastering.[22]

Fletcher also felt uneasy about the inevitable partisanship involved in having charge of one particular group of pupils. He might have felt differently, of course, if his first headmastership had included a board-ing house: it was difficult now to add this extra care and responsibility after eight years at Marlborough without it. But in 1924 the opportunity came to buy a large house and estate next to the school and Fletcher grasped it with enthusiasm. Here was an ideal headmaster's residence plus an additional fifty acres of breathing space and playing fields.

The house system at Charterhouse is as idiosyncratic as any. To start with in London the gownboys, or scholars, were the only pupils and those who boarded lodged together within the school. As the school's reputation grew, fee-paying boys were added and some were accommodated in the headmaster's house, later named Saunderites after Augustus Saunders, headmaster from 1832 to 1853. A third boarding house was built and named Verites after its first housemaster, Oliver Walford, whose nickname was 'Old Ver'. These houses, Gownboys, Saunderites and Verites, were replicated among the new buildings at Godalming and incorporated within the main block. The rapid increase in numbers under Haig Brown made more boarding houses essential. Eight were added and again named after the master who founded them – Girdlestoneites, for example, after Mr F. K. W. Girdlestone (though then and since called Duckites after Girdlestone's sobriquet 'Duck' which mocked his ungainly walk), Hodgsonites after the Revd J. T. Hodgson and Pageites after Dr T. E. Page[j] (-ites was borrowed from the Canaanite tribes in the Old Testament: Amorites, Hittites, Jebusites). These eight masters had paid out of their own pockets for the conversion or construction of their houses and ran them independently of the school, making what profits they could from the fees they charged for board and lodging. 'Without doubt this is the origin of the position and power of the housemasters at Charterhouse which long survived; they have often been compared to the barons of feudal days.'[23] There is no doubt too that Fletcher weakened this power when, after the war, he brought the houses under more central control and reformed the way in which housemasters were paid, replacing the profits of a hotelier with a fixed annual salary.

Conditions within all the houses were not much better than they had been at Marlborough. Apart from ten or twelve seniors who had their own studies, the boys still slept in unheated dormitories and spent their waking hours in what was called 'long room' where they worked, socialised and ate their meals. Only two small rooms were set aside for

---

[j] All these houses except Girdlestoneites were demolished in the early 1970s and replaced by new houses.

changing into sports kit, and washing and sanitary arrangements were meagre and primitive. Nonetheless, the house system at Charterhouse and Rugby had advantages over the hostel system at Rossall and Marlborough. With houses the school was broken down into manageable (though often exclusive and contentious) units, making for better discipline. There was better pastoral care too, at least when the housemaster took an active role in his house. Most housemasters, however, preferred to remain on their private sides and to delegate the running of the house entirely to the monitors. That, of course, often meant fagging, beatings and misery for the younger boys. In Fletcher's time some improvements were made to the physical condition of the houses and caning was restricted to head monitors. In rules drawn up in 1925 the latter were instructed to 'remember that corporal punishment should only be administered in such cases as seem to them to render it absolutely necessary, and that in beating they are bound to exercise great care and moderation'.[k] Such a method of discipline is anathema today and it is easy to overlook how liberal Fletcher's reforms were; in the 1920s the restrictions he imposed were positively progressive.

Although Fletcher was never comfortable combining the roles of headmaster and housemaster he was determined to be a successful and exemplary housemaster, however difficult that might be. He had no choice but to leave his senior boys in charge and he rarely trespassed onto the boys' side unless accompanied by a monitor. Nonetheless, he often lunched with the boys in long room and presided at prayers in the evening, and he made sure too that he kept the monitors up to the mark. He was fortunate in his first head monitor, Douglas Vernon. Fletcher described him as 'a boy of exceptional character and gifts of leadership, under whom a house which for many years had been singularly unsuccessful and was not without reason ill-spoken of made remarkable strides towards recovery'.[24] Vernon was an outstanding footballer, scoring the only and winning goal in extra time in the house finals at the end of Fletcher's first term. It was a triumph that helped to restore the house's self-respect and signalled a new start under Fletcher. Vernon went up to Oxford in 1912 where he won two football blues. He was commissioned into the Grenadier Guards at the start of the war and was killed on the Somme two years later. In his memory his parents donated one of the four porches of the new chapel.

Fletcher made good use too of house tutors, especially Humphrey

[k] The third of seven rules drawn up at Fletcher's request by J. C. S. Hale, head monitor, 1925–6.

Grose-Hodge whom he appointed to the staff in 1920. He had been in Fletcher's classical sixth at Marlborough, had won a first at Cambridge, and served as a captain in the Indian Army during the war (a younger brother was killed at Ypres). He was liked and respected by the boys and Fletcher praised his 'stimulating wit and admirable teaching'.[25] Though Fletcher was sorry to see him leave in 1928 he was delighted with his appointment as Headmaster of Bedford, the same post Fletcher had applied for twenty-five years before.

Fletcher's relentless workload was taking its toll and there were further attacks of pneumonia. By 1924 he had been at Charterhouse for thirteen years and during this time he had reordered and revived the school after Rendall, steered it through the First World War, and campaigned for and driven the building of the new chapel – and all this in addition to the routine work of a headmaster which at Charterhouse included teaching the classical sixth and running a boarding house. Dorothy was becoming increasingly concerned about his health and when the opportunity came to move out of Saunderites and into a more private house she urged Fletcher to take it.

The governors of Haig Brown's time had purchased a site of seventy acres. This was extraordinarily capacious after London and by Fletcher's time additional acres had been acquired. Meanwhile the school had quadrupled in number, buildings had spread and most of the land had been converted into games-fields. When in 1924 an adjoining fifty-acre estate with an admirable house came onto the market, Fletcher and the masters were determined that the school should have it. The governing body took fright at the price and procrastinated. So the masters forced the issue by borrowing the money in the hope that the governors would re-purchase from them at their own price. 'We decided on this one afternoon at a meeting in my house. Realizing at tea-time that a measure of governing body sanction was needed I motored up to Oxford with another master, interviewed the Provost of Oriel,[1] chairman of the finance committee, and obtained his assent, returned the same evening to Charterhouse, and made a firm offer by telephone next morning to the vendor's agents. As a result of this deliberately impulsive action the governing body obtained for £10,000 an estate whose actual price was £16,000.'[26]

The additional land with its uninterrupted views south-west to the

---

[1] Lancelot Phelps was educated at Charterhouse (Fletcher described him as 'a Carthusian of Carthusians') and spent 64 years at Oriel, 15 as provost.

blue hills of Hindhead made a very considerable difference to the school.[m] Northbrook House on the edge of the estate is an elegant late-Georgian white plastered building of classical proportions. In Fletcher's time it stood in its own grounds of five acres with two tennis courts, a kitchen garden and greenhouses. The house contained eight bedrooms, two bathrooms, a billiard room and a servants' hall.[n] The move out of Saunderites and into Northbrook in January 1925 provided a fresh lease of life for Dorothy as well as for Frank, and she was soon hard at work turning what had become a rather shabby farmhouse into a gracious and attractive headmaster's residence. Dorothy took the gardens in hand too and added this work to the improvements she was making elsewhere in the school grounds. Here she was helped by the landscape gardener Russell Page, who in executing his scheme needed all the support the Fletchers could lend. 'Every tree,' he wrote, 'every path, every short cut was sacrosanct to a whole series of taboos (based on all sorts of ritual distinctions) rigidly maintained by the conservatism of boys and masters. All these I knew, since I myself had been at school there. My problem was to rationalise the physical relationship of the various buildings and open areas with the problems of circulation, as well as to take into account the traditional use of every square yard. Any proposal to cut down an old tree or plant a new one required endless lobbying.'[27] In the gardens Dorothy was helped by the celebrated Surrey gardener Gertrude Jekyll, who had become a good friend of the Fletchers. Gertrude Jekyll was in her seventies and eighties during the Fletcher's time at Charterhouse and nearly blind. She lived alone across the valley at Munstead in the house the architect Edwin Lutyens had designed for her.[o] She had already laid out the garden at Saunderites and Lutyens had built its fine summer-house and double dry stone walls which still support an abundance of plants and flowers. At Northbrook House Jekyll turned a workaday farmhouse garden into an admirable example of her distinctive naturalistic style of planting.

The Fletchers' new life at Northbrook was exciting and rejuvenating, and they took every opportunity to enjoy its advantages and to

[m] For many years the school maintained a small farm on the estate which the boys helped to run; today the farm has been replaced by the school's golf course.

[n] The house is now named Great Comp and is the school's sanatorium.

[o] Lutyens was twenty-six years younger than Jekyll but theirs was a distinctive and prolific collaboration which included the British First World War cemeteries in France and Belgium.

share them with the school. In his report six months after the move Fletcher reassured the governors that 'Northbrook has proved convenient in every way: it is easily accessible and there is no feeling of remoteness; at the same time the amenities and the greater privacy are a great boon to my wife and myself and have not, I hope, diminished our efficiency.'[28] Life at Northbrook was redolent of that unhurried, leisurely life enjoyed in the 1920s and '30s by those who could still afford it. Breakfast parties and black-tie dinners in the winter, and in the summer, croquet, tennis and raspberries and cream in the garden. All this formed strong and treasured memories. In a volume of reminiscences presented to Fletcher on his eightieth birthday, a pupil looks back on his time at school which started in 1925:

> Much of the memories of those years centre around Northbrook; and indeed I wonder whether any Carthusian who did not know Northbrook in those days ever truly savoured the *douceur de vivre*. On an Irishman their impact was perhaps even more forceful than it would have been on one who was familiar with the country-house life of the South of England. In all events, the dinner-parties there, at which we learned to like claret and were treated as adults, the lazy Wednesday afternoon tennis-parties, at which our hostess did not think it absurd to talk about Jane Austen or the Impressionists, the background of sweet pea and delphiniums and well-mown lawns – these produced an atmosphere in which in retrospect I can luxuriate, and which at the time did much to turn us into civilized beings.

The Shakespeare Society met each month after dinner in the drawing room. Its members were twelve carefully selected boys and four masters, plus the headmaster. A play was chosen and cast and read from start to finish in an evening. Dorothy was an additional and enthusiastic member and would commandeer the best female parts (her favourite was Cleopatra). From time to time the Oxford University Dramatic Society put on open-air plays in front of the house with the school as spectators, sitting on the lawns. The Charterhouse Masque was performed there in 1929 and again on the eve of Fletcher's retirement in 1935. 'On such occasions house and garden were for weeks beforehand the scene of varied activities, of rehearsals and preparations of every kind. Boys young and old co-operated, whether as performers or assistants, painting the scenery, helping with the electricity arrangements, and doing the various odd jobs which such performances entail.

The whole community came together as one family, with Northbrook as the centre.'[29]

Dorothy was a charming and energetic hostess, engaging her guests in conversation about themselves and paying scrupulous attention to arrangements. She was helped by Albert Humphries and his wife who lived with the Fletchers at Northbrook. Albert had started in 1908 as the garden boy at the Master's lodge at Marlborough and the Fletchers had brought him with them to Charterhouse as gardener and handyman. He soon married a Godalming girl who worked as a maid in the school and she became the Fletchers' housekeeper in both Saunderites and Northbrook. Though cars were becoming popular Fletcher never learnt to drive and Albert became his chauffeur. Albert and his wife were devoted to the Fletchers and worked for them for fifty years. Their only child was born in Saunderites in 1920 and was christened Dorothy after Mrs Fletcher and both she and Frank looked on her almost as a daughter.

The war memorial chapel took five years to build and Saturday 18 June 1927 (the fifty-fifth anniversary of the start of the first term in Godalming) was set aside for its consecration. Past and present pupils, parents, masters and governors, contributors to the fund and relatives of those who had been killed were all invited. The service was conducted by the Bishop of Winchester in the presence of Randall Davidson, Archbishop of Canterbury, and eight other bishops. General Sir Robert Baden-Powell was there with General Sir Archibald Montgomery-Massingberd who had also been a boy at the school, and had been chief of staff to Lord Rawlinson[p] in France. Field-Marshal Lord Plumer[q] was present to inspect a guard of honour of the OTC and to address the large crowds inside and outside the chapel. Plumer was an Etonian not a Carthusian but his long and distinguished military career, his rank and war record gave him an almost unrivalled authority to represent the armed forces; this was, after all, not just a school's memorial chapel but one of national significance and 'perhaps the noblest of all the memorials raised in England to those who have fallen in the war'.[30] Among other distinguished guests was the architect, Sir Giles Gilbert Scott. He had been knighted in 1924 and Fletcher had written him a postcard congratulating him 'on Liverpool and on your new honour – very welcome to all who know you and your work'.[31]

[p] General in command of the 4th Army at the Battle of the Somme.
[q] Viscount Plumer of Messines had commanded II Army Corps at 3rd Ypres in 1917.

A long procession formed in the South African Cloister outside the old chapel and moved at 3 o'clock to the west end of the memorial chapel. A congregation of 1,000 was already seated and there were nearly 3,000 assembled outside. When the procession reached the chapel the first verse of the national anthem was sung and Fletcher addressed the company in carefully chosen words:

> Carthusians and friends of Charterhouse, and you especially who have become in a very real sense Carthusians in virtue of a son or brother's name recorded within this building, we have opened our ceremony to-day by dedicating ourselves, in the singing of the National Anthem, to our King and Country, associating the School loyalty which binds us together with the wider patriotism of national service: and we shall proceed later to unite and conse-crate them both to the highest service of which the symbol is this Chapel of ours, which we have laboured with anxious thought to make a worthy memorial of our dead.[32]

Fletcher informed his audience that for every ten boys then in the school there were eleven names recorded on the screens just inside the chapel behind him. He then called on Lord Plumer 'to speak in memory of our Carthusian dead'. First, Plumer spoke of General Morland who had been present five years before for the laying of the foundation stone but who had since passed away. He spoke of sad memories that are also beautiful 'because the gloom of our mourning is dispelled by our pride in their sacrifice'. He spoke too in praise of the contribution the public schools had made to the war: 'Our Allies were surprised – our enemies certainly were – at the number of men who came forward and were able, after rudimentary instruction, to assume positions of great responsibility and display wonderful powers of leadership.'[33]

After a hymn the procession made a circuit of the chapel before entering through the west doors. As the choir and dignitaries walked round outside, slowly and solemnly, all eyes were drawn to the build-ing. What was most striking now that the scaffolding was down and the chapel completed was the building's height, its simple and soaring lines and the brightness of its honey-coloured stone which was almost too dazzling in the midsummer sunshine. For Fletcher these were moments of almost overwhelming emotion – of triumph and relief mixed with apprehension (the ceremony had only just begun) and that sadness he would always feel when entering the chapel and remember-ing those whose short lives it embodied.

Back at the west end the procession halted for the bishop to knock three times on the doors with his crozier. The doors were opened and the procession made its way through the chapel. First they passed the names and leaving dates of nearly 700 Carthusians engraved in red and gold on grey stone screens. Gilbert Scott had been right about the light – the sunshine was pouring through the glass making the yellow stone look almost white. 'Those who had prophesied that the building would be dark found an interior flooded with light,' noted Fletcher.[34] The length of the chapel, and the time it took the procession to reach the sanctuary, was striking too, especially after the cramped conditions of the old chapel.

High above the altar, in front of the two panels of the window, was suspended a massive cross of carved and gilded wood and beneath it was a marble sarcophagus guarded by two golden angels. The theme of sacrifice was reinforced in the stained glass which showed two knights, one kneeling to dedicate his sword before an altar and the other receiving a crown at the hands of an angel. But Fletcher was not alone in finding the east end a disappointment, both in its busy jumble of styles and features, and in the Victorian sentimentalism of the chivalry. The motto, 'WHO DIES IF ENGLAND LIVE' (from Kipling's *For All We Have and Are*) which appears on a scroll in the window caused heated controversy. Many of the masters found it triumphalist, jingoistic and careless of those whose sacrifice the windows were there to commemorate. Fletcher sympathised with these objections though in a sermon he did his best to point out that, when taken in context and preceded as they are in the poem by the words 'What stands if Freedom fall?', they were unexceptional. On another occasion, and to a smaller audience, Fletcher confided that he rather hoped that the picture was so obscure and the lettering so badly spaced that little notice would be taken of them.

The consecration service was a glorious and dignified crowning of thirteen years of hardship, sacrifice and determination. Afterwards the Fletchers received a host of congratulatory letters from those who had been present. Sir Michael Sadler, art patron and Master of University College, Oxford wrote a particularly perceptive letter to Dorothy:

The Chapel is the greatest of modern Gothic buildings. And I have felt in it what I feel in no other modern building, very great as some of them are. It is austerely brave and yet compassionate. It strikes me more and more, and encourages one deeply because it is

not reminiscent but prophetic. There is nothing 'copy-cat' about it
… Every time I go into it, or walk near it, I feel the power and
tenderness of it. It is European, not American: scientific, communal and austere, with all the best modern things but also catholic,
reverent and personal.

What a grand thing it must have been to share in getting this
masterpiece made.[35]

Among the most treasured of the letters was one from Leonard
Furneaux, Fletcher's English master at Rossall, who after retirement
had moved to Godalming. 'My dear Fletcher,' he wrote, 'I must write a
line to congratulate you on the brilliant success of what must have been
about the greatest day of your life.'[36] Indeed it was, and it marked too a
profound moment of renewal. The following day, Sunday 19 June,
there were three services in the chapel: holy communion at eight with
the Bishop of Winchester as celebrant, matins at ten-thirty and even-
song at seven at which Fletcher preached. 'It is of little value', he
concluded the sermon, 'to build noble Chapels unless some nobleness
of life goes with them: and the true dedication of this Chapel must be
the dedication of our own lives.'[37]

Thirty years later in 1957, after final additions to the furnishings, an
inscription was carved above the headmaster's stall:

CARTHUSIANS
REMEMBERING WITH GRATITUDE
THE LIFE AND SERVICE
OF
FRANK FLETCHER
(HEADMASTER 1911–1935)
HAVE NOW COMPLETED
A WORK THAT HE INSPIRED

8

Charterhouse 3

1927–1935

By 1927 Frank Fletcher had been a headmaster for twenty-four years. His wisdom and experience were highly regarded and were drawing him increasingly into the wider world of education. His chief forum for discussion and influence was the annual Headmasters' Conference. Fletcher had been a member since 1903; the following year he was elected onto the committee where he remained for over thirty years. He was chairman of the Conference on ten occasions, including 1927 when the headmasters met at Rugby. Fletcher found himself presiding in the same room where he had taught his first form in 1894: the headmasters, he wryly observed, were 'a more orderly but less interesting gathering'.[1] The year before though he had written to Ralph, his nephew and godson, then aged nine: 'Tomorrow I have to go down to Brighton to keep a lot of headmasters in order. They're much more trouble than boys!'[2]

The Headmasters' Conference was founded in 1869 by Edward Thring, Headmaster of Uppingham. The Conference had its origins in a smaller gathering earlier in the same year of headmasters of endowed grammar schools – Sherborne, King's Canterbury, Uppingham, Repton, Tonbridge and Oakham among them. They met to defend themselves against a government commission and what was soon to become the Endowed Schools' Act which threatened to restrict their freedom from government control. The decision was taken at that first meeting in London to join with other public school headmasters every year at Christmas to discuss common experiences and problems. The headmasters would take it in turn to host the meeting and Thring offered Uppingham for the first Conference. 'Came back from London to-day,' he wrote in his diary. 'By far the most satisfactory thing to me was that I have got a school congress to meet every year at a school, and next Christmas at Uppingham (D.V.) the first will be held. May God bless this great working step … This may and will, please God, be the beginning of a great work, which may have more beneficent power than any

Acts of Parliament.'³ Thirty-seven headmasters were invited by Thring, including those of the nine great Clarendon schools. He was particularly concerned to include these schools but in the event none of them were among the twelve headmasters who attended. The next year thirty-four headmasters met at Sherborne, including Winchester, Westminster, Charterhouse and Shrewsbury. In 1871 the number had risen to fifty, Eton among them.

By the time Fletcher joined in 1903 over a hundred headmasters were members of the Conference though not all attended every meeting. From 1904 until 1937 membership was limited to 150. Topics debated during Fletcher's thirty years included the tiresome and perennial matters of salaries, pensions and fees, and what are today dated issues like the O.T.C., schoolmasters in holy orders, and, on one occasion, 'noxious literature'. Other matters discussed (inspections, examinations, teacher training and a changing curriculum) are still high on the agenda. Fletcher was not only an assiduous committee man with a scrupulous concern for procedure; he was also a frequent and carefully prepared contributor to debate and he relished the chance to revive his talent. He always enjoyed these two-day conferences, not least because they provided an opportunity to visit other schools and keep in touch with other headmasters who, as time went on, included some of his former pupils. When Fletcher was chairman for the second time in 1914 his Rugby pupil, William Temple, was still secretary though he had just been succeeded at Repton by Fletcher's Marlborough pupil, Geoffrey Fisher. When Fletcher presided for the ninth time in 1931 the meeting was held at Charterhouse. Three of his Marlborough pupils were among the ninety-five headmasters present – Geoffrey Fisher, Humphrey Grose-Hodge and George Turner, now Master of Marlborough.

The survival or not of Greek as an essential subject in the public schools' curriculum was a frequent topic on the Conference's agendas. As early as 1877 headmasters were expressing their anxiety that Oxford and Cambridge might do away with Greek as a compulsory subject for admission. The concern proved premature, though by the time Fletcher joined the Conference the universities were giving serious consideration to its abolition. Greek at the start of a boy's time at public school had also been under threat. In 1906 a resolution 'That in the interest of the general education of young boys, it is advisable that the study of Greek should be postponed until the age of 13 or 14, and that Greek should not be a subject of entrance examinations in schools represented by the Conference' was passed with twenty-six votes for and only four against. Fears were expressed by some headmasters that this would mean the end of Greek in their schools since no boy would want to take it up from scratch when they arrived. The Headmaster of Shrewsbury (H. W. Moss) warned that if members of the Conference 'did not resist these attempts to interfere with the study of Greek, first above and then below, the result would inevitably be the disappearance of Greek from the curriculum of English education'.[4] Fletcher reinforced this view, as did H. A. James of Rugby, invariably the Conference's prophet of gloom. Fletcher supported an amendment that at least the rudiments of Greek should be taught at preparatory schools but the amendment was lost. Nonetheless, Greek continued as a part of the classical curriculum throughout Fletcher's time as headmaster (though fears that it faced extinction were frequently raised at the Conferences). 'We who believe in the Greek language and literature as a great educational instrument and an essential element in European civilization have been able to maintain it in our schools, not indeed in the old privileged position of unchallenged supremacy, but none the less holding its own. If it is moribund, which I do not believe, it is an unconscionable time in dying.'[5]

Another hotly debated perennial which today seems remarkably trivial was the question of Latin pronunciation. Fletcher had moved the following resolution in 1906, and though it was carried by thirty-two votes to eleven, the debate rumbled on until the thirties: 'That this Conference is of opinion that the system of Latin pronunciation recommended by the Classical Association should be adopted by all schools represented on the Conference with as little delay as possible.' Fletcher's own experience had been one of confusion. He had been taught the old pronunciation at Rossall and Oxford. At Rugby boys were taught the old in the junior part of the school but the new in the sixth[a]. In the lower bench of the sixth, J. L. Paton used the new while the headmaster, Dr James, taught the old. Fletcher was happy to conform to James's methods but when he moved to Marlborough he found that the school was used to the new 'and I willingly and without difficulty adopted it'.[6] Not surprisingly, he felt very strongly that there had to be uniformity between the Conference schools, and it was for

---

[a] The difference between the two is considerable – e.g. for *vitae* the old pronunciation is *vytee* and the new *weetye*.

this pragmatic reason that he moved the resolution and stoutly defended it in the years to come.

Though the proposal was carried and acted on in most if not all the schools, the decision was regularly revisited, notably in an acrimonious debate at the Conference in 1926. The instigator of the debate was Fletcher's contemporary, Cyril Alington, Headmaster of Eton. Alington had been a scholar at Marlborough under George Bell and returned there to teach after Oxford where he had won a fellowship at All Souls. He moved to Eton in 1899 where he was ordained and appointed master-in-college.[b] Despite his quick mind and prodigious memory Alington was not a precise scholar like Fletcher and his knowledge of the classics was never as detailed or thorough. 'Even as a young man his teaching was rapid, superficial, jocose, at any rate in the eyes of a clever boy.'[7] Alington was a maverick – witty and amusing but at times opinionated and supercilious. He and Fletcher were very different characters and they had scant regard for each other.

A month before the 1926 Conference, Alington had broken ranks and written to preparatory schools to say that the new pronunciation was no longer necessary. Alington's letter encouraged a few headmasters to raise their own uncertainties about the decision taken twenty years before. On the other hand Cyril Norwood, Fletcher's successor but one as Master of Marlborough and by 1926 Headmaster of Harrow, gave a strong defence of the *status quo* in an impromptu speech which was not without a hint of Harrow v. Eton rivalry:

> At Eton, by their own admission, apparently they have never tried the reformed pronunciation, and, therefore, do not know what they are speaking of ... It seems to me that the reformed pronunciation is reasonable, and the old method is unreasonable. It is reasonable because it is very much in line with the pronunciation of French, Italian and Spanish. It has authority, because it was a considered scheme drawn up by the best scholars of the Cambridge school ... The system has the backing of the Classical Association, it has been adopted by the Board of Education, it is now at last uniform in this country to the extent of about 99 per cent. of the students, and I do ask you with no uncertain voice to turn down this Motion. I am sure that this Conference is not going to support this very unfortunate letter which proceeded from Eton.[8]

[b] Housemaster of the scholars' house.

Fletcher summed up the debate from the chair and issued another appeal for uniformity. The motion 'That the "reformed" pronunciation of Latin, having now had a fair trial, has failed to justify itself by results' was lost by thirty-eight votes to nine. That was still not the end of the matter so far as Alington was concerned. Five years later when the Conference met at Charterhouse and Fletcher was chairman again, Alington made a long and pompous speech on his favourite topic, the education of the average boy. He took the opportunity for a swipe at Fletcher when declaring that the change in Latin pronunciation had put a serious stumbling-block in the way of such a boy. 'But even the head-master of Eton', mused Fletcher, 'cannot put the clock back effectively, though he may damage the works.'[9]

The 1920s and '30s were decades of considerable change and modern-isation to the curriculum and the details were often the subject of discussion and debate at the Conferences. Looking back, Fletcher could not recall a single alteration to the pattern of study during his nine years at Rugby and the timetable had been constructed in the 1870s. There were then only two main subjects, 'classics in the morning, mathematics in the afternoon',[10] and these took up three quarters of the time. Other subjects were taught under these headings: classics embraced languages, literature, history and scripture, and mathematics covered science (though Fletcher regretted that he had never learnt any science at Rossall). By the time he was Master of Marlborough new specialisms were reorganising the timetable and challenging the long supremacy of Latin and Greek. Writing in 1936, Fletcher describes this evolution with a clear note of regret:

> On the linguistic and literary side modern languages, modern history, and 'English' have been separated off. Each claims its own pigeon-hole, and the pigeon-holes have tended more and more to be watertight compartments. On the non-literary side first chem-istry, then physics, asserted themselves as separate entities: then biology came into the field, regarded by the other two as Cinderella was by her older sisters... Now as one born out of due time has come geography; it is still uncertain to which of the two main classifications it belongs... I once hoped that it might supply the much-needed bridge between the literary and the non-literary subjects. But it came in as an additional subject, to add to the

complexities of the time-table and the despair of teachers who are struggling to lay broad foundations.[11]

Fletcher's objection was not so much to a range of separate subjects but to the choices that pupils had to make if specialist subjects were to be allowed space in the timetable. That was at the expense of the general education which he valued: an educated man, in his view, was an expert in one subject but a good listener in as many others as possible. Specialisation also meant the end of the old form-master system whereby, at the junior level at least, a master taught a variety of subjects to his own class. This allowed him to get to know the boys well and to have a broader sense of their academic inclinations and ability. 'Verbs of teaching, both in Latin and Greek, take two accusatives: you teach a boy and you teach a subject. For the form-master the personal accusative is necessarily, as indeed it should be for all schoolmasters, the more important.'[12]

Alongside specialisation was the growth of modern sides to rival and soon surpass the classics. One of the tasks the Charterhouse governing body set Fletcher when he was appointed was to organise the modern side so that it became a more respected and efficient part of the school. He had done this already at Marlborough, and at Charterhouse he managed again to combine his own strong preference for the classics with a determination that the modern side should not be regarded as inferior. This had always been a danger because the cleverest boys invariably chose Latin and Greek. Edward Bowen at Harrow had been asked by his headmaster in 1869 to establish a modern side which became the model for other schools. From the start Bowen argued 'that it was necessary to discriminate between two alternative conceptions: on the one hand that of a branch of the school which should aim at the best attainable teaching, and rank as far as possible on an equality with the classical school; on the other that of a division which should be professedly inferior, should welcome the duller boys, and bring the teaching to as low a level as was necessary for their training. I was willing to undertake the task on either hypothesis: Dr. Butler chose the former.'[13] At most other schools, including all four of Fletcher's, the modern side was certainly seen and treated as inferior. At Charterhouse in Haig Brown's time, 'Quite a lot of mobbing went on between the members of C Form (Modern side, as they were then called), and the Classical side; a sort of feud went on between them. The Classical side thought the others were socially inferior and so looked down on them.

Some in passing the C Form members would hold their noses and make a detour.'[14] Such snobbery was still in evidence when Fletcher was headmaster and in order to discourage it he did away with any separation between classical and modern in the lower part of the school. He also insisted on Latin being taught to all boys until they reached the sixth and could choose for themselves.

Fletcher's championing of Latin is no surprise and he remained convinced throughout his career that there was no subject to take its place. His reasons were not literary or historical but linguistic: 'It has been organized for centuries as an instrument of grammatical and linguistic training such as our uninflected English language cannot give: it is the basis of French, Italian and Spanish: it has influenced the framework of German: it has supplied directly or indirectly a large part of the vocabulary of English. It is the master key which unlocks many linguistic doors.'[15] Making Latin compulsory had the additional advantage of ensuring that preparatory schools did not recommend to Charterhouse duller boys who were ignorant or incapable of learning the language.

The end of the war and the passing of the 1918 Education Act brought a significant increase in secondary education and an improvement in the status, salaries and security of teachers. The nation had lost an entire generation of men, especially those from the public schools, and the country was in desperate need of educated and trained young men and women to rebuild the nation and ensure its place in the modern world. Many of the old social divisions had been destroyed in the trenches and increasingly the state and the public schools were looking for ways to co-operate in support of the national system. All this was welcomed by Fletcher whose own background had never allowed him to feel comfortable with the exclusive and privileged nature of the great boarding schools. 'It is a real loss', he wrote, 'to the old foundations like Charterhouse or Winchester or Rugby that their boys come from a limited class, that a large and valuable section of the nation is excluded from them for financial reasons... I have no wish to see the characteristic features of our public schools disappear from our education. Such a disappearance would be a national disaster, at which only the daughters of the Philistines would rejoice and the children of the undiscerning triumph. But I emphatically do *not* regard social distinction as one of those essential characteristics.'[16]

The public schools' relation to the national system of education was a major preoccupation of the Headmasters' Conference throughout Fletcher's long membership, and one in which he took a strong personal interest. Three months before Fletcher retired from Charterhouse in 1935, H. A. James's successor as President of St John's College, Oxford had called on the older public schools to do more to support the State. In reply Fletcher, as chairman of the Conference, wrote a long and defensive letter to *The Times*[17] in which he recounted what had at least been attempted since the end of the war. He explained that a proposal made in 1918 had 'aroused the suspicions of headmasters of the newer and State-aided secondary schools. They thought that the older boarding schools were proposing to skim off the cream of their scholars by enticing away at 13½ the most promising of the ex-elementary schoolboys whom they had taken at 11.' As a result, 'the well-intentioned but ill-considered proposal came to nothing.' The letter continues:

> It was not long after this (I write away from my records and cannot give the exact date) that I went, as chairman of the H.M.C., to the President of the Board of Education[c] with a definite offer of service from the older public schools, taking with me the Headmaster of Eton, Dr. Alington, and Dr. Norwood, then the Master of Marlborough... We were told at the time that there was no demand for places in our schools for ex-elementary schoolboys, but that the Board appreciated our willingness and desire to co-operate, and would call on us if need and opportunity arose.

Fletcher goes on to explain that though there was a strong desire among many headmasters to open their schools to all boys, there were problems for boarding schools whose fees were necessarily high. 'The admission to them of boys whose parents cannot afford any contribution bristles with difficulties.' Nonetheless, Fletcher concludes the letter with three bold statements:

> (1) It is eminently desirable, both for our schools and for our country, that such boys should be admitted by us.
> (2) The opposition to their admission has not proceeded from the 'public' schools.
> (3) The obstacles to their admission are practical and financial, not social.

[c] The meeting took place on 3 April 1919 with H. A. L. Fisher, President of the Board of Education (1916–22) and architect of the 1918 Education Act.

The matter was raised again four years later when Fred Bramley, secretary to the TUC, came to discuss with the Conference committee the relation of public school training to industrial appointments. Fletcher was particularly intrigued and encouraged by this initiative and his own industrial roots helped him to forge an understanding with Bramley who was more than willing to see public school men taking more posts of responsibility in industry. But if they were to do so, they should 'throw open the doors of that education as widely as possible'.[18] Bramley added that the trades unions were considering the possibility of funding places for working-class boys but here, of course, was the difficulty. Fletcher regretted that 'Mr. Bramley's interesting suggestion has borne no practical fruit as far as the older public schools are concerned. Financial and administrative difficulties have blocked the way.'[19]

Despite his many responsibilities Fletcher never lost his love of teaching and his conviction that, even for a busy headmaster, teaching must come first. Throughout his forty years at Rugby, Marlborough and Charterhouse Fletcher taught the clever boys of the classical sixth. 'Work remained a delight up to the last lesson that I taught.'[20] The delight was shared by his pupils: for William Temple at Rugby he was supreme and for George Turner at Marlborough he was, before all else, a great teacher:

> Not all fine scholars – and his scholarship was superlatively fine –
> are good teachers, and of those that are, some make their names
> as teachers as much by dramatic performance as by their learning.
> But no man was less of an actor than Sir Frank: his power as a
> teacher came straight from his intellect and from his heart; and it
> was the integrity of both, his lucid mastery of what he taught and
> his keen desire that those whom he taught should understand, that
> made us eager to learn from him.[21]

Harold Hanbury started at Charterhouse with Fletcher in 1911. He had won the third scholarship and went on to read law at Oxford where he was a fellow of Lincoln College for thirty years before being elected Professor of English Law. 'I was privileged to come very close to (Fletcher) during my two years in the Sixth Form,' he wrote in a retrospective article in *The Carthusian*. 'He was a brilliant classic and most inspiring teacher.'[22]

Fletcher shared his sixth form teaching with A. L. Irvine, known, despite his weakness for sarcasm, as 'Uncle'. The dramatist Sir Ronald Millar remembered him as 'pink, plump, shy, and Dickensian, with a head like an egg'[23] while Fletcher thought of him as a 'kind friend and untiring worker'.[24] Irvine came to Charterhouse from Bradfield in 1914 and was the third generation of his family to teach there. F. S. Porter, his predecessor as sixth form classics master, had been appointed to succeed the legendary T. E. Page shortly before Fletcher arrived. He was not a success and after three years Fletcher transferred him to a junior form to make way for Irvine. Fletcher and Irvine complemented one another both as teachers and personalities. 'Irvine was a great enthusiast, widely cultivated, he could easily be diverted from the work in hand to talk of William Morris or stained glass, for instance ... Fletcher was something more; he had a touch of genius; he was a scholar with a particular interest in Aeschylus's *Agamemnon* ... Though small, he had a commanding presence and his delivery was impressive. Both he and Irvine taught us English for two hours a week; but whereas Irvine might go on pleasantly about, say, Browning's *Pippa Passes*, Fletcher took us through the best parts of great works like *The Faerie Queen* and *Paradise Lost*.'[25] When Irvine started to teach the sixth he was struck by how little English literature they knew. So, 'through all my thirty-two years the hour's school on Tuesday afternoon after Corps parade was made sacred to English. We could not read much, but it was possible to whet the appetite.'[26] Fletcher also taught as much English as he could manage, in addition to Greek and Latin composition, translation and the study of works of classical literature. Browning, of course, was always a favourite, as were Shakespeare, Milton and Tennyson.

In an age before constant public examinations, league tables and tightly packed timetables there was scope for a teacher to diversify and pursue enthusiasms. Fletcher and Irvine each taught half the same boys' lessons and they were free to plan their syllabuses in a way unimaginable today. In his memoirs, *Sixty Years at School*, Irvine describes one of the advantages of teaching the sixth as not being too strictly bound by a timetable:

If occasionally it seemed good to lay by Demosthenes or Tacitus for an hour while I read the trial of Mr. Pickwick, or the dinner-party at Mr. Dilly's, or Cobden's Over, or the description of the gorge of the Adonis from *The Golden Bough*, I am sure it was quite as good education ...

I declined at all times to think much about examinations, and hated the idea of any special preparation for scholarship-hunting. Perhaps that is why so many got them: they generally went up fresh. But once I did have to face the question of examinations, when in 1926 I persuaded the headmaster to let go the very useless Higher Certificate and have an examination with subjects and examiners of our own choice ...[27]

In Fletcher's time classics enjoyed an enviable record of scholarships at Oxford and Cambridge. In 1928 A. B. Ramsay, the Master of Magdalene College, Cambridge was the examiner at Charterhouse. He told Cyril Alington how impressed he had been by the standard of work and was asked in return why it was then that Charterhouse did not win scholarships. This was untrue: since 1914 forty-seven had been awarded at Oxford and twenty at Cambridge, and in time Cambridge came to take a larger share, especially at King's, Trinity and Magdalene. No pupil of Fletcher's at Rugby, Marlborough or Charterhouse had followed him in winning the coveted Ireland Scholarship at Oxford until in 1924 it was awarded to Thomas Webster who had been senior scholar at Charterhouse. Like Fletcher he took a first in greats and also won the Craven and the Derby, and ended his career as Professor of Greek at University College, London. He had gone up from Charterhouse to Christ Church because Irvine did not think he was good enough for Balliol!

Fletcher and Irvine shared a classroom in Gownboys, the central boarding house which in London had accommodated the scholars. The room was small, dark and stuffy and at last in 1931 a new sixth form room was built. It was in a better position, next to the library, and was built in Tudor style with an adjoining archway flanked by oriel windows. The room was used not just for classics teaching but also for monitors' meetings, and Irvine persuaded Fletcher that it deserved better than the previous dreary desks and benches. Oak furniture was specially designed by Christopher Green who had been head of school in 1919 and had recently helped his father to design the interior of the Dorchester Hotel. Irvine was a passionate admirer of the poetry and designs (though not the politics) of William Morris. He took every opportunity to enthuse about Morris and after showing the sixth form some of his textiles, one pupil suggested that they had Morris curtains for the room and that the form would pay. Material of crimson and black was chosen and Irvine records that 'with the clean furniture, the curtains and the pictures, the room was one it was a pleasure to inhabit.

The walls were free for the formation of a picture gallery, which grew from two Medici prints to thirteen, derived from various sources and ranging from Leonardo da Vinci to Charles Furse. And very useful they were. Everyone was expected to have an adequate knowledge of them and occasionally that knowledge was tested on paper.'[28]

After leaving Saunderites in 1924 Fletcher had limited contact with pupils other than the monitors and his pupils in the classical sixth. To most boys he seemed a distant, stern and daunting figure, despite the fact that he was often seen walking around the school and would stop when he met a boy and ask about his family, his work or his games. He regularly saw every junior member of the school for 'calling over' which still happens at Charterhouse today. 'Each form stood in line in turn in front of the Head and the list of their current places in the form were laid in front of him. He discussed their progress with the form master, and every now and then would crook his finger and a boy would come up onto the dais and speak, or be spoken to by the Head ... it gave every boy a sense of belonging – sometimes an uncomfortable one, and it made clear to all that each boy did matter to the school and to the Head.'[29] 'Calling over' gave Fletcher a chance not only to see and be seen by every boy below the sixth but also to scrutinise their academic progress. He was able too to know how forms (and formmasters) were performing and to offer what encouragement, remedy or censure was required.

Brooke Hall, the masters' common room, was also housed in Gownboys when Charterhouse moved to Godalming. Again it soon proved inadequate and in 1910 when Henry Silver bequeathed £5,000 to the school it was decided to erect a separate building with several rooms for the masters. Silver had left Charterhouse in 1844 and later became a friend of Thackeray when they were both contributors to *Punch*. The new building was positioned at one of the entrances to the school, incorporating an archway with lodgings for the school sergeant on one side and the masters' rooms on the other. It is a handsome building with battlements, stone mullioned windows and, above the arch, carved faces and six painted coats of arms, including Silver's, Thackeray's and Fletcher's. Fletcher's had been granted to his father in 1913, the year Brooke Hall was completed. The shield is azure blue with a white cross and three familial arrows in each of the quarters.

The new facilities of Brooke Hall encouraged a lively companionship and conviviality among the masters unknown in other schools. Fletcher valued this for the good influence it had on the school and he dined with his colleagues as often as he could:

> The Brooke Hall of to-day is a happy mixture of a common room and a club, in which masters united by the bond of common work ... meet daily in casual intercourse, and may, if they will, meet twice a week to dine. The institution has acquired in course of time a sort of personality, and makes a valuable contribution to the efficiency and the pleasantness of Charterhouse ... A stranger who is privileged to join in a Brooke Hall dinner ... finds himself in a society resembling the high table of a college or the officers' mess of a good regiment, but with this advantage over both, that the members dine together more rarely and are therefore more mutually interesting.[30]

Fletcher enjoyed the masters' company at Charterhouse more than he had at Marlborough. This was certainly due in part to the opportunities Brooke Hall gave to meet them off duty. He was older too and more confident and relaxed with colleagues.

Max Beerbohm was a boy at Charterhouse in the 1880s and he discovered his talent for caricature by sketching the masters. The best known shows Haig Brown on his Sunday afternoon walk with two housemasters, F. K.W. Girdlestone and T. E. Page.[31] It is a delightful pen and ink cartoon depicting three Victorian eccentrics of various shapes and sizes dressed in frock coats and high hats and deep in conversation. This trio took their Sunday stroll together for twenty-four years and it remained an institution after Haig Brown retired. Rendall declined the invitation so another master, William Moss, took his place. Fletcher joined as soon as he arrived and the perambulation continued until 1933 when Page, after sixty years of Sunday walking, found his legs were no longer equal to the task.

When Fletcher started at Charterhouse Page had just retired after nearly forty years. Girdlestone had one more year to go, making fifty years at the school, including ten in London, five as a boy and five as a master. Girdlestone had returned to teach three years before Fletcher was born and was a housemaster for over forty years. 'His life was a model of regularity, mapped out by the clock, with a time and a day for everything. Regularly on two days a week I used to see him going down past my study window to play fives or rackets, a striking bearded figure, on his head the house-cap he had worn as a boy, moving with that peculiar walk which earned him the nickname of 'Duck'. On Sundays with equal regularity he walked, in a top-hat, with Page and Moss and the headmaster, always taking the same round.'[32] Girdlestone was approaching seventy when in July 1912 he wrote to Fletcher to say 'I think the time has arrived, when, as they say in Devonshire, I ought to be declining business, or (in other words) retiring ... I have delayed writing this letter till somewhat late; but, to speak the honest truth, after so many years' connection with the school, I much wish to avoid a prolonged period of farewells, and all demonstrations or testimonials of every sort and kind.'[33] At the assembly at the end of term Fletcher asked the masters to leave and in their absence, and to much cheering, he sang the great man's praises. Girdlestone retired to his native Devon and never returned to Charterhouse.

Girdlestone and Page were very different schoolmasters. While Girdlestone was pedantic, unambitious and devoted to detail, Page was a towering figure, intellectually brilliant, passionate, and with interests that stretched far beyond Charterhouse. 'It is not, I think,' wrote Fletcher, 'an exaggeration to say that he is the most distinguished man I have ever known ... He combined to a peculiar degree the qualities of the scholar and the man of the world.'[34] After Shrewsbury Page had won every prize at Cambridge including a congratulatory first and a fellowship. He preferred schoolmastering to university teaching and came to Charterhouse in 1873 as sixth form classics master, a position he maintained until he resigned aged 60 in 1910. 'It is a tragedy', wrote Sir Ronald Storrs in his memoirs, 'that T. E. Page, one of the few who could inspire as well as teach, was not, in the prime of life, appointed a University Professor of Latin or of Greek or the Master of some great college. But it is a tragedy of which no sixth-form Charterhouse boy can complain, and for which some of us must always feel and express, though we can never repay, an infinite debt of gratitude.'[35]

Though Page left Charterhouse six months before Fletcher arrived, they became close personal friends. He had welcomed Fletcher's appointment and wrote to say so, offering his help and advice. He respected Fletcher's scholarship and the fact that he was not in holy orders. Page had applied for the headmastership himself when Rendall was appointed and blamed the fact that he was not selected on his being a layman. This had embittered him and he became a trenchant critic of governing bodies, headmasters and the Headmasters' Conference alike. When retired he lived near the school and was often seen walking past and through the grounds. His height and stoop, his dishevelled appearance and his grave, lugubrious expression, reminded the boys of an Old

Testament prophet. Osbert Lancaster was at Charterhouse in the 1920s and remembered the vivid impression he had made:

> Immensely tall with long hair falling over his coat-collar and a growth of stubble on his massive chin, which never reached a point where it could quite qualify as a beard, he was the one personage connected with the school whose reputation extended beyond its boundaries. Reputedly a grandson of George IV he was undoubtedly one of the great classical scholars of his day whose edition of the Aeneid I believe still holds the field. Many, many years previously he had purchased a large roll of light grey Donegal tweed, which had become legendary even in my father's time, from which all his trousers had subsequently been cut. Although a permanent and much appreciated feature of the Carthusian landscape he was by no means immobile and was likely to turn up in the most improbable spots; on one occasion I found myself opposite him in the restaurant car on the Blue Train, on another I encountered him strolling down Bond Street with Mrs. Asquith on his arm.[36]

Page began a new, varied and eminent career after leaving Charterhouse. He was appointed editor-in-chief of the Loeb Classical Library with its Greek and Latin texts printed in parallel with new translations. Page was an exacting editor, correcting the typescript of his translators as if it were a sixth form exercise, with careful explanations in the margins. He was also a gifted orator, an enthusiastic if independent Liberal, and a friend and admirer of Herbert Asquith. He was invited to give the speech at the Reform Club in Pall Mall (of which he was the doyen) when in February 1925 the club gave Asquith a dinner to mark his translation from the Commons to the Lords. Page proposed Fletcher for membership and he was seconded by Henry Phillipps who had been a pupil of Page's at Charterhouse and was by then a leading Liberal, having been private secretary to Asquith, chief whip and chairman of the party. Fletcher was elected in February 1928 and enjoyed evenings and dinners at the club and a wider circle of friends than Brooke Hall could provide. Fletcher was present when the club presented Page with his portrait which hangs today in the Strangers' Room beside those of Dickens, Thackeray and Gladstone. He was there too when a dinner was given in 1934 to celebrate Page's being made a Companion of Honour by King George V; Fletcher was among eleven members who gave speeches, including two members of the cabinet.

Fletcher inherited three masters who had been Page's pupils: A. H. Tod, Frank Dames-Longworth and A. F. Radcliffe whom Fletcher eloquently described as 'a master of graceful scholarship and kindly culture'.[37] Dames-Longworth was an Irish aristocrat and typical of a snobbish, clever, games-playing, extrovert breed of public school-master. After Cambridge (where he took a first in classics and won blues in rackets and tennis) he taught at Marlborough for a year before returning to Charterhouse in 1886 to teach the fifth form. He was an inspiring teacher, an even more inspiring rackets coach, and a jealously devoted housemaster. According to Irvine, Dames-Longworth was 'a man with much of Irish charm and a good deal of Irish unreasonable-ness – not always an easy colleague, especially to headmasters.'[38] Certainly he and Fletcher were very different in background and temperament and did not get on. The cricketer R. C. Robertson-Glasgow remembered the war years as 'a struggle being fought out between an old idea and a new, of which, at Charterhouse, the respec-tive champions were Frank Dames-Longworth and Frank Fletcher, the headmaster. Conservative v. Liberal; Trinity, Cambridge v. Balliol, Oxford; champagne, if you like, v. tea. They were united only in their love of classical learning, and both were scholars of the first order. But they differed utterly and from the roots in their conception of scholar-ship. Fletcher loved learning because it was learning; Longworth loved it rather because it was something without which no gentleman was quite complete, a polite adjunct of the finished social article.'[39]

Another master whom Fletcher distrusted was Alfred Tressler, and again partly for political reasons, though this time at the other end of the spectrum. Tressler was a socialist and in the war years he had been outspoken in his disapproval of nationalism and the OTC. Actually this had more to do with his German ancestry for which he was badly treated by the boys in the years before and during the war. He bore his persecution with admirable *sang-froid* and won the boys round. In the end he became very popular and was bitterly disappointed when Fletcher refused to make him a housemaster. Tressler was an energetic and eccentric teacher of German, French and English and he was also a fine classical scholar. Harold Hanbury remembered 'an occasion when neither Fletcher nor Irvine was available to take the Sixth in Homer and Tressler's aid was invoked. How we all enjoyed that hour! His idea always was that the only way to get the best out of Homer was to race through the text picking up especial points of beauty on the way.'[40] Tressler was a keen cyclist and in the holidays he took boys with him to the Continent. The informality and daring of these adventures made them most unusual. 'The memory of the tours is one of growth and discipline and freedom. One's first bathe in a Southern sea; making friends with German students in youth hostels; eating fried frogs' legs in the moonlight by Diocletian's palace; seeing veiled Moslem women in the oriental market at Sarajevo, among the hookahs and rose leaf jam.'[41]

Fletcher was always so busy and settled at Charterhouse that he never thought seriously of leaving. The mastership of an Oxford or Cambridge college would have been the most obvious appointment and he had been considered by Magdalene, Cambridge in 1925 when the Master, Arthur Benson, died (Benson had been Mallory's tutor). Fletcher was soon rejected though on the grounds that he was an Oxford man. Eight years later he was one of several names considered by St Catherine's, Cambridge. He was approached, as was Cyril Norwood, Headmaster of Harrow, but both declined. The post would have meant a substantial drop in salary but by 1933 Fletcher was getting close to retirement so this was not an obstacle. He felt, however, that he had rejected a university career at the start and had no wish to change his mind forty years later. Only Balliol might have persuaded him and there had indeed been a chance in 1924, the year when Fletcher was elected an honorary fellow and when A. L. Smith, Strachan Davidson's successor as Master, died after half a century at the college. In the running were three fellows, all friends and contemporaries of Fletcher – Cyril Bailey, A. W. Pickard-Cambridge and 'Sligger' Urquhart. Instead A. D. Lindsay, Professor of Moral Philosophy at Glasgow and an active member of the Labour party, was elected and stayed until 1949.

Headmasters do not as a rule make good heads of colleges and Fletcher was aware of this. Even today, independent school heads exercise a level of power and patronage that has vanished in every other profession.[d] College heads, on the other hand, have never been more than first among equals, unable to exercise authority without the agreement of the fellows. Very few former headmasters have managed to adjust to this. G. G. Bradley left Marlborough in 1870 to become Master of University College, Oxford which he soon set about reforming with the same zeal he had employed at Marlborough. 'His first

[d] The educational historian, A. F. Leach, observed in 1913: 'There is probably no position in English civic life where a single individual exercises such uncontrolled power as does the headmaster of a successful public school.'

address to the undergraduates had a decidedly headmagisterial tone, and was described as "mealy" by a diarist among them, whose first impressions of the new Master were not favourable.'[42] Neither the fellows nor the undergraduates cared for Bradley's interventionist style and they made his life a misery. Both Fletcher's headmasters at Rugby had bad experiences as heads of Oxford colleges. H. A. James was appointed President of St John's and confessed that he 'felt throughout that a considerable part of it could have been done by an intelligent secretary or clerk'.[43] John Percival went from Clifton to Trinity, Oxford in 1878. Immediately he tried to root out undergraduate idlers and he rode roughshod over the independence of the fellows. He had his followers, Charles Gore among them, who 'felt that a great, strong, righteous will was expressing itself among us, with profound astonishment at our being content to be such fools as we were; and this to me was very bracing.'[44] But Percival was delighted when the invitation came to leave Oxford for Rugby.

Though Fletcher was clear that the mastership of St Catherine's was not for him he found the approach unsettling. He was sixty-three and had been at Charterhouse for over twenty years. There was no fixed age limit (Haig Brown had retired from the school at seventy-three) but Fletcher decided that sixty-five would be the right time to go and in November 1934 he went to Lambeth Palace to tell the Archbishop of Canterbury, Cosmo Lang, that he intended to leave at the end of the summer term. They discussed potential successors and the archbishop's note on the meeting says that Fletcher 'could not think of any ordained man in England who was of the first rank'.[45] (Lang's reply is not recorded!) Instead Fletcher recommended his pupil, George Turner, if he could be persuaded to leave Marlborough. Fletcher wrote a formal letter of resignation at the end of January: 'I cannot hope, at the age of 65 to retain the freshness & initiative which the work calls for; & I feel that the necessary time has come for me to hand over to a younger man.'[46] The governing body was informed at their February meeting and the following day Fletcher told the school at the beginning of the service in chapel. As it happened, the psalm that morning was the 121st. 'It seemed like an answer of goodwill when they sang the concluding verses, and especially the last of all: "The Lord shall preserve thy going out and thy coming in, from this time forth for evermore!"'[47]

Turner refused to apply, though twelve years later he was to become Fletcher's successor-but-one. Fletcher vented his disappointment by interfering in the selection process. He was particularly incensed to discover that the governing body was considering an application from Robert Longden, a fellow of Christ Church.[e] He was too reminiscent of Rendall and furthermore he was a bachelor. In an impassioned and revealing letter to Lang, Fletcher wrote:

> I regard a young unmarried don who has never been a school-master, whatever his academic distinctions or personal attractive-ness, as quite unqualified for the work of this Headmastership ... Charterhouse suffered grievously, more grievously than outsiders can realize, from the appointment after Haig Brown of a man of academic distinction with no school experience ... I owe every-thing to my training on the Rugby staff. It was that, and not acad-emical distinctions, that qualified me, so far as I was qualified, to be Master of Marlborough ... The school which has had Mrs Haig Brown and my wife deserves and looks for a good Head-master's wife ... I should have been quite lost at Marlborough without my wife.[48]

The governors ignored Fletcher's advice and included Longden on a short-list of three who were called for interview. The others were the Headmaster of Fettes, A. H. Ashcroft, and Robert Birley, a thirty-two-year-old history master at Eton. Fletcher determined to champion Birley's cause, despite the fact that he had overlooked him when he had applied for a history post a few years before. Birley appealed to Fletcher for a variety of reasons: he was much the same age as Fletcher when he started at Marlborough; he had a Lancashire background and, extra-ordinarily enough, Birley's great-great-uncle had led the cavalry charge at Peterloo when Fletcher's great-grandfather read the Riot Act. Furthermore, Birley had been a boy at Rugby in G. F. Bradby's house and an undergraduate at Balliol where Fletcher's friend Cyril Bailey was his tutor. Birley's breadth and energy of intellect, as well as his great height and physical ungainliness, reminded Fletcher of William Temple, and indeed the two men shared much the same social conscience and were both products of Rugby and Balliol. Birley had proved himself at Eton as a brilliant and inspiring teacher, but of history not classics. Fletcher was not deterred by this but recognised in Birley a modern breed of headmaster. 'The conviction is growing on me', he wrote to

[e] Longden was appointed Master of Wellington where he was killed in a bombing raid in 1940. Another Christ Church tutor had applied for the Mastership of Marlborough when Fletcher left.

Lang, 'that it will probably be necessary to break new ground and take someone of the post war generation which is just on the verge of being ready. The man I have in mind is Robert Birley, who has been for eight or nine years a master at Eton. Elliott describes him as 'alpha+' and tells me that when Alington left there was a strong desire in the staff that Birley should be his successor ... Birley was in Godfrey Bradby's House at Rugby: so he has more than an Eton training ... I know of no one else available who would be welcomed here or whom I should care to see appointed.'[49] The governing body reached the same unanimous conclusion and Birley was appointed in March 1935.

The Fletchers were dreading their final few months at Charterhouse but in the end they were cheered by the kindness of all concerned and by their own feelings of thankfulness for the past. William Temple was by now Archbishop of York and both he and the Archbishop of Canterbury came on separate occasions to Charterhouse during Fletcher's final term to preach and stay for the weekend at Northbrook. Senior boys were invited to join them for dinner and one recalls Fletcher and Archbishop Lang exchanging memories of Jowett and Balliol. While he was staying, Temple gave an address to the upper forms on Christian evidences. Fletcher had not given him any previous notice but nonetheless 'the clearness & fluency, not without touches of humour, with which he spoke, held the boys' attention & left many of them with the conviction that they had understood every word that he said. It was a remarkable tour de force, enjoyed equally by both speaker and audience: both the eloquence & the enjoyment were characteristic.'[50]

The Charterhouse Masque was performed again in June in front of Northbrook House, partly to celebrate the Silver Jubilee of George V and partly to mark the headmaster's retirement. The writer and war correspondent Sir Philip Gibbs happened to visit Charterhouse when the masque was being rehearsed. He was there to research his book *England Speaks*, 'Being Talks with Road-Sweepers, Barbers, Statesmen, Lords and Ladies, Beggars ... and All Manner of Folk of Humble and Exalted Rank.' The book is a nostalgic 'Panorama of the English Scene in this Year of Grace 1935', and in the section on The Public Schools, Gibbs gives a fascinating vignette of the Fletchers' last summer at Charterhouse, and of a vanished age:

It was a summer day in June, with a blue sky overhead and a warm sun on the fields, whose haymaking was beginning. I drove through deep lanes, overhung by the heavy foliage of tall elms, with a tracery of sunlight and shadow across the roads. Foxgloves were growing tall in the hedges, and the elderberry blossom was like snow on the bushes. For the way to Charterhouse lies through a pleasant countryside, not yet spoilt, though terribly in danger because of a by-pass road which came with a clean gash through its loveliness.

I enquired the way to the main entrance of the school of one of the Charterhouse boys, who was riding a bicycle. He was kind enough to turn round out of his way – which was probably towards a tuck shop – and ride ahead of my car to show me. 'Good form,' I thought. 'That boy has nice manners. There's something to be said for Charterhouse.'

There was a lot to be said for Charterhouse. I had met old Carthusians, as they call themselves, in many parts of the world. Many of them were officers in a World War, and laughed a little and sighed a little when they talked of these places, which they wanted to see again and mostly never did. The day I went to their old school was given up to a pageant. They were having a dress rehearsal when I arrived, as was explained to me by the sergeant porter who undertook to find the Head Master for me.

We walked through the big archway, past the new chapel by Gilbert Scott. The school buildings, ivy-covered and stately, are in a noble setting. Beyond them the playing fields stretch away, smooth and green, to a vista of tall trees, heavy in foliage, and to the surrounding hills of Surrey. The first and second elevens were playing cricket, and I stood to watch them for a few seconds. The sergeant porter discovered the whereabouts of the Head Master. He was watching the rehearsal of the pageant, from which he led me a little way for a quiet talk under the trees. 'This is my last term,' he told me, with a moment's sadness. 'I have had a longish innings. I've been here for twenty-four years.'

Fletcher of Charterhouse is a famous name all over the world among old Carthusians. He was the Head Master of the boys who heard one day in August that their elder brothers were wanted for a war. 'Your King and Country need you,' they were told, and they didn't need telling twice. 'How do you compare the present vintage of boys with those of the pre-war years?' I asked. Fletcher of Charterhouse glanced over at the crowd of boys sitting on the benches above the pageant ground, and a smile softened his thin

lips. 'They're all right. We're back to normal now. There's nothing wrong with this lot. For a time after the war the boys were
nervy and difficult. Some of them were inclined to be cynical and
hard. The war left its mark on them. It cast a shadow over them.
Now we've got beyond all that.'

He took me over to the pageant ground, and I stayed for an
hour or so watching the rehearsal. On the benches behind me
were rows of boys in old costumes. I looked at their faces and saw
in them the line of heredity back to Elizabethan England, and
beyond. In front of us was a canvas screen representing old walls
with a gateway, through which the actors came and went. They
were performing a masque bringing to life again old scenes in the
history of Charterhouse, from the days when the monks were
turned out of their monastery by orders from the King.[51]

In July there were farewell dinners in a marquee on the Northbrook
lawn – one for masters and their wives and matrons and another for
forty members of the works department and domestic and grounds
staff who presented Frank with a silver pocket watch and Dorothy with
a silver card case. Brooke Hall gave them a beautiful thirteenth-century
Chinese porcelain dish. A presentation fund was set up by Old Carthusians: over 1,000 subscribed and raised nearly £1,000, half of which
was spent on a bust of Fletcher by Jacob Epstein. This was given to the
school and Dorothy was given a replica (now in the library at Rossall).
Fletcher had so disliked his portrait at Marlborough that he was only
prepared to sit for a sculptor. Epstein was a bold choice – his work was
innovative and controversial and his personal reputation notorious. He
stayed with the Fletchers for a week in order to study Fletcher at close
hand and it is hard to imagine what this rebellious, bohemian New
Yorker with his scandalous private life had to say to a man so
completely his opposite. But Fletcher had chosen him and was fascinated by his work.

1935 was the same year that Epstein created perhaps his most
controversial statue, the massive *Ecce Homo*, the figure of Christ
brought bound before Pilate. The work was savaged by the critics:
G. K. Chesterton described it as 'one of the greatest insults to religion I
have ever seen'.[52] The sculpture was never sold and was finally installed
amid the ruins of Coventry Cathedral, close to Epstein's *St Michael and
the Devil,* on the wall of the new cathedral. 'I always knew you were a
man of courage', a friend wrote to Fletcher, 'but the man who has his

bust done by Epstein deserves the Victoria Cross.'[53] But Fletcher enjoyed the experience of three weeks of daily sittings. 'It was a delight to watch a great artist at work, and to listen to his accounts of the people who had sat to him – descriptions as vivid and candid as his portraits. No one who has seen him at work could dismiss him as a *poseur* or fail to credit him with earnestness and sincerity. "I cannot flatter," he said: "I wish I could."'[54] The bust is of bronze and life-size with Epstein's characteristic rough and rugged surface. Fletcher's expression is benign and it is certainly, as the The Times's critic called it, a 'portrait of astonishing vitality'.[55]

On the last Sunday of the term at the end of July the school gathered in the afternoon in front of Haig Brown's statue. The boys had raised enough money to buy the Fletchers a small Austin motor-car which was driven up by the head boy. Fletcher walked along the lines, shaking hands with every boy, before being driven round the block. Evening chapel followed with the closing service and its jubilant singing of 'Jerusalem'. In his valedictory sermon, Fletcher looked back to the consecration of the chapel eight years before, and forward to a future inspired by everything the chapel stood for.

9

Retirement

1935–1954

Two more farewell dinners were given in London in October. Fifty men who had been boys in Saunderites when Fletcher was their housemaster gave a dinner at the London Charterhouse where they presented Frank with a silver cigarette-box and Dorothy with a cheque to spend on a Saunderite corner in their new garden. A committee representing Rossall, Rugby, Marlborough and Charterhouse had arranged a white-tie dinner the next evening at the Connaught Rooms in Great Queen Street. The Archbishop of York, William Temple, was in the chair and eighty guests were present, including Fletcher's brothers, Ernest and Clement. J. R. White, a master who had taught at Rossall in Fletcher's time, was there, as well as nine headmasters, all of whom were Fletcher's pupils or headmasters of Fletcher's four schools: George Turner was both. In proposing the toast Temple referred to his own time at Rugby where he and Fletcher 'formed a friendship which both of us have treasured from that day to this, and which we find among our most abiding delights'. In replying, Fletcher looked back to Rossall, with its windswept shore and devoted masters; to Percival, James and Bradby at Rugby who had taught him the art of schoolmastering; to Marlborough, the foremost of the great Victorian schools with its magnificent setting; and to Charterhouse, 'a great community, which makes every master who serves it feel that life in a school is indeed life worth living'.

The decision to live in Devon in retirement was easily made. Dorothy was a devoted Devonian and could speak its dialect, while Frank had come to appreciate the county and relished the chance to live near the sea. Soon after they started at Charterhouse the Fletchers had a holiday home built at Woolacombe in north Devon, designed by the Surrey architect William Green who was A. L. Irvine's brother-in-law. They had spent most of the school holidays at the house and it had provided a welcome retreat. But it was not right for a permanent home and when the opportunity came to buy a plot of land near Dartmouth the Fletchers decided to move south and have another house built for them. They knew the spot already because it belonged to their friend the actor Cyril Maude who had been a boy at Charterhouse in the 1870s. This time the Fletchers chose the architect Hubert Worthington[a] who had studied under Lutyens. He created a large and beautiful house (the Fletchers named it Sutton Close) and managed to blend Lutyens with the local Devon style. The house had pale cream walls, blue louvred shutters at the windows, and a large sleeping-balcony attached to the main bedrooms. It was situated in an old walled garden at the head of the combe, looking down to the sea, with terraces and gardens in front and fir trees to the side. Though the Humphries family moved with them and lived in a cottage nearby, there were rooms in the house for two resident maids. Indeed the Fletchers lived here in considerable style and Dorothy became something of a *grande dame* with her nine-inch cigarette holder and a voice that was sounding more and more like the actress Edith Evans. She spent her days entertaining guests, painting and gardening, and taking an interest in the affairs of Stoke Fleming, the local village.

Fletcher's transition to retirement was eased by a very busy first two years. In 1936 James Darling (who had left Brooke Hall in 1929 to become Headmaster of Geelong Grammar School) invited Fletcher to attend a meeting of the Australian Headmasters' Conference. Fletcher had made similar educational visits before – in 1907 he had been to Germany at the request of the Board of Education to investigate the German method of teaching classics, and in 1930 he went to Canada with fifteen other headmasters to visit universities. Dorothy accompanied him to Australia and caused the Darlings some concern. 'Frank was his own kind and unassuming self and Mrs Fletcher was kind also, but she … rather expected everything to be just right, that is, as it would be in England. It took her a long time to understand that in Australia a bathroom door is always open if there is nobody in it and when it is shut it means that it is occupied. The lack of locks on the inside of such doors filled her throughout the tour with horrible apprehensions.'[1] Nonetheless, the Fletchers enjoyed the visit and the long voyage there and back. Frank was reminded of a saying of T. E. Page: 'I know nothing pleasanter than to do something you want to do, to feel that it is your duty to do it, and to do it at someone else's expense!'[2]

---

[a] Worthington's commissions included the remodelling of the Old Bodleian Library and the Radcliffe Camera at Oxford.

While they were away in Australia Fletcher's volume of sermons and addresses, *Brethren and Companions*, was being prepared for publication. A housemaster at Charterhouse, the Revd L. J. Allen, undertook the proof-reading: Fletcher had made the selection but most of the sermons were in manuscript and the printing needed careful scrutiny. Fletcher started to write his memoirs, *After Many Days: A Schoolmaster's Memories*, on the voyage there and back and they were published the following year. He explains in his preface that the book is not an autobiography or a treatise on education but 'a volume of reminiscences, personal and educational, set in an autobiographical framework'.[3] Despite its precise and rather formal prose, the style is surprisingly humorous, intimate and anecdotal. A review in *The Times* described the book's clarity and unpretentious wisdom: 'These reminiscences are, above all, a chronicle of human contact; they are recorded simply, allusively, almost casually, yet they make a whole, and the sense of gratitude and permanence shines through.'[4]

Fletcher finished the book on new year's eve 1936. Early in 1937 a telegram from Downing Street enquired whether he would accept the honour of knighthood for a lifetime's services to education. It came as a complete surprise: Fletcher was the first headmaster to have been offered such a distinction. Naturally he felt proud and gratified that his work, especially for the Headmasters' Conference, had been so acknowledged but he had also inherited a scepticism and unease about public awards and decorations. In his memoirs he commends his great-grandfather's decline of a baronetcy and remarks approvingly 'that my father would have done the same, if his services to Church and State had been similarly recognised. He found the reward in the work he did.'[5] Dorothy though was delighted and urged Frank to accept. He did not take much persuading and at 11 o'clock on Friday 11 June 1937 Fletcher was knighted at Buckingham Palace by the new king, George VI. Hundreds of congratulatory letters and telegrams from past pupils and colleagues, headmasters and friends poured into Sutton Close. One was from Cyril Norwood who had retired from Harrow the year before Fletcher. He was knighted too in 1938, the second headmaster to receive such an honour. Fletcher liked to think that he had started a trend but he was privately pleased that he had been chosen first and Norwood second.

In the next two years Fletcher was invited to be a guest lecturer on Hellenic Travellers' Club cruises. In 1938 he and Dorothy made it a family occasion and the party included their nephew Ralph, then up at

Balliol, and two nieces, Ralph's sister, Barbara, who was also at Oxford at St Anne's, and Cicely, who was reading classics at Lady Margaret Hall. The cruise lasted a fortnight and included visits to the Acropolis and Parthenon at Athens, to its rival city of Sparta, to Agamemnon's Mycenae, to the great amphitheatre at Epidauros and to Delos, the birthplace of Apollo; the sea had been too rough to visit Troy. The boat, SS *Letitia*, was small and hardly luxurious but the food was adequate and the opportunity to see so much in so short a time was ample compensation. Next year Frank and Dorothy took only Cicely. The lecture Fletcher gave on 'Tiryns, Argos, Mycenae in Legend and Literature' was later published.[6] Cicely had been studying Homeric archaeology and did not agree with all Fletcher's theories. Fletcher though was trying to excite an audience of passengers who were interested rather than learned and who wanted to be informed about the associations of places they were about to visit. In this context he felt that it made sense to exaggerate links between the stories told by Homer and the sites and ruins they were about to explore. 'So when we visit the palace-foundations of Tiryns and Mycenae I believe that we are standing by Homeric chieftains' castles: we interpret the ground-plan by the houses and palaces described in Homer, and may regard the incidents of Homer as having taken place in similar surroundings.'[7] Cicely was not convinced but Fletcher teased her by sticking to his guns; arguments over the dinner table were heated.

Fletcher was especially fond and proud of Cicely. By her own admission she was not a scholar and expected only a third in mods. She rashly promised to write Frank a Latin poem if she achieved a second. She did and Frank replied in kind in a playfully chauvinistic poem composed in alcaics, Horace's favourite metre: 'Uncle Frank joyfully sends his greetings to that learned girl, Cecilia; recently, while sailing across the deep sea, she feared neither the threatening waves nor the lashes of her uncle's tongue; now she has won new honours for Lady Margaret, for her father and for her family, triumphing in Oxford mods, in that she, a woman classicist, emerged on a par with men classicists. What a great girl you are – shining far above all other girls!'

Rumours of war caused Fletcher as much concern as anyone who had lived through the First World War just twenty years before. A German battleship anchored off Palermo was a troublesome sight and a sign of the German-Italian axis which was soon to begin its assault on Greece. The invasion closed the Aegean to travellers and made the Fletchers' second cruise the last Hellenic tour until the war was over. Fletcher worried about Birley who would have to see Charterhouse through another world war and he despaired that so few lessons had been learnt. In October 1938 William Temple asked him to add his signature to a letter to *The Times* calling for world unity. Other signatories included H. G. Wells and the scientist Sir Richard Gregory, editor of *Nature*. Their plea was well meant but naïve and redolent of League of Nations idealism:

> In order rightly to direct the normal day-to-day relations between nations a sustained plan is necessary, and in the formulation of such a plan the tenets of the New Testament must be translated from terms which embrace individuals into terms which embrace nations. To love thy neighbour as thyself, in the wider setting, clearly implies that the welfare of humanity and the interests of the whole community of nations must be placed before the narrower interests of any individual nations. Here is a guiding principle to which the actions of all Governments should conform.[8]

The Headmaster of Clayesmore School in Dorset was called up in 1940 and Fletcher was asked to take his place for the duration of the war. Dorothy was reluctant to leave Devon but Frank agreed to do his duty. His heart was not in the work though and Clayesmore was not his sort of school. Founded in 1896 it embodied a revolutionary ideal in which cultural activities and manual work ranked alongside academic endeavour. Edward Thring would have approved, especially of the school's emphasis on each pupil finding ways to express his particular talents, whatever they might be. The Fletchers were both unhappy and Frank felt unable to lead the school as he would have wished. 'A tactful legend was circulated that the Dorset air did not suit Lady Fletcher and, with a friendly, sad and rather apologetic letter, he quietly withdrew from the scene.'[9] Fortunately the pupils took the legend at face value and the school magazine paid tribute to Fletcher's 'wise and tactful handling of what might have been a difficult time of transition ... We sympathise with Lady Fletcher for the illness which has prevented her from sharing much of our life, and we regret it particularly since it means that she and Sir Frank are forced to leave.'[10]

William Temple's translation from York to Canterbury in 1942 was greeted with enthusiasm throughout the country and filled the Fletchers with especial pride and rejoicing. Fletcher had always followed his progress with interest and admiration (he collected first editions of all thirty-five of his books) and he had managed to keep in contact through letters and visits. Temple's broadcasts had already established him as a wartime leader and in his tragically short time at Canterbury he won the nation's affection as 'the people's archbishop'. But the strain of war, a massive workload and an inability to say no broke his health, and just two and a half years after his enthronement Temple collapsed and died, aged sixty-three. It was a tragic blow, not just to those like the Fletchers who knew and loved him, but to the nation and indeed to the world. It is hard today to imagine just what a towering figure an archbishop could be. His friend R. H. Hodgkin, then Provost of Queen's College, Oxford where he and Temple had been fellows together, wrote that his sudden death 'seemed to shake the western world as if one of its pillars had been removed'.[11] 'Many primates have ruled the Church with vigour and distinction,' wrote Temple's biographer, 'one or two have helped to determine the course of its history, and a few have wielded an appreciable influence over one section or another of the life of England. But of none except Temple, since the Reformation, can it be said that the *world* was the poorer for his passing.'[12]

Temple's death in the dark days of war plunged Frank and Dorothy into an unusual depression. They were both expert at keeping a sense of proportion and were well used to maintaining a stiff upper lip. But Frank was now in his seventies and the sudden loss of a much-loved friend and pupil who was also so important to the country proved a heavy burden. Their spirits were revived though by the announcement that Geoffrey Fisher was to succeed Temple: Fletcher's star Marlborough pupil was to follow his star Rugby pupil on the throne of St Augustine, just as (with Fletcher's help) he had followed him as Headmaster of Repton thirty years before. Though Temple had wanted Fisher to succeed him he was not an obvious choice and for the Fletchers it was a wonderful surprise. Again they watched his achievements with fascination, culminating the year before Fletcher died with the coronation of Queen Elizabeth II. The ceremony was to be televised for the first time and the Fletchers' was one of many households to obtain a set in order to watch the service. It was another extraordinary moment for Fletcher when he watched his pupil raise the crown of St Edward and place it on the sovereign's head.

For years Temple had been encouraging Fletcher to join the Church

Assembly. He had refused because he knew that he could not give the responsibility the attention he felt it deserved. But in retirement he was, as he put it, 'available for such unpaid jobs as I knew (and have since found) are always waiting to be done by those who have nominally "given up work"'.[13] The Church Assembly owed its inception in 1919 to William Temple as much as anyone. He had resigned the fashionable and lucrative living of St James's, Piccadilly to become the first secretary of the 'Life and Liberty' movement which was campaigning for more freedom for the Church from government control. The new Church Assembly was the movement's most important achievement, bringing more independence and democracy to the running of the Church.

Fletcher represented the Exeter diocese in the house of laity and was conscientious about attending the Assembly whenever it met in its building in Dean's Yard next to Westminster School. The Archbishop of Canterbury presided and Fletcher found himself sitting before two successive chairmen who had been his pupils. He was never in awe of either of them and on one occasion he took Fisher to one side and told him not to smoke when taking the chair! Much of the business was financial and routine and not dissimilar to the agendas of the Headmasters' Conference – pensions and stipends, funding for training, and matters of patronage and clerical discipline. Larger issues of Church unity and Church and State were debated too. The white paper which preceded 'Rab' Butler's 1944 Education Act was scrutinised and discussed at length and Temple's passionate advocacy of a new national system of education added to the strains which shortened his life. Fletcher was particularly useful here and his views in support of collective worship, religious instruction and the role of Church schools were listened to with considerable respect.

Fletcher had resisted repeated invitations to join his brothers Clement and Ernest on Rossall's council. He had certainly been tempted: he was devoted to his school, his father had also been on the council, and William Temple had joined when Bishop of Manchester. But when his Charterhouse pupil Charles Young was appointed headmaster in 1937 Fletcher agreed to join and remained a governor until 1948 when ill-health forced him to resign.

Despite Fletcher's very proper belief that 'a school council has two main functions, to choose the best Headmaster they can get and then to give him the freest possible hand'[14] these were demanding years for the governors. Lancashire had been badly affected by the industrial depression of the 1930s and numbers in the school were falling to such an extent that the preparatory school was sold and amalgamation with another school considered. Then in 1937 Rossall's sea-wall was shattered after a spate of heavy gales and high tides. The defences had to be rebuilt immediately, and though Fleetwood came to the rescue and shared the cost, the expense to the school was still considerable. As soon as war was declared the school buildings were commandeered to house a government department and the council had to find alternative accommodation. After an anxious search the Countess of Carlisle offered to lease Naworth Castle at a favourable rent and the school spent 1940 there. Beautiful and rich in history though it was, the castle was not suitable and the council managed to persuade the government to allow the school to return on condition that it shared its buildings with another evacuated school. Alleyn's arrived from Dulwich and stayed for the remainder of the war.

To add to the council's concerns the Battle of Britain encouraged the headmaster to offer his services to the RAF. Charles Young had left Charterhouse in 1914 and enlisted with the Royal Flying Corps: his experience was needed now to train young pilots. He was away for two years and the school was run by the bursar. As soon as he returned in 1942 the chairman of the council, Dr Herbert, Bishop of Blackburn, was translated to Norwich and had to resign. He had enjoyed his difficult five years at the helm, not least because he had been a pupil at Rugby under Rossall's headmaster, H. A. James. Fletcher was asked to succeed him and happily agreed: it was sixty years since he had started there as a boy and he was the first Old Rossallian to have occupied the chair.

The school's centenary was in 1944 but war postponed the celebration. Fletcher chaired the centenary committee which met first in October 1946. Having been present at the golden jubilee in 1894 he was able to draw on his memories of what had happened then. The time was fixed for the following October and there was again to be a concert (this time the guest conductor was Sir Thomas Beecham who had played in the school orchestra at the jubilee). The 1894 celebrations had happened in June so cricket gave way to rugby and this time the service was broadcast by the BBC. The Earl and Countess of Derby attended: the thirteenth earl had been patron of the school at its foundation and all four of his descendants had taken a close interest in the school. Despite heavy responsibilities as secretary of state for war and ambassador in Paris, the present earl had been a frequent visitor and had been instrumental in the school's speedy return from exile at Naworth. He was now eighty-two and Fletcher was seventy-seven. 'When Sir Frank Fletcher, Chairman of the Rossall Council, slowly advanced to greet Lord Derby, President of the Rossall Corporation, a silence of respect, admiration and pride fell upon the gathering. Here were two great men, in their different ways very great benefactors of Rossall, who in spite of age and affliction had come to honour her Centenary.'[15]

In 1946 Fletcher was elected the forty-fifth president of the Classical Association, founded in 1905 to promote classical education and scholarship. The association's custom was to choose for its president alternately a classical scholar and a man of eminence outside the classics. Fletcher belonged to the former category, though he was the first schoolmaster to have been elected. His predecessors among the latter included two prime ministers, Asquith and Baldwin; three distinguished pro-consuls, Curzon, Cromer and Milner; a lord chief justice, Lord Hewart; and a great archbishop, William Temple. Fletcher gave his presidential address on *Our Debt to the Classics; A Retrospect* at the annual meeting which in 1946 was held conveniently for Fletcher at Exeter. The shadow of war hangs obtrusively over Fletcher's apologia for the classics:

> The classics are, I believe, more than ever needed to-day, and more than ever relevant. They are needed as an antidote to the materialist outlook encouraged by purely scientific and vocational training, and to insular nationalistic views such as those which have led the world to disaster. They are relevant because the conditions in which youth to-day is growing up are far more akin than the days of our boyhood to those in which the great Latin and Greek writers lived.
>
> Theirs was no stable world. They grew up among wars and rumours of wars, when sudden reversals of fortune were common, amid recent memories of a troubled past and fears for an uncertain future. Virgil's description of his own times – 'right and wrong confounded, world-wide wars, crime rampant in many shapes, fighting in the East, and in the West Germany stirring up war' (*movet Germania bellum*) strikes a familiar note to us.[16]

So Fletcher deplores the drift away from the classics and defends them as a means 'to preserving for a further period the standards, the virtues and the living breath of civilization among the wrecks of a shattered world'.[17]

Fletcher's contributions to classical scholarship were confined largely to his teaching and to the sixth form pupils he encouraged and inspired. He produced only two slim volumes, both school commentaries on classical texts and both written in retirement. The first on the sixth book of Virgil's *Aeneid* was published by Oxford University Press in 1941. It is an iceberg of a book with the range and depth of Fletcher's scholarship largely concealed but discernible beneath the surface. In his preface Fletcher explains that his edition 'is not overburdened with irrelevant learning, but supplies, I hope, sufficient information to enable the student to discover for himself and appreciate the meaning of what he reads'.[18] Though the emphasis is on the detail of the text, complex ideas are explained clearly and difficult phrases translated.

In 1949 Basil Blackwell published Fletcher's *Notes to the Agamemnon of Aeschylus*. To Fletcher, *Aeneid* vi was the high-water-mark of Virgil's greatest work and similarly the *Agamemnon* was the finest of the Greek tragedies. In his presidential address to the Classical Association he had interpreted it in the same context of war: 'The *Agamemnon* is no longer for us just a play about an unfaithful wife and a murdered husband. It is a dramatic and infinitely sympathetic presentment of what war, even successful war, means in the way of unhappiness to all sorts and conditions of men and women, to the soldiers at the front, to deserted wives at home, to old men like the poet himself left behind while the young go out to fight ...'[19] Fletcher's notes have neither a text nor an introduction. The detail is there again and so too is the depth of scholarship but these are clearly teaching notes tidied and expanded for a wider audience. Some of Fletcher's style and qualities as a teacher are evident: an ear for the sound of the Greek words, an insight into the characters and an eye for the staging of the drama. Fletcher offers a wide range of comparisons to other classical texts and also to the Bible, Shakespeare, Browning, Coleridge and Tennyson. His constant desire to educate his pupils in English as well as classical literature is clear.

In the spring of 1947 Fletcher suffered a serious stroke which badly disabled his right side and forced him to write with his left hand. Producing the *Agamemnon* notes for publication, limited though they were, was a considerable achievement. So too was the visit to Rossall for the centenary just a few months later. Fletcher's determination to

minimise his disability was helped by Dorothy who shared his uncomplaining courage and resolve. She recognised that he needed to be near
Charterhouse again where George Turner was soon to succeed Birley
as headmaster and where Fletcher would be able to revive old friendships and take a new interest in the school. So she sacrificed her native
Devon and found a spacious house with a large garden at Eashing, just
one and a half miles' drive from Charterhouse. The Humphries family
moved with them and lived in a cottage in the grounds. Albert's devoted
service came into its own as he supported Frank on his daily exercise
around the garden, helped him in and out of the bath, and drove him to
and from chapel on Sundays, and in the afternoons to watch the games.
Former colleagues and friends were welcome at their home and enjoyed
the Fletchers' interest in their lives as well as their relish for news and
gossip. Fletcher's mind was relatively unaffected and he continued to
read and complete *The Times*'s crossword in twenty minutes. His
powers of speech though were damaged and he found it easier to listen
than to talk. William Veale, who had lived all his life at Charterhouse,[b]
was a regular visitor and he remembered how 'reminiscences afforded
Sir Frank great pleasure. He would sit back in his arm-chair on his half
of the hearth, as he called it, sitting opposite Lady Fletcher, always
there. When recalling some occasion, he would partially close his eyes,
as if to picture only that. If one, by chance, mentioned a happening that
he had forgotten or which was new to him, he would be all alert, and
lean forward as if not to miss any detail.'[20]

Fletcher's eightieth birthday in May 1950 was a very special occasion. Dorothy invited a host of former pupils and colleagues, friends
and family to a party at Eashing. A beautifully-bound volume of nearly
eighty essays, verses, quotations and reminiscences was presented, the
first of which, written in his own hand on Lambeth Palace notepaper, is
signed 'Geoffrey Cantuar':

My Dear Frank,
  Here is a tribute of great affection and gratitude from some of
your old pupils, Rugbeian, Marlburian and Carthusian, which
comes to greet you on your eightieth birthday: and I am allowed
the honour of saying the first word.
  It shall be in plain English. You know how little able I was to
write Latin or Greek: witness the wriggling lines in red ink which

---

[b] Veale's father was Haig Brown's butler. He started full-time work at Charterhouse in
1889 when he was fourteen and retired fifty-six years later.

used to underscore the most part of my compositions. But if you could not teach me to be a 'pure scholar', you taught me more valuable things which remain with me to this day ...

I wish your other Archbishop pupil were still here to give his greeting to you. For him as for myself, & for all who have in any way & another come under your influence, I acknowledge our common debt to you to which each one of us adds his own secret store of personal loyalties and of grace received.

Three years later Fletcher suffered a second stroke and it was clear after a spell in hospital that neither he nor Dorothy would be able to cope if he returned home. He was moved instead to Stoneycroft nursing home in Hindhead. Dorothy, now seventy-seven, was driven to see him every day but other visitors were now less frequent. Fletcher's mind and memory had been affected and he found it hard to recognise people or have any kind of communication. Mercifully this twilight existence did not last for long and Fletcher died in his sleep on 17 November 1954. Austere and restrained to the last, he had given strict instructions that he was to be cremated privately, that no flowers were to be sent, and that his ashes were to be scattered in the grounds of the crematorium.

Fletcher had said nothing about a memorial service and a fortnight later a packed and moving service was conducted in the chapel he had done so much to build. One of the prayers used at the consecration was included and Archbishop Fisher, as chairman of the governing body, gave the address. Exactly fifty years before he had been a member of Fletcher's sixth form: 'always for me', he said in his eulogy, 'he is the Master and I the eager and clumsy pupil.'[21] After the service, when Dorothy was being driven away, she wound down her window and called out imperiously to Fisher, 'Geoffrey!', and he came running across to her in his archiepiscopal robes as though still Frank Fletcher's senior prefect.

APPENDIX I

Sermon Preached at the Annual Founder's Day Service in the Chapel at the London Charterhouse, 12 December 1918

'It is good for us to be here.' – Luke IX. 33

Year after year, for more than three centuries now, in obedience to our ancient statute, Carthusians have met in this Chapel on this day to renew old associations, and to dedicate themselves afresh to the service of God and man in memory of what Charterhouse has done for them. To-night more especially we are met to give thanks; first for the munificent bounty and wise foresight of our Founder, whose body lies there 'buried in peace', who 300 years ago built so much greater than he knew: secondly, for the lives and examples of all faithful Carthusians, and those especially who in these last four years have borne the burden and heat of the day in the service of their country, of whom the greater part remain unto this present, but some, more than 600, have fallen: and lastly, as on this occasion I am more particularly bound to add, for a month of unexpected, long-hoped-for, peace.

For all these things 'it is good for us to be here'. But it is especially with reference to the last of the three that I have chosen for text these words of Peter, his first impulsive utterance when he and the other disciples awoke on the Mount of Transfiguration. They were the words of one still dazed by a wonderful experience, hardly knowing what he said. What that experience had been I do not pretend to explain. Dream, vision, revelation, call it which you will. But to them it meant that they had seen One whom they knew as their friend and daily companion revealed in a new dazzling light as equal to, nay, greater than, the great heroes of old. They cannot realize what it means, can only feel vaguely that it has been good for them to be there, in that high atmosphere, on that mount of vision. They could not understand at the time, we are told. But afterwards they remembered.

We too have been lately on our Mount of Transfiguration. We have seen our country, our school-fellows and pupils, all classes of our countrymen, transfigured by a great light of common endurance and sacrifice, lifted to the level of what seemed the unbelievable horoisms of old. For more than four years we watched them, through days of darkness and disappointment, anxiety and defeat: and as we watched, we asked ourselves humbly, we whom age or infirmity or duty forbade to share their dangers, whether we should have borne them so nobly, if the call had come to our generation and to us.

And then, with a bewildering suddenness, the end came: and for the first time for day or night since August, 1914, along the whole Western Front the guns were silent. None of us here, young or old, are likely to forget the day when that news came. None of those who in past years have met here in our Founder's honour have ever come with such a memory in their heart since the time of those who first sat in those seats, the Brothers who could remember the defeat of the Spanish Armada.

It was good to be an Englishman that day; good, too, to be a Carthusian; good above all to be with the School at Charterhouse. None who were present will easily forget our service held an hour after hostilities ceased, when not only boys and masters and masters' families, but the workmen on the buildings and estate, and the women working in the laundry, thronged to Chapel to sing the Te Deum and join in thanksgiving. It was a wonderful service: and hardly less inspiring was another which was held in the evening by special request of the servants of the households who could not come earlier – in which more than a hundred of them joined, helped by the boys' choir, who are with us here to-night. For once at least our Chapel was the centre and expression of our highest and strongest feelings and of our common Charterhouse life. For once at least we had met together, high and low, young and old, rich and poor, one with another, to give thanks with one accord to Him Who maketh wars to cease in all the world, Who is to be praised both for the living and the dead.

For the dead: for that day we knew that they had not died in vain. They were very near to us then, those boys and masters of ours who had fallen. Every week of each quarter throughout the war, we had commemorated them in short voluntary services, reading out the weekly toll of wounded and missing, prisoners and killed, and praying for them and for ourselves, that we might be worthy of the example and name they had left us, and might stand with them unashamed at the last in the presence of the Master. And now we could think of them, not without sorrow indeed, but with thankfulness, knowing that their sacrifice had not been wasted, that the right for which they gave their lives had prevailed.

But if we praised God for the dead, with even fuller hearts we gave thanks for the living. For more than four years, day after day, I had looked round the School Chapel, with the knowledge that of the 600 faces before me many would before long be looking upon the sordid horrors of war, silently asking myself how many, before a year was passed, might be lying dead on some battlefield. We had prayed in our hearts for them that, if it were possible, the cup might pass from them: and now, suddenly, we knew that it had passed, and that that nightmare of anticipation was lifted.

All that is a month ago now. We have felt the first thrill of relief pass: we have seen the first freshness and glory of it fade into the light of common day. If I have tried, perhaps vainly, to recapture it for a moment this evening, it has been in order to blend the memory of it with the thanksgivings and inspiration of this our ancient service.

Even now it is hard to recapture. We have come down already, like the disciples, from the Mount of Transfiguration into the doubts and difficulties, the faithlessness and failures, of ordinary life. It must be so: the hard work of the world, by which alone men's evils are cured, cannot be done if we remain on the heights. But can we not bring into it some of the vision that we have seen? Surely, if our feelings in those four years, and on that great day of solemn thankfulness, were more than mere excitement, mere sentiment, mere emotional admiration of those who had fought and fallen and conquered. If so, they will have left some lasting inspiration behind, some real resolve that, God helping us, we will meet the perilous opportunities of peace with a little of the courageous self-forgetfulness that our brothers showed on the battle-field. We have had our 'hours of insight', glimpses of a united nation kindled by a new spirit of comradeship and sacrifice. Can we do nothing to keep that flame alive?

Comradeship, or, if I may use the warmer term, brotherhood; – where should we find the inspiration for it if not in the life of an English Public School? Where above all if not here at Charterhouse, which has almost a hereditary right to the word? As long as 550 years ago a brotherhood, a Carthusian brotherhood, was first settled on this spot: and we claim the title for ourselves still. Brother Carthusians, and you not least who bear here the honourable title of Brothers of the Charterhouse, it is to strengthen and renew bonds of brotherhood that we meet here on our Founder's Day. I need not remind you who know what it is to belong to a Carthusian community, what privileges of mutual helpfulness that name implies. You who live in this Hospital, no less than we on our Surrey hill, know how much depends on charity and forbearance, on laying aside all petty jealousies and unworthy self-assertion. Unless we can do that, each for himself in his own community, we frustrate by our own selfishness the great purpose of our Founder.

It is the great glory of an English Public School that it links together all who belong to it in a great brotherhood, in a fellowship which does not end with our schooldays. All of us, boys and masters and old Carthusians, have learnt by experience, 'how good and pleasant a thing it is to dwell together in unity'. Of all the gifts of our ancient Foundation, there is none greater than this. And two commandments it lays on us in return. The first is, that we be true to that spirit in our relations to one another, putting aside personal rivalries, and bearing one another's burdens. And the second is like unto it; we are called upon to extend the same to others also who are not of our own class and circle, to be, if I may say so, missionaries of brotherhood to the world outside.

There we have to my mind the great Public School problem of the future. Rightly or wrongly, perhaps inevitably – of this I am not sure – our boys during their period of education are set apart, fenced off in separate and somewhat exclusive communities. Can they break down afterwards the barriers that have shut them in? Can they go down and bear the burden and heat of the day in the midst of their fellow-men without pride, without self-consciousness, above all without conde-scension? To that infinitely important question many of them in these last few years have given their answer, an answer to thank God for. Among the happier omens for the future has been the simple natural relation between public school boys and others with whom they have recently been thrown into special contact, whether private soldiers, or officers raised from the ranks, or agricultural labourers on the fields. They have claimed no privileges, shirked no responsibility, despised no form of useful labour. As we think of what they have done, we may thank God and take courage for the difficult years that lie before us.

For difficult they will certainly be – a searching test of the character which it is our boast that our schools develop. We of the so-called Public School class shall be asked to make any sacrifices. It will not be easy: there will be prejudices to be flung overboard, and cherished privileges to be surrendered. But the reward is proportionately great, the

The Fletchers' wedding party, August 1902

LEFT Fletcher in 1903: the new Master of Marlborough   RIGHT Fletcher on the right,
looking much the same age as his senior prefect (centre)

Marlborough College from the playing fields with the chapel on the right
and the white horse behind

The Master's Lodge at Marlborough

Fletcher's common room at Marlborough in 1908: M. H. Gould is sitting left of Fletcher and 'Pat' O'Regan is seated on the ground on the left

Charterhouse: Hardwick's new buildings at Godalming

LEFT Beerbohm's caricature of Page, Haig Brown and Girdlestone
RIGHT Robert Graves as a new boy at Charterhouse

George Mallory

LEFT The Verite fire: Fletcher is standing at first floor level and to the left of Tod
RIGHT Fletcher at the end of the First World War

Brooke Hall in 1920: on the left of the second row from the back is Grose-Hodge with Irvine three along and P. C. next but one along from Irvine. Two to the left of Fletcher is Dames-Longworth and between them is Tod

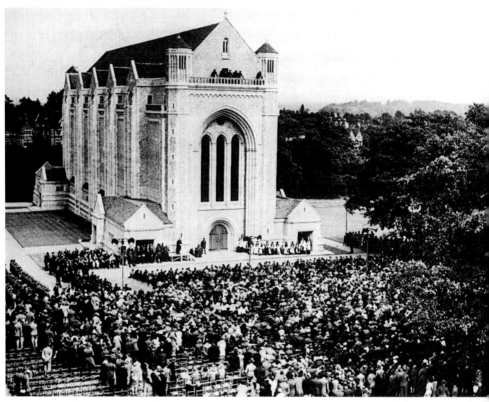

Fletcher addressing the crowd at the consecration of the Memorial Chapel

Fletcher teaching the sixth form at Charterhouse in 1935; his nephew Ralph
is in the centre of the front row

Epstein's bust

Dorothy in retirement

Fletcher's retirement dinner at the Connaught Rooms: at the table by the window (right) Fletcher is standing to the left of William Temple, George Turner is sitting beside Fletcher, and Robert Birley is on the left

The Hellenic cruise in 1938: Barbara is standing to the left of Frank and Cicely is standing to the right of Dorothy and next to Molly; Ralph is standing second on the left next to his mother

Dorothy and Frank at Sutton Close

prize of a fuller and a wider brotherhood than any that we have yet known. Faith will be needed to take new ventures: and foresight to know what to sacrifice and what to keep. But who should know better than Carthusians how old things and new may be blended? Who should have faith to face change if not members of the School that, guided by the strong faith and wise foresight of William Haig Brown, made the great venture of its history forty-six years ago? There are voices encouraging us, full of inspiration: – the call of our Founder, whose motto[1] bids us give back to men what God has so liberally given to us: the call of our fallen brothers, young men who had great possessions, of life, health, and hope, yet did not turn away sorrowful when the summons came to them: and above all, heard through and behind both, the voice of our Master Himself, inviting us to deny ourselves, ignore ourselves, so that others, and we with them, 'may have life, and have it more abundantly'.

1 Deo Dante Dedi.

APPENDIX II

Presidential Address Delivered to the Classical Association at Exeter, 9 April 1946

OUR DEBT TO THE CLASSICS
A RETROSPECT

There is a grim story, which some of you will remember, told by Herodotus, that pioneer of historians and prince of story-tellers, about the Persian Sisamnes and his son Otanes and how King Cambyses dealt with them. The father, one of the royal judges, was found to have taken bribes. The king had him executed, and from the dead man's skin made thongs of leather, with which he covered the chair of judgement. He then appointed the son judge in his father's place, and charged him μεμνῆσθαι ἐν τῷ καθίζων θρόνῳ δικάζει 'to remember in what chair he was sitting'. The circumstances of succession of your presidential chair are fortunately of a less grisly character; but the reminder is one which every new President may well apply, *mutatis mutandis*, to himself, when he reflects on the great and good men whom he so unworthily succeeds.

The reflection was emphasized for me when our admirable secretary, Mr. Bridge, whose services to our Association we gratefully acknowledge, sent me a list of the forty-four former presidents, together with copies of forty of their addresses. I understand that it is proposed to publish a selection of these as a volume when paper can be spared, from income-tax forms which no one welcomes and government pamphlets which no one reads, for less ephemeral and more attractive publications. They have, we believe, something more than a temporary value as a testimony to the world of the debt which eminent and learned men of very varied careers and characters acknowledge that they owe to their classical education.

Dr. Gilbert Murray, *quem honoris causa nomino*, observed in the opening of his presidential address of 1918 that 'it is the general custom of this association to choose as its President alternately a classical scholar and a man of wide eminence outside the classics'. We may note in passing that the two categories are not mutually exclusive: he is himself a notable instance of their combination. The recent occasion of his eightieth birthday has given his many admirers a chance to show how greatly that combination of public service with academic work is appreciated: and you will not consider it inappropriate to our meeting or irrelevant to my argument if I take this opportunity of associating our Association with the congratulations and good wishes that were expressed, and record the pride with which we claim him as a champion of our cause and a living witness for its defence.

I am told that this is the first occasion on which a mere schoolmaster has been chosen for President. As such I must be counted among the professional scholars; and I greatly appreciate the honour you have done me in associating me with a list which is headed by the famous name of that most attractive of scholars, Henry Butcher, which recalls the charming and scholarly personality of men like Warde Fowler and Mackail, and includes many living scholars of high reputation and learning.

One name in the list calls for a special tribute on this occasion. The Association has lost during the year one of its most distinguished members whose writings and personality were an eloquent testimony to the classical studies with which he was throughout his life so closely identified. The death of John William Mackail at the end of last year removed a veteran supporter of the cause for which our Association stands. Many who knew him only from his writings were stimulated and inspired by them to study and appreciate the great writers of the past: those who heard his occasional speeches at our meetings remember the grace and charm of his voice and language and appearance: and we who had the pleasure of his personal acquaintance think of him as one whose character was permeated with the beauty of the poetry which he studied and interpreted. *Abeunt studia in mores*: he seemed a living example of the qualities which, in the words of another of our ex-presidents, we connect with classical studies, 'the philosophic temper, the gentle judgement, the interest in knowledge and beauty for their own sake'. His speeches in this Association and elsewhere were distinguished by a scholarly felicity of phrasing which enlivened and illuminated our discussions. His presidential address in 1923 was a graceful and eloquent tribute to what Greece and Rome have given to the world – 'the Greek genius for asking the right question, and the Roman faculty of finding the practical answer'. Again: 'The Classics', he claimed, 'are a standard and example of right things done in the right way. With the doing of wrong things in the right way we are familiar; it is what is known as the doctrine of efficiency.' I recall how at another meeting of this Association he brightened a debate on the dull subject of books in School Certificate examinations by describing the issue as a choice 'between the tyranny of the set book and the anarchy of the excerpt'.

Two other quotations I have a personal reason for recalling. Balliol men of my generation are grateful to him for the tribute he paid to the memory of Evelyn Abbott, the paralysed tutor of our time, who had borne (he said) his lifelong affliction 'with more than Greek philosophy and more than Roman fortitude'. And a letter which I received from him in the year before his death, when he could write only with difficulty, closes with words that we may take as his message to our meeting to-day, in which he spoke of the 'substantial contribution' which scholars can make 'to preserving for a further period the standards, the virtues and the living breath of civilization among the wrecks of a shattered world'. In that contribution he took his full share. For it is the 'living breath' of the humanities that inspires the scholar and enables him to inspire others.

That is an essential feature of true classical education. It brings the student into direct personal contact with the greatest minds of the past. He does not merely read about them: spirit communicates with spirit and mind with mind across the gulf of centuries. True, the sound of the living voice is lost; no learning can recover for us the actual pronunciation of ancient Greek and Latin, though we may affirm with confidence that Greek was not pronounced by Demosthenes as now by the modern Athenian, and that the vowel sounds of Horace's Latin were not those of modern English, as some reactionaries still pronounce them. We may sympathize with the vain longing of R. L. Stevenson: 'If but some Roman would return from Hades and tell me by what conduct of the voice these thundering verses should be uttered, *Aut Lacedaemonium Tarentum*, I feel as if I should enter at last into the full enjoyment of the best of human verses.' But there is no voice, nor any that answers. As vainly might we wish that we could call up, like Odysseus, the ghost of Tiresias, to answer the question about Homer's pronunciation which that very great scholar and shrewd critic, T. E. Page used to ask, whether his famous epithet of the sea πολυφλοίσβοιο represents by its sound the roaring of ocean or the lisping of the waves.

The sound of the living voice is lost for us: but everything else remains: it is no dead language in which these writers speak. The words and thoughts are alive: the form and structure of the languages, the rhythms and the metres live. After all, how near, I wonder, can we get to the actual pronunciation of Shakespeare's Elizabethan players? Are you sure that he would recognise or even understand his own lines if he heard us reciting them? The pronunciation of a language is its most transitory feature. To call Greek and Latin 'dead' is a gross misuse of words.

The classical scholar will not merely, like the historian, read about great men of the past and their actions: he can speak with them face to face. Nor will he be dependent on translations, however brilliant, for his knowledge of the immortal writers whose noble thoughts are wedded to noble words in a union which no man may put asunder. They cannot be divorced without loss of that direct personal touch which is the joy of reading, which no version in an alien language can give. Translations of great literature may be a help to the understanding of the originals: they can never be a substitute for them.

To the lifelong interest and fuller pleasure which this direct contact can bring, speaker after speaker in our Association and its various branches have borne witness.

So far I have called my witnesses only from the professional scholars who have presided over us. But the public, the jury whom we wish to impress, are more likely to be convinced by the evidence of the other half of our list, the men distinguished in other walks of life who have professed their belief in the classics and their gratitude for what they have gained from them, than by academic scholars, however eminent, for whom, in the words of Dean Gaisford, the study has 'led not infrequently to positions of considerable emolument'. We have had for Presidents in the past Prime Ministers, Asquith and Baldwin; three great pro-consuls, Curzon and Cromer and Milner; ambassadors like Bryce and Crewe; Sir William Osler, an eminent doctor of medicine; Walter Leaf, a great banker; a Lord Chief Justice, Lord Hewart; and a great Archbishop, William Temple, whose premature death two years ago removed from our midst a great thinker and inspiring leader. To these, who are no longer with us, we can add others, happily still living: the famous name of Dean Inge, most intellectual of ecclesiastics; Leopold Amery, Cabinet Minister in many Governments; and a notable representative of modern literature, Mr. T. S. Eliot. These are impressive witnesses; and they are representative of many besides themselves. They speak for a great multitude of ordinary men and women for whom the

Greek and Latin which they were taught in youth have had no direct connexion with their subsequent careers, but who none the less believe that they owe to those studies not only a mental training which has made other learning easier, but (what they value still more) a wider outlook and a fuller enjoyment of some of the best and greatest things that life can give. The grown man, looking back upon the studies of his boyhood, recognizes this and acknowledges his debt, as he comes upon his old school-books:

> Here's an Odyssey – that came later –
>   Made one feel, in a hazy way,
> Life had gifts that were even greater,
>   Once achieved, than success in play;
> Till, as we stumbled over the grammar,
>   Skipping words that were hard to find,
> Unawares we had caught the glamour,
>   Homer's world, and the soul behind.
> Virgil, Oedipus at Colonus,
>   Did we fret till the hour was done?
> Merely grunt as the pearls were thrown us,
>   Longing so for the air and sun?
> Even so, when the limbs were aching
>   Most and worst for the fields again,
> All unknown you were slowly waking
>   Strange new music within the brain.[1]

We have called our witnesses for the defence. But we must not forget that there may be a case for the prosecution. It is an impressive list; but our critics may ask the question which, Cicero tells us, Dionysius of Syracuse asked in the temple of Venus Marina when he was shown the votive offerings of voyagers who had vowed to the goddess in perils of shipwreck and been saved: *Ubi sunt nomina eorum qui perierunt?* 'Where are the names of those who were drowned?' What of those who in the past have been diverted from more congenial studies by the tyranny of the classics forced upon them? What of those others who have been alienated from great literature by 'The drilled dull lesson, forced down word by word?' Byron, who wrote that line, went on to complain that Horace had been spoiled for him: 'Then farewell Horace, whom I hated so!' and we are told that the poet Gray could not enjoy

1 G. F. Bradby.

the beauties of Virgil till he was released from the duty of reading him as a task. Our critics, too, may not without reason complain of what one of our presidents called 'the unequal dominance of classics' in the past, which left many non-scholars with a pathetic sense of failure, such as was sympathetically voiced by the schoolboy poet thirty-five years ago:

> We are the wasters, who have no
>   Hope in this world here, neither fame,
> Because we cannot collar low
>   Nor write a strange dead tongue as well
> As strange dead men did long ago.[1]

We need not, in defending our cause, identify ourselves with all that is affirmed by some of its most ardent supporters. We shall not take too seriously the claim advanced recently by an Oxford tutor in a letter to *The Times*, that efficiency in washing up – a very necessary accomplishment in these days – was a direct result of his classical training, or the statement made by the wife of another that if she had not read 'Greats' she would not have adapted herself so well in middle life to the art of cooking. But neither shall we sympathize with the wife who wrote complaining that two terms spent by her at school in learning Greek might more profitably have been spent in learning to cook.

'We are concerned', as Professor Butcher said in his presidential address in 1907, 'in retaining as a civic possession the most potent instrument that has yet been found for the awakening and enlargement of the mind.' It is perhaps an old-fashioned belief, but one which I am old-fashioned enough to hold, that to have been grounded in Latin and Greek, even for those who do not keep them up afterwards, has real educational value. 'My life', wrote one such, a Colonel in the Royal Engineers, 'consists now of modern languages, mathematics, science, etc. But I wouldn't swop my classical education for anything, and don't regret it one jot or tittle. Having been grounded in them it's much easier to learn anything else.' University teachers of other subjects, even of those which are not literary, have been known to bear the same testimony: they prefer for pupils students who come to them with a good linguistic and history training, such as classical education in the past has given. It is a matter for regret that in the development of secondary education which has taken place since 1902 premature specialization

---

1 Charles Sorley.

in science and mathematics has tended to crowd out literary subjects and these latter when provided have too often been of a non-classical type. I cannot believe that modern history or modern languages or specialized 'English' can provide either the foundations for subsequent learning or the key to wider enjoyment that our generation gained from the older learning. It may be too much to say, as a teacher in a place where classical studies had to struggle against modern subjects said at one of our meetings about a non-classical education, that 'if a man is not clever he seems to learn little from it; if he is clever you feel what an enormous amount he has missed'. But I cannot help regretting it when a boy or girl with literary or linguistic gifts is not given in youth the keys that open the doors to the two languages and literatures that have meant so much to generation after generation of Europeans.

The classical education of my day left gaps in our knowledge, especially of scientific subjects, gaps which I regret. But it did not exclude modern languages or history, or encourage us to make a false distinction between ancient and modern, or to think that history began with 1066 and all that. And though we never had 'English' lessons, we were learning all the while, in school and out, to write English and to read and appreciate English literature. There is an element of nostalgia in the retrospect, when I compare the wider education that was the normal standard then with the over-specialization of to-day, which has distributed the subjects of literary education among a number of mutually exclusive pigeon-holes, and has deprived those whose inclinations or careers divert them to scientific subjects of the training in language which the old system afforded, leaving them 'with wisdom at one entrance quite shut out'. We, too, may ask the question of Dionysius – *Ubi sunt nomina eorum qui perierunt*? What of the boys and girls in schools where Greek is not taught, who might have profited by it? Which is the greater tragedy, that a few students for whom the classics are uncongenial should have them forced upon them, or that one who might have derived from them the inspiration and stimulus and happiness which they can give, and might have made a real contribution to their study, should have no opportunity of learning them? How many mute inglorious Murrays and Mackails are passing out of our schools to-day?

I am not normally disposed, in spite of my age, to praise the past at the expense of the present. But I am bound to deplore the drift away from the classics of which there are many signs to-day in our universities and schools. In schools known to me, once strongholds of scholarship, the numbers taking the classical course have sadly diminished, and in my university more and more even of the scholars are being diverted from Literae Humaniores to easier lines of study, modern languages or history or the course called by the specious name of 'Modern Greats', which seems to include nothing that Greats in our day excluded, and to omit so much of eternal value that it gave us.

Yet the classics are, I believe, more than ever needed to-day, and more than ever relevant. They are needed as an antidote to the materialist outlook encouraged by a purely scientific and vocational training, and to insular nationalistic views such as those which have led the world to disaster. They are relevant because the conditions in which youth to-day is growing up are far more akin than the days of our boyhood to those in which the great Latin and Greek writers lived.

Theirs was no stable world. They grew up among wars and rumours of wars, when sudden reversals of fortune were common, amid recent memories of a troubled past and fears for an uncertain future. Virgil's description of his own times – 'right and wrong confounded, world-wide wars, crime rampant in many shapes, fighting in the East, and in the West, Germany stirring up war' (*movet Germania bellum*) strikes a familiar note to us. So, too, does his description of 'fields, whose farmers have been removed, gone to weeds' (*squalent abductis arva colonis*) which for us in South Devon who lived in or near the battle-training area has a special relevance. We knew also what it meant to suffer, or like Virgil be threatened with, eviction in favour of an alien soldiery:

> *Impius haec tam culta novalia miles habebit?*
> *barbarus has segetes?*

The poetry of Virgil begins with that experience of war and its aftermath. It ends with the account, in the last part of the *Aeneid*, of war as it seemed to the civilian poet, 'a chaos of horror and muddle'. Like Aeneas and Achates in the hall of Dido we feel, as we read, the kinship of a common experience. Here are *lacrimae rerum* and a heart touched by man's mortality, the heart of a poet:

> *majestic in his sadness*
> *at the doubtful doom of human kind.*

The same experiences that make Virgil more real to us increase our sympathetic understanding of Greek literature, especially of the tragedians. The pessimism and pathos of Euripides, the serenity and artistic perfection of Sophocles, and above all the prophetic grandeur and deep human sympathy of Aeschylus, stand out against a background of insecurity and war, in the midst of which they lived. To read the tragedies in times of war and crisis is to see a deeper significance in them and feel a closer kinship with the writers. The greatest of them all, the *Agamemnon*, is no longer for us just a play about an unfaithful wife and a murdered husband. It is a dramatic and infinitely sympathetic presentment of what war, even successful war, means in the way of unhappiness to all sorts and conditions of men and women, to the soldiers at the front, to deserted wives at home, to old men like the poet himself left behind while the young go out to fight, to all those who wait anxiously for news, to the homes to which sons, husbands or brothers will never return, to captive women whose unregarded fate is far more pitiful and tragic than the death of a victorious king in the hour of his triumph.

Aeschylus, like Virgil, writes from personal experience, and it is an experience which to-day we can in great measure share. To read the two poets is to be brought into direct contact with men who were born into a troubled and unstable world, yet never lost their vision of beauty or their faith in the potential greatness of the spirit of man. So much the more must we regret anything which lessens the number of their possible readers.

When this Association was founded forty-one years ago the controversy about so-called 'compulsory' Greek was exciting Oxford and Cambridge. It is worth while remembering that it was not a clear-cut issue of classics against science. There were scientists and mathematicians who voted for the retention of Greek as a condition of entrance to the university because they valued the modicum of Greek which they had been enabled thereby to acquire. A Cambridge science professor of my acquaintance, a prejudiced opponent, when I first knew him, of classical education, was converted by a visit to India, where he found how much their classical memories meant to the Indian Civilians: and he voted, when he came back, for the retention of Greek. On the other hand there were classical scholars and teachers who voted for its abandonment, some of us, I think, because we were afraid of being called reactionaries if we opposed this, some from a genuine belief that the change could be brought about with no educational loss. And there were some who prophesied that if the demand for Greek as a condition of entrance to the two oldest universities were abandoned, 'in twenty years' time Greek in our schools would be as dead as Hebrew'. The Ides of March came, and passed, with the gloomy prophecy unfulfilled. Greek lives, but for a smaller proportion of students. We cannot say that there has been no loss. In this context I would commend to you some wise words of Dr. Mackail. The aim, he said, of our Association is 'to bring the classics themselves more largely and more effectively into national life, to induce that contact with them which kindles imagination, quickens intelligence, and brings joy'. But this contact ... 'is not a thing to be imposed by compulsion, but a gift to be placed within reach, a privilege to be widely extended. Compulsory Greek and Latin are phrases as irrelevant as compulsory warmth and light. Such things are not compulsory, they are only necessary. But it is our business to endeavour that there shall be, so far as possible, no compulsory ignorance of them.'

Those words were spoken twenty-three years ago. If we compare the position to-day with what it was then, can we say that in the schools which profess to give higher education, whether those which are called 'grammar schools' or even the so-called 'public schools', we have protected our boys and girls from that 'compulsory ignorance'?

An Australian headmaster, addressing his fellow-teachers on the responsibilities of their calling, reminded them in a significant sentence that 'a Grammar School headmaster taught William Shakespeare English'. But how did he teach him? A Grammar School in those days was what the dictionary still defies it as being, 'a school in which grammar, especially Latin grammar, is taught; a higher school in which Greek and Latin are taught'. I should be glad to think that Shakespeare's successors in the grammar schools of to-day were given similar opportunities and would make similar use of them. We may accept Ben Jonson's statement that he had 'small Latin and less Greek' – a remark that is full of encouragement for those whose knowledge of those two languages had advanced only a short distance – but the difference between 'small' or 'less' and 'none' is a difference not of degree but of kind. Even an elementary knowledge of Greek makes it easier to get the heart out of a work translated from the language, and to use it as Shakespeare used North's Plutarch: even the small Latin with which he was credited enabled him to construct Antony's great speech in *Julius Caesar* out of one Latin phrase in Cicero's 2nd *Philippic* and a brief reference in North. Would a local grammar school have given him as much to-day?

A study of the records of our Association during the forty-two years of its existence leaves no doubt as to the keenness of our members and our faith in the cause which we support: it leaves also the impression of a cause which needs support now more than ever before. The earlier addresses strike a note of confidence in the position of classics in education which sounds strangely at the present time. In the first of them which has been preserved, Henry Butcher, our President of 1907, could declare that we were in the full swing of a new classical renaissance, while at the same time warning us against the 'host of educational reformers' who urged us to 'give up Greek', and reminding us that 'Latin divorced from Greek is a maimed and impoverished study'.

The warning note is repeated in the addresses of subsequent presidents, who find it increasingly necessary to justify the claims of classics to a predominant position in English education. Sir Frederic Kenyon, in 1914, defends them as 'the widest and most liberal form of preparation for every-day life'. 'We are concerned', he says, 'to preserve *for the average man and woman* those imaginative elements which redeem life from being a mere routine of material desires and their gratification.'

The four years of war that followed were less disastrous for the cause of classics than the seven years since 1939 have proved, though it may be noted that in one year (1916) there was no presidential address. (The Association may reflect with pride that there has been no such gap in any year of the recent war.) The influence of the crisis is observable in the address of 1915, when Professor Ridgeway vigorously denounced the excessive deference paid to German scholarship, and T. E. Page supported him with a speech, the concluding words of which are as applicable for us to-day as they were to his audience then. 'In that new era' (after the war), he said, 'this Association will have a great work before it, *to see that the study of classical literature shall remain, as it always ought to be, an integral part of English education*, and that perhaps, having got rid of some of that encumbering mass of Teutonic learning, we may go back to that good honest English system of trying to appreciate what is the real soul and spirit of the ancient writers.'

I venture to digress at this point to observe how relevant to the present day are some of the reflections made by the scholars and public men who addressed our Association in those years. The great doctor of medicine, Sir William Osler, who was President in 1919, is constrained to remind us that scientific men are not more brutal than their fellows, while confessing with shame that having in 1916 denounced reprisals, in 1918 he had been prepared to demand the bombing of Berlin. And he speaks of the hopes and fears of the time in words which we might echo to-day: 'Our fears are lest we fail to control the fretful forces of

Caliban; our hopes are to rebuild Jerusalem in this green and pleasant land.'

Three years later, in a memorable meeting, Lord Milner delivered the presidential address, and the vote of thanks was seconded by Mr. Asquith, his political opponent, who at college had been his friendly rival for the highest classical honours of the university. Milner asked in his address 'where will it all end, in a Paradise of wealth and comfort, in which there will be no such thing as poverty, and all the harder and more distasteful forms of labour will be performed by mechanical means, or in the total overthrow of our civilization by stupendous new engines of destruction?' And Asquith's comment is even more significant. 'I would far rather trust for better feelings among the more civilized races of mankind to the humanities than to a more extensive knowledge of the exact composition of the atom.'

The words seem strangely prophetic to-day. Now, twenty-four years later, men are asking the same questions with even greater urgency. Now more than ever there is need to maintain those 'humanities' which have no national frontiers and are the common inheritance of civilized men. Now more than ever there is need of an Association like ours, when material force seems to govern the world and we are called upon, in education as in war, to hold up hands of surrender to the efficiency of science, *efficaci dare manus scientiae*.

In the presidential address of 1923, when we were slowly recovering from the first German war, Dr. Mackail could declare that classical studies were advancing steadily in the recognition which they commanded. 'The tide', he said, 'has begun to flow.' I wish that your President of to-day could give as hopeful a report. But the tide which was advancing then seems now to be ebbing,

> *and now we only hear*
> *Its melancholy long withdrawing roar.*

We who urge a return to the classics are reproached as reactionaries: we are told that we are 'fighting a rearguard action', that we are 'knocking our heads against a brick wall'. For my part, I stand before you as an unrepentant apologist for the cause. Let me recall the famous retort made by a headmaster of Uppingham to an obstructive member of his Governing Body. 'But, Mr. Thring, you are knocking your head against a brick wall.' 'That, my lord, is precisely what I intend to do.' Rearguard actions, as recent years have taught us, may be a prelude to final victory, and it is no lost cause or impossible loyalty that we maintain when we profess year by year in our meetings our belief that the Greek and Latin classics are an eternal treasure, a κτῆμα ἔς αἰεί whose value does not diminish with the passing of time, an inheritance which we are concerned, amid all the changes and chances of modern education, to preserve for those who come after us.

APPENDIX III

Archbishop Geoffrey Fisher's Address
at Sir Frank Fletcher's Memorial Service
in the Chapel at Charterhouse,
3 December 1954

In trying to speak to you of Frank Fletcher, I recall at once how supremely good he was himself when it was required of him to speak words in memory of some distinguished member, master or old boy, of the school community. In the simplicity and restraint with which he used then to speak, in the reverent clarity with which a career was evaluated and a character revealed, in the warm tribute of human sympathy and appreciation, were clearly to be discerned his own qualities of mind and spirit. The attempt to do for him what he could do with such sureness of touch and truth for others makes me once more conscious that always for me he is the Master and I the eager and clumsy pupil.

Most of you, I expect, remember him in the setting of Charterhouse to which the greater part of his life's work and devotion was given, and from which his influence went out to bear fruit by his own vision and leadership in the world of education, and in the world at large through those whom he had taught and inspired. I had glimpses of him in that setting from time to time and after his retirement. Towards the end of his working life it came about, that I, the pupil, as Chairman of the Governing Bodies Association presided over him as a member of its Executive Committee and had to call him to order who had first taught me what order was. From such scattered memories of fifty years I could try to construct for you some generalized picture of Frank Fletcher and his career. Your recollections of him are all intensely personal; and I can speak best of him by going back to my personal memory of what I received from him when he came to Marlborough a young Headmaster, eager to prove himself in his first post of independent responsibility.

I remember vividly his first meeting with the Sixth Form. As we stood awaiting him expectant and slightly hostile towards the unknown, he came in unheralded and went quietly from one to another

shaking hands with each of us. There were no obvious marks of authority or command in his manner or appearance; and yet at once everyone
there felt that here was a person to be reckoned with, a power to be
reckoned with: there was evident at once to some of us a quality in him
which invited an instinctive loyalty. Perhaps it was the fearlessness with
which he took our respect for granted and assumed our friendship.
Certainly he was no respecter of persons or of public opinion or of
popular favour. He had a measuring rod of his own by which to form
his judgements: and having formed them (carefully, as we came to
know, and not always easily), he acted upon them with a quiet inflexibility.

At Marlborough he went through a period of some unpopularity,
and I expect the same was true at Charterhouse. But from the beginning he had the utter devotion of those who, not yet understanding
quite what he was trying to do, gave him their trust and unhesitating
loyalty. At Marlborough, and I expect here too, he began by finding his
way to his goal with the same disciplined courage and judgement which
made him earlier an Alpine climber. In both schools he soon became
accepted, and trusted, as only great Headmasters are. But the outline of
his character never changed. He was at Marlborough what a distinguished Carthusian found him in later years and admirably put into
such words as these:- Majestic yet friendly, Olympian yet intimate,
rugged yet polished, in the clouds yet firmly planted on earth, and with
a strength which was tremendous.

I must mention next the excitement of learning from him, and learning always far more than we then realised. He taught as the masters of
teaching always do, not chiefly by his great learning but by his temper
of mind. If he was no respecter of persons, he was no respecter of ideas,
until they had been examined and scrutinised. When the facts were
sufficiently assembled, he would make us search for their meaning or
explanation. His constant method was to ask Why? and again, Why?
Relentlessly he pushed on and on until he could find sure ground and
the truthful answer, or at least the direction in which it lay. He engaged
us in the search because he was searching for it himself. And when the
answer was found it was valued not because it was orthodox and traditional (though generally it was) but because it was true, or true so far as
it went. As often as not the answer would run off into a quotation from
Browning or Plato or the New Testament: but it never ran away into
sand. The questioning never became destructive. It rested on the
assumption, made daily more valid and secure, that truth was there to

be found, that in a measure it was already found and was its own reward, and that there were reserves of truth which 'for our unworthiness we dare not, and for our blindness we cannot ask' to perceive, but which the divine light may reveal to those who search faithfully. So what we learned of him was always a moral truth, matching his moral courage, whether the field of its exercise was Greek composition, or Aeschylus or an intellectual idea or a question of words, or a current political situation or some school problem. And this combined pursuit and practice of truth was not only interesting but exciting, and the very stuff out of which loyalty to the art of living and especially to the art of living in and for the community was made.

And one other quality I would specially recall – his ability to understand and so to enter into terms of friendship with all kinds of boys – the younger as well as the older, the stupid as much as the able, the ill behaved as much as the well behaved – once they allowed him in, so to speak. Some, of course, refused: there are always refusers and he would not push his way in. But as my experience of him grew, I came to marvel at the way in which boys of all sorts and conditions were won by him to give him their trust, and took their place in his affections. I know what I owed thus to him myself; I understood later how gently he had led me on from my uncritical and crude devotion to deeply held conventional orthodoxies, so that I came not to outgrow them but to rediscover them through friendship at a higher level of truth and power. It would have been so easy to shock, to injure, to disappoint or to destroy my fledgling enthusiasm. This delicacy in his understanding of boys of all kinds sprang perhaps from two things – first from the vivid interest in everyone which made him a master of friendship, and then from his reverence for the personal worth of each which enabled him to triumph over natural impatience at the perversities of boys and men, and to have a pastoral care for all.

It was through all these elements at once that he taught us what the Christian Faith meant to him: all that we received from him through loyalty and friendship, through the discipline of learning, through the stringency of his standards of moral and intellectual truth, and through the inspiration of his own interpretation of life, found (for some of us at least) its explanation and its completion when in his sermons in Chapel and in his expositions of St. Paul's Epistles, he allowed us to perceive what the knowledge of God and the service of God meant and when some word or chance event would afford to us a sudden glimpse of the depth and power of his dedication to our Lord.

When physical failure came to limit so severely his powers of communication with us, we must all have felt something like indignation, that he who was always so competent, so master of every situation, so rich in friendships and in the interchange of mind and spirit, should be cut off from us, that one on whom we all depended should become altogether dependent upon others. Loss indeed there was: but it is the manner of bearing it that reveals God's love and man's highest reaches. And few were so well equipped to bear this crippling loss as Frank Fletcher; few have borne it so freely. He knew (he taught something of it to me) how to accept cheerfully what could not be mended, and how to surrender without complaint what could not be kept. Moral courage, contempt of circumstances, the power that comes from trusting truth even when its answer is beyond our sight, the comfort of undoubting faith in the friendship of Christ and the wisdom of God, humility, self-disregard, – all these means of grace were ready to his hand. The life of this beloved community which he had served with all his powers as teacher and friend, the consecration of that life in this Chapel which he dreamed of and saw to fulfilment, were to the end his joy and comfort. And present to the end was the partner of all his life's service, who had been so gloriously proud of him in those early days at Marlborough and had so eagerly contributed her creative share to his achievements, no less proud of him and partner in all his work for Charterhouse, and perhaps proudest of all of him in the patience of his endurance when all she could give to him was her ceaseless offering of companionship and care and love.

So release came to him at last. His zest for friendship will find larger fulfilment beyond. He who so loved and served this community here will be taken up into the greater company of the faithful. His reverence for all truth and all life will have its reward. To his questions there will be the inexhaustible answer of the Divine Word, at once Light and Love, to master which will be the exercise and the joy of God's people through all eternity. As we commend him to the life in Christ beyond, thankful for every thought of his comradeship with us here, may we not fitly say 'Blessed are the pure in heart, for they shall see God', and 'Thanks be to God, which giveth us the victory through our Lord Jesus Christ.'

Source Notes

AMD refers to *After Many Days*, Frank Fletcher's memoirs published in 1937

CHAPTER I

1 Sir James Darling, *Richly Rewarding*, p. 83.
2 Quoted by Fletcher, *AMD*, p. 108.
3 Lambeth Palace Library: Fisher Papers, vol. 141, f.13 – see Appendix III, p. 239.
4 Frank Fletcher's obituary in *The Times*, 18 November 1954.
5 *AMD*, p. 43.
6 Illustrations, i, p. 2.
7 Illustrations, i, p. 3: Colonel Ralph's obituary in *The Gentleman's Magazine* explains that 'A liberal subscription was raised in the town & vicinity of Bolton for the painting of his portrait, which was executed in masterly style.'
8 *AMD*, pp. 43f.
9 See Pauline Gregg, *A Social and Economic History of Britain 1760–1963*, p. 47.
10 *Ibid.*, p. 141.
11 William Cobbett, quoted by David Thomson, *England in the Nineteenth Century*, 1950, p. 12. Cobbett was a self-taught son of a labourer who became the radical agriculturalist, essayist and politician.
12 Quoted by Florence and Kenneth Wood, *A Lancashire Gentleman: The Letters and Journals of Richard Hodgkinson 1763–1847*, p. 13: Richard Hodgkinson managed the financial and estate concerns of the Atherton Gwillym family.
13 E. P. Thompson, *The Making of the English Working Class*, p. 536.
14 Gregg, *op. cit.*, p. 91.
15 Thompson, *op. cit.*, p. 743.
16 Gregg, *op. cit.*, p. 92: the figure of 80,000 is an exaggeration.
17 Robert Walmsley, *Peterloo: The Case Reopened*, pp. 217f.

18 W. Brimelow, *Political and Parliamentary History of Bolton*, vol. i, 1882: quoted by F. and K. Wood, *op. cit.*, pp. 4f.
19 Kenneth Wood, *The Coal Pits of Chowbent*, p. 74.
20 *AMD*, p. 43.
21 *Ibid.*, pp. 41f.

CHAPTER 2

1 See J. R. de S. Honey, *Tom Brown's Universe*, p. 126.
2 *AMD*, pp. 13f.
3 Lord Ernle, *Whippington to Westminster*, 1938, p. 30: quoted by Honey, *op. cit.*, p. xi.
4 Quoted by G. R. Parkin, *Life of Edward Thring*, 1898, vol. i, p. 66. Thring was appointed to Uppingham in 1853 where he proved an innovative and humane headmaster. He founded the Headmasters' Conference in 1869.
5 *AMD*, p. 40.
6 *Ibid.*, p. 41.
7 *Ibid.*, p. 46.
8 *Ibid.*, p. 44.
9 *Ibid.*
10 *Ibid.*, pp. 45f.
11 W. Furness (ed.), *The Centenary History of Rossall School*, p. 4.
12 *Ibid.*, pp. 4f.
13 A. G. Bradley *et al*, *A History of Marlborough College* (1893), revised 1923, p. 199.
14 Quoted by Furness, *op. cit.*, p. 5.
15 *AMD*, p. 31.
16 From *The Orchards, the Sea, and the Guns* by F. W. Harvey, a pupil 1902–5.
17 *AMD*, pp. 31f.
18 See Honey, *op. cit.*, p. 43.
19 Dr Woolley's Rule, 1844 or 1845: quoted by Honey, *op. cit.*, p. 44.
20 Honey, *op. cit.*, p. 44.
21 Quoted by Furness, *op. cit.*, p. 6.
22 *Ibid.*
23 *Ibid.*, p. 12.
24 *AMD*, p. 29.
25 *Ibid.*, p. 13.
26 *Ibid.*, pp. 24f.

27 Frank Fletcher, 'H.A.J.', chapter iv, Furness, *op. cit.*, p. 34.

28 *AMD*, p. 26: the 'someone' was Edward Lyttelton, Headmaster of Eton, 1905–16.

29 Quoted by Peter Bennett, *'Rossall Will Be What You Make It'*, p. 26.

30 Fletcher, *op. cit.*, pp. 30f.

31 *Ibid.*, note, p. 31.

32 Furness, *op. cit.*, p. 224.

33 *The Rossallian*, 24 July 1884, p. 14.

34 *AMD*, pp. 26f.

35 *Ibid.*, p. 27.

36 Quoted by Fletcher, *op. cit.*, p. 35.

37 *Ibid.*

38 *Ibid.*, p. 28.

39 Quoted by Bennett, *op. cit.*, p. 26.

40 *AMD*, p. 22.

41 Quoted by Bennett, *op. cit.*, p. 31.

42 *AMD*, p. 21.

43 *Ibid.*, pp. 22f.

44 *The Carthusian*, October 1886 (vol. iv, pp. 229f.): 'he who brought us here' is William Haig Brown.

45 Furness, *op. cit.*, p. 49.

46 *The Rossallian* 22 November 1886, p. 9.

47 *Ibid.*, 25 July 1887, p. 11.

48 *Ibid.*

49 *Ibid.*, 19 March 1889, p. 11: his one argument was that there were sufficient immigrants in London and elsewhere already.

50 *AMD*, p. 35.

51 *Ibid.*, pp. 35f.

52 *Ibid.*, p. 36.

53 Furness, *op. cit.*, p. 49.

54 *AMD*, p. 29.

55 *Ibid.*, p. 30.

56 *Ibid.*

57 *The Rossallian*, 27 July 1889, p. 1.

CHAPTER 3

1 *AMD*, p. 47.

2 Noël Annan, *The Dons: Mentors, Eccentrics and Geniuses*, p. 61.

3 Quoted by J. G. Lockhart, *Cosmo Gordon Lang,* p. 26: Lang became Archbishop of York in 1909 and Archbishop of Canterbury in 1928.

4 Quoted by John Jones, *Balliol College: A History*, p. 207.

5 Evelyn Abbott and Lewis Campbell, *The Life and Letters of Benjamin Jowett*, vol. i, p. 273.

6 Peter Hinchliff, *Benjamin Jowett and the Christian Religion*, p. 73.

7 Quoted by Jones, *op. cit.,* p. 200.

8 10 October 1870 (Lambeth Palace Library: Tait Papers, vol. 88, f. 163).

9 Sir Leslie Stephen, 'Jowett's Life', *The National Review*, 1897.

10 *AMD*, p. 59.

11 *Ibid.*, p. 47.

12 Viscount Samuel, *Memoirs*, 1945, p. 9.

13 *AMD*, p. 48.

14 Goldwin Smith, *Reminiscences*, 1910, p. 83.

15 Lewis Carroll, *Alice's Adventures in Wonderland*, 1865; Puffin Classics edn., 1994, pp. 44f.

16 John Prest, 'Balliol, For Example', *The History of the University of Oxford*, vol. vii, ed. M. G. Brock and M. C. Curthoys, p. 163.

17 Illustrations, i, p. 5.

18 *AMD,* pp. 57f.

19 *Ibid.*, p. 63.

20 *Ibid.*, p. 55.

21 *Ibid.*, p. 52f.

22 Quoted by Janet Howarth, 'The Self-Governing University, 1882–1914', Brock and Curthoys, *op. cit.*, p. 601. In replying, Gladstone described this as 'the highest compliment that can be paid to a human being'!

23 *AMD,* p. 55: for a more detailed eyewitness account see C. R. L. Fletcher (no relation), *Mr. Gladstone and Oxford 1890*, 1908, pp. 60f.

24 *Ibid.,* p. 51.

25 Quoted by H. S. Jones, 'University and College Sport', Brock and Curthoys, *op. cit.*, p. 529.

26 *AMD*, p. 51: Paravicini was a product of Bradley's Marlborough (see ch. 5).

27 *Ibid.*, pp. 66f: Hardie returned to Edinburgh in 1895 as Professor of Humanity.

28 *Ibid.*, p. 30.

29 M. C. Curthoys, 'The Colleges in the New Era', Brock and Curthoys, *op. cit.*, p. 135.

30 *AMD*, pp. 30f.

31 *Ibid.*, p. 30: the colleague referred to was George Smith, later Headmaster of Merchiston and Dulwich. The description is remarkably similar to that of Mr M'Choakumchild in Dickens's *Hard Times*: 'If he had only learnt a little less, how infinitely better he might have taught much more!'

32 *Ibid.*, p. 70.

33 See W. H. Fremantle (ed.), *College Sermons*.

34 A. M. M. Stedman (ed.), *Oxford: Its Life and Schools*, p. 85.

35 Richard Jenkyns, 'Classical Studies, 1872–1914', Brock and Curthoys, *op. cit.*, p. 328.

36 *AMD*, pp. 68f.

37 Letter to Lord Lansdowne: quoted by A. L. Rowse, *Oxford in the History of the Nation*, 1995, p. 188.

38 'In memoriam Sir Frank Fletcher', *Alpine Journal*, vol. 60, May 1955, p. 153.

39 *AMD*, p. 26.

40 *Ibid.*, pp. 59f.

41 See Curthoys, *op. cit.*, p. 139.

42 *AMD*, pp. 61f: it was Urquhart who shouted 'Shame!'.

43 *Ibid.*, p. 63.

44 Quoted by S. Paget, *Henry Scott Holland: Memoir and Letters*, 1921, p. 33.

45 Quoted by Peter Hinchliff, *op. cit.*, p. 147.

46 Peter Hinchliff, 'Jowett and Gore: Two Balliol Essayists', *Theology*, 87, 1984, p. 251.

47 Quoted by David Newsome, *Godliness and Good Learning*, p. 231.

48 Quoted by James Carpenter, *Gore: A Study in Liberal Catholic Thought*, 1960, p. 8. Herbert Hensley Henson was Bishop of Hereford and then of Durham. Gore was successively Bishop of Worcester, Birmingham and Oxford.

49 G. L. Prestige, *The Life of Charles Gore*, p. 9.

50 W. H. Fremantle, *Reflections*, 1921, p. 110.

51 *AMD*, pp. 63f.

52 *Ibid.*, p. 64.

53 Quoted by Prestige, *op. cit.*, pp. 38f.

54 *AMD*, p. 65: incarnation was the central doctrine in *Lux Mundi*.

55 See Peter Hinchliff, 'Benjamin Jowett and the Church of England:

or "Why really great men are never Clergymen"', *Balliol Studies*, ed. John Prest.

56 *AMD*, p. 73.

57 W. H. Fremantle (ed.), *College Sermons*, p. 347.

58 *AMD*, p. 71: Margot Tennant, the socialite daughter of a wealthy Liberal baronet, married Asquith a year later – hence Fletcher's regret.

59 Harold Hartley, 'The Successors of Jowett', in H. W. C. Davis, *A History of Balliol College* (revised).

60 *AMD*, p. 72.

CHAPTER 4

1 William Temple, *Life of Bishop Percival*, p. 105.

2 *AMD*, pp. 73f.

3 J. B. Hope Simpson, *Rugby since Arnold*, p. 5.

4 Letter from Mrs Arnold to her sister, 19 November 1839: quoted by J. R. de S. Honey, *Tom Brown's Universe*, p. 16.

5 J. H. Simpson, *Schoolmaster's Harvest*, p. 46.

6 *AMD*, p. 88.

7 *Ibid.*, pp. 47f.

8 *Ibid.*, p. 88.

9 *Ibid.*, pp. 88f.

10 G. F. Bradby: quoted by Temple, *op. cit.*, pp. 123f.

11 Temple, *op. cit.*, p. 116.

12 Quoted by J. R. de S. Honey and M. C. Curthoys, 'Oxford and Schooling', *The History of the University of Oxford*, vol. vii, ed. M. G. Brock and M. C. Curthoys, p. 557.

13 A. P. Stanley, *The Life and Correspondence of Thomas Arnold*, vol. i, p. 93.

14 H. C. Bradby, *Rugby*, p. 54.

15 G. F. Bradby, Preface to *The Lanchester Tradition*.

16 *Ibid.*, pp. 7f.

17 'Headmaster', *The Spectator*, 12 August 1960.

18 Basil Willey, *Nineteenth Century Studies*, pp. 59f.

19 Thomas Hughes, *Tom Brown's Schooldays*, 1857, Puffin Classics edn., 1994, p. 371.

20 Peter Hinchliff, *Benjamin Jowett and the Christian Religion*, p. 27.

21 Stanley, *op. cit.*, p. ix: Stanley's recumbent effigy in Rugby Chapel lies immediately beneath Arnold's.

22 Willey, *op. cit.*, p. 61.

23 Stanley, *op. cit.*, p. 93.

24 Michael McCrum, *Thomas Arnold, Head Master*, p. 15.

25 Quoted by David Newsome, *Godliness and Good Learning*, p. 38.

26 McCrum, *op. cit.*, p. 121.

27 *Ibid*, p. 66: in one of Arnold's most famous sermons he speaks of public schools as the seats and nurseries of vice – 'It may be unavoidable, or it may not; but the fact is indisputable. None can pass through a large school without being intimately acquainted with vice; and few, alas! very few without tasting too largely of that poisoned bowl.'

28 Stanley, *op. cit.*, pp. 150f: Thomas Hughes paints much the same picture as Stanley who describes how he and C. J. Vaughan used to nudge each other with delight as Arnold mounted the pulpit steps.

29 The author, 'Only the best is good enough now', *The Daily Telegraph*, 29 September 1999.

30 Stanley, *op. cit.*, pp. 105f.

31 Quoted by Terence Copley, *Black Tom*, p. 121.

32 Illustrations, i, p. 5.

33 *The Meteor*, 13 February 1897, pp. 10f.

34 Quoted by David Newsome, *op. cit.*, p. 218.

35 Quoted by Honey, *op. cit.*, p. 325.

36 T. W. Jex-Blake, 'Rough Notes for an Autobiography' (manuscript): quoted by Hope Simpson *op. cit.*, p. 102.

37 Quoted by Hope Simpson, *op. cit.*, pp. 103f.

38 *Ibid.*, p. 112.

39 *Ibid.*, p. 114.

40 See G. L. Prestige, *The Life of Charles Gore*, p. 23.

41 *AMD*, p. 75.

42 Temple, *op. cit.*, p. 101.

43 F. A. Iremonger, *William Temple, Archbishop of Canterbury*, p. 23.

44 Temple, *op. cit.*, pp. 102f: Temple quotes G. F. Bradby.

45 *Ibid.*, p. 103.

46 *Ibid.*, p. 105.

47 *Ibid.*, p. 106.

48 *AMD*, pp. 76f.

49 *Ibid.*, p. 79.

50 *Ibid.*, p. 80.

51 Quoted by Hope Simpson, *op. cit.*, p. 131.

52 *Ibid.*, p. 136.

53 *AMD*, p. 80.
54 Hope Simpson, *op. cit.*, p. 153.
55 *AMD*, p. 91.
56 *Ibid.*, p. 92.
57 *Ibid.*
58 *Ibid.*, pp. 90f.
59 *Ibid.*, pp. 92f.
60 *Ibid.*, p. 94.
61 *Ibid*: the friend was T. E. Page, the brilliant classical scholar and sixth form master at Charterhouse. If this was James's club it would have been the Athenaeum; if Page's, the Reform.
62 Simpson, *op. cit.*, p. 66.
63 *AMD*, p. 78.
64 *Ibid.*, p. 83.
65 Temple, *op. cit.*, p. 105.
66 *AMD*, pp. 85f.
67 *Ibid.*, p. 86.
68 H. C. Bradby, *op. cit.*, pp. 155f.
69 *AMD*, p. 95.
70 *Ibid.*, pp. 95f.
71 *Ibid.*, pp. 97f.
72 Illustrations, ii, p. 6.
73 'What should England do to be saved?', *Westminster Review*, June 1901: quoted by Donald Read, *England 1868–1914*, 1979, p. 379.
74 Rugby School archives.
75 See p. 33.
76 See p. 34.
77 Peter Bennett, '*Rossall Will Be What You Make It*', p. 66.
78 *The Meteor*, 11 July 1899, p. 84: the marble statue by Thomas Brock stands in front of the Temple Reading Room.
79 *Ibid.*, p. 85.
80 *Ibid.*, p. 86.
81 H. C. Bradby, *op. cit.*, p. 160.
82 *AMD*, p. 89: this was the first time that Rugby had achieved two Balliol scholarships (both in classics) in the same year (1898) and James awarded the school two extra days' holiday.
83 Rugby School archives.
84 *AMD*, p. 69.
85 *Ibid*: Tawney's father, however, asked him how he 'proposed to wipe out this disgrace'!

86 Iremonger, *op. cit.*, p. 3.

87 *Ibid.*, p. 12.

88 *Ibid.*, p. 38.

89 *Ibid.*, p. 475.

90 *Ibid.*, p. 14.

91 *AMD*, pp. 89f.

92 Anthony Wright, *R.A. Tawney*, 1987, p. viii.

93 Ross Terrill, *R.H. Tawney and His Times*, 1973, p. 23.

94 Quoted in Frank Fletcher's obituary in *The Times*, 18 November 1954.

95 Quoted by Iremonger, *op. cit.*, pp. 46f. As Headmaster of Repton, Temple presented a complete Browning to every boy who reached the upper sixth.

96 *AMD*, p. 90: Fletcher had said that he did not suppose that St Paul had written his letters, like Cicero, with an eye to posterity.

97 Quoted by Iremonger, *op. cit.*, p. 37.

98 Willey, *op. cit.*, p. 78.

99 *AMD*, p. 101.

100 Frank Fletcher's obituary in *The Alpine Journal*, vol. 60, May 1955, p. 151.

101 T. G. Longstaff, 'Fifty Years Ago', *ibid.*, vol. 62, November 1957, p. 134.

102 *AMD*, pp. 102f.

103 Dorothy Fletcher's obituary in *The Carthusian*, July 1958, p. 230.

104 *AMD*, p. 103.

105 *Ibid.*

CHAPTER 5

1 Noël Annan, *Roxburgh of Stowe*, pp. 6f.

2 *AMD*, p. 104.

3 *Ibid.*, p. 112.

4 Bernard Palmer, *A Class of Their Own*, p. 3.

5 *Pall Mall Gazette*, 2 October 1891, p. 7.

6 *AMD*, p. 111.

7 *Ibid.*, p. 108.

8 *Ibid.*, p. 105.

9 *Ibid.*, p. 106.

10 *Ibid.*, p. 105.

11 Marlborough College Council minutes, 2 April 1903 (Marlborough College archives).
12 *AMD*, p. 107.
13 *Ibid.*
14 *Ibid.*
15 *Ibid.*, pp. 107f.
16 Thomas Hinde, *Paths of Progress*, pp. 109f: G. G. Bradley was Master from 1858 to 1871.
17 J. R. de S. Honey, *Tom Brown's Universe*, p. 315.
18 *The Times*, 19 June 1903.
19 *Ibid.*
20 *AMD*, p. 109: the archbishop was the newly enthroned Randall Davidson.
21 *The Meteor*, 28 July 1903: the two day match at Lord's was a draw.
22 Frank Fletcher, '*Genius Loci*', Brentnall and Kempson, *op. cit.*, p. 31.
23 *Ibid.*
24 Charles Sorley, 'Rain', first published in *The Marlburian*, 31 October 1912.
25 Louis MacNeice, *The Strings Are False*, p. 86.
26 Sorley, *op. cit.*
27 *AMD*, p. 115.
28 F. M. Heywood, 'The First Hundred Years', Brentnall and Kempson, *op. cit.*, p. 2.
29 *Ibid.*
30 Thomas Hughes, *Tom Brown's Schooldays*, 1857, Puffin Classics edn, 1994, p. 139.
31 David Newsome, *Godliness and Good Learning*, pp. 56f.
32 Quoted by A. G. Bradley *et al*, *A History of Marlborough College*, p. 168.
33 Annan, *op. cit.*, p. 10.
34 Quoted by James A. Mangan, *Athleticism: A Case-Study of the Evolution of an Educational Ideology*, appendix ii (Marlborough College archives).
35 11 July 1870: Stanley had introduced Bradley to Jowett.
36 Bell's eulogy, *The Marlburian*, 21 March 1903, pp. 28f.
37 Heywood, *op. cit.*, p. 4.
38 Quoted by Bradley, *op. cit.*, p. 223. Hallam's twin brother Lionel was sent to Eton on the grounds that he was not tough enough for Marlborough.

39 Hugh Kingsmill, *After Puritanism*, 1929: quoted by J. R. Townsend, introduction to the 1971 Hamish Hamilton edn. of *Eric*, p. 12. *Tom Brown's Schooldays*, published the year before *Eric*, presented a more up-to-date and certainly a more attractive hero.

40 *AMD*, pp. 114f: see also Fletcher, *op. cit.*

41 *Ibid.*, p. 31.

42 *Ibid.*, p. 116.

43 Niall Hamilton, *A History of the Chapel of St Michael and All Angels*, 1986, p. 28.

44 *AMD*, p. 112.

45 *The Marlburian*, winter 1954, p. 60.

46 21 March 1935 (Lambeth Palace Library: Lang Papers, vol. 132, f. 212).

47 *AMD*, p. 119.

48 Dorothy Fletcher's obituary by George Turner, *The Marlburian*, summer 1958, p. 47.

49 A poem in *The Marlburian* by one of Bell's boys: quoted by Hinde, *op. cit.*, p. 105.

50 *AMD*, pp. 121f: Edward Bowen started his teaching career at Marlborough in 1859 but moved to Harrow after less than a term in order to earn a decent salary. He spent the next forty-two years there as a reforming and devoted master, and the author of over thirty of the school songs, including the famous 'Forty Years On'.

51 MacNeice, *op. cit.*, pp. 83f.

52 Quoted by Jean Moorcroft Wilson, *Charles Hamilton Sorley*, p. 52.

53 *Ibid.*, p. 53: Sorley's form-master was F. A. H. Atkey.

54 Quoted by Bevis Hillier, *Young Betjeman*, p. 101.

55 *AMD*, p. 122.

56 *Ibid.*, p. 118.

57 *Ibid.*

58 *Ibid.*, p. 119.

59 *Ibid.*, p. 120.

60 *Ibid.*

61 *Ibid.*

62 See Mangan, *op. cit.*, p. 25.

63 *AMD*, pp. 123f.

64 *Ibid.*, p. 124.

65 Quoted by Wilson, *op. cit.*, p. 53: Sorley was cynical about both sides of the divide and came to despise the whole system.

66 Marlborough College prefects' book, Lent Term 1906 (Marlborough College archives).

67 *AMD*, p. 125: Fisher recalled that the holiday was spent at Ballachulish in Scotland.

68 Fletcher's speech at his retirement dinner in the Connaught Rooms, 8 October 1935.

69 Letter from Fletcher to George Turner, 27 August 1910 (Marlborough College archives).

70 *AMD*, p. 126.

71 *Ibid*, p. 262.

72 Quoted by William Purcell, *Fisher of Lambeth*, pp. 41f.: Fletcher was 33 not 32 when he started.

73 *AMD*, p. 127.

74 Quoted by Mangan, *op. cit*: the real founder and organiser of the modern side was J. Franck Bright, a master at Marlborough from 1856–72 and afterwards Master of University College, Oxford.

75 MacNeice, *op. cit.*, pp. 82f.

76 *AMD*, pp. 126f.

77 Fletcher, *op. cit.*, p. 36.

78 MacNeice, *op. cit.*, p. 80.

79 L. E. Upcott, 'The Middle Years', Brentnall and Kempson, *op. cit.*, p. 22: Fletcher and Upcott shared the classical sixth teaching.

80 Quoted by Miranda Carter, *Anthony Blunt, His Lives*, p. 19.

81 Fletcher, *op. cit.*, p. 35.

82 Marlborough College Council minutes, 18 June 1902 (Marlborough College archives).

83 The Red Book, 22 March 1906 (Marlborough College archives).

84 *Ibid.*, 25 October 1909.

85 *Ibid.*, 3 November 1903.

86 *Ibid.*, October 1904.

87 Letter to A. C. B. Brown, 24 April 1908 (Marlborough College archives).

88 *Ibid.*, 27 April 1908.

89 MacNeice, *op. cit.*, p. 89.

90 *AMD*, p. 131.

91 *Ibid.*

92 *Ibid.*, p. 134.

93 G. C. Turner, 'Scattered Memories', *The Marlburian*, Lent Term 1966, p. 22.

94 Quoted by Wilson, *op. cit.*, p. 59.

95 *AMD*, p. 134.

96 Quoted by Wilson, *op. cit.*, p. 66.

97 *Ibid.*, p. 74: Bickersteth married Sorley's sister.

98 *AMD*, p. 136.

99 Annan, *op. cit.*, p. 150.

100 *AMD*, pp. 128f.

101 *Ibid.*, p. 116.

102 *Ibid.*, p. 138.

103 A. R. Pelly, *My Masters*, 1993, p. 79.

104 *AMD*, pp. 138f.

105 Quoted by Fletcher, *ibid.*, p. 140.

106 *Ibid.*, p. 141.

107 *Ibid.*, p. 144.

108 *Ibid.*, p. 147.

109 Quoted by Edward Carpenter, *Archbishop Fisher – His Life and Times*, p. 15.

110 Marlborough College Council minutes, 31 May 1911 (Marlborough College archives).

111 *Ibid.*, 27 June 1911.

112 *Ibid.*

113 *The Marlburian*, 21 October 1911.

114 Letter to Geoffrey Fisher, 12 July 1911 (Marlborough College archives).

115 Frank Fletcher's obituary, *The Marlburian*, winter 1954, p. 60.

116 *The Marlburian*, Christmas 1958, pp. 47f.

117 Letter to George Turner, 27 July 1910 (Marlborough College archives).

118 *AMD*, p. 137.

119 James Hilton, *Good-bye, Mr Chips*, 1934, p. 127: it may be relevant that Fletcher was suffering from mumps when he took the scholarship examination at Rossall.

CHAPTER 6

1 *AMD*, p. 139.

2 Quoted by Fletcher, *ibid.*, p. 31.

3 Quoted by E. P. Eardley Wilmot and E. C. Streatfield, *Charterhouse: Old and New*, p. 8.

4 Quoted by Anthony Quick, *Charterhouse, A History of the School*, p. 1.

5 Eardley Wilmot and Streatfield, *op. cit.*, p. 13.

6 Quoted in *The Carthusian*, September 1932 (vol. xv, p. 1080).

7 Quick, *op cit.*, p. 41.

8 *Ibid.*

9 *Ibid.*, p. 71.

10 Harold E. Haig Brown (ed.), *William Haig Brown of Charterhouse*, p. 109.

11 *The Times*, 6 June 1945.

12 W. H. Holden (ed.), *The Charterhouse We Knew*, pp. 37f.: the words of Aurelius are from *Meditations* x 15.

13 Sir Ronald Storrs, *Orientations*, 1937 p. 11.

14 Letter to John Graves, 6 July 1914: quoted by R. P. Graves, *Robert Graves, The Assault Heroic*, p. 105.

15 Robert Graves, *Goodbye to All That*, Penguin edn., 1960, p. 38.

16 *Ibid.*

17 *Ibid.*, p. 39.

18 *Ibid.*, pp. 37f.

19 *Ibid.*, p. 42.

20 An Aristophanic parody quoted by Noel Annan, *Roxburgh of Stowe*, p. 11.

21 Robert Graves, *op. cit.*, p. 43.

22 *Ibid.*, p. 44.

23 Sermon preached at the London Charterhouse, 12 December 1918, *Brethren and Companions*, p. 23 – see Appendix I, p. 223.

24 Holden (ed.), *op. cit.*, p. 59.

25 G. L. Thorp, 'Frank Fletcher in 1911', *The Carthusian*, July 1935 (vol. xvi, p. 998).

26 *AMD*, pp. 153f.

27 Appendix III, p. 240.

28 A. L. Irvine, *Sixty Years at School*, p. 99.

29 *The Carthusian*, November 1911 (vol. x, p. 510).

30 *AMD*, p. 151.

31 *Ibid.*, p. 154.

32 Fletcher's paper on the monitorial system, July 1912 (Charterhouse archives).

33 *AMD*, pp. 161ff: Graves was one of these intellectual rebels.
34 Robert Graves, *op. cit.*, p. 52.
35 Letter from J. S. Shields, 14 July 1992 (Charterhouse archives).
36 Diary of Graves's father, 10 October 1911: quoted by R. P. Graves, *op. cit.*, p. 75.
37 Robert Graves, *op. cit.*, p. 48.
38 Virginia Woolf, 'Old Bloomsbury' (*c.*1922), *Moments of Being*, ed. Jeanne Schulkind, 1978 edn., p. 201: Virginia Stephen married Leonard Woolf in 1912.
39 Letter, probably autumn 1919: quoted by R. P. Graves, *op. cit.*, p. 85.
40 David Robertson, *George Mallory* 1969, p. 80.
41 Robert Graves, *op. cit.*, p. 41.
42 *Ibid.*, p. 50.
43 *AMD*, p. 139.
44 *The Carthusian*, February 1914 (vol. xi, p. 226).
45 *AMD*, p. 188.
46 *Ibid.*, pp. 189f.
47 Letter to Geoffrey Young, 22 November 1914: quoted by Peter and Leni Gillman, *The Wildest Dream*, p. 124.
48 *AMD*, p. 194
49 *Ibid.*, pp. 194f. and Charterhouse archives.
50 *Ibid.*, p. 196 and Charterhouse archives.
51 *Ibid.*, p. 192.
52 Quoted by Gillman, *op. cit.*, p. 127.
53 *Ibid.*, p. 130.
54 28 December 1916: *AMD*, p. 251.
55 Robert Graves, *op. cit.*, pp. 54f.
56 Appendix I, p. 223.
57 *The Carthusian*, June 1916 (vol. xi, p. 603).
58 *AMD*, p. 147.
59 Charterhouse archives.
60 *AMD*, p. 200.
61 Holden (ed.), *op. cit.*, p. 73.
62 A. H. Tod, 'The Verite Fire', 1938 (Charterhouse archives).
63 *AMD*, pp. 202f.
64 *Ibid.*, p. 208.
65 *Ibid.*, p. 207.
66 Appendix I, p. 222.

CHAPTER 7

1   W. H. Holden (ed.), *The Charterhouse We Knew*, p. 38.
2   Headmaster's report to the governing body, May 1912 (Charterhouse archives).
3   Frank Fletcher 'The Public School Chapel', *The Architectural Review*, July 1927, p. 43.
4   *Ibid.*, p. 43.
5   The letter was also published in *The Carthusian*, October 1917 (vol. xii, pp. 136f.).
6   *AMD*, p. 210.
7   Fletcher, *op. cit.*, p. 43.
8   *The Carthusian*, March 1918 (vol. xii, p. 193).
9   *AMD*, pp. 210f.
10 *Ibid.*, p. 213.
11 Quoted by Fletcher, *ibid*.
12 *Ibid.*, pp. 219f.
13 *Ibid.*, p. 221: the Cenotaph in Whitehall was designed by Sir Edwin Lutyens.
14 *Ibid.*, p. 215.
15 *Ibid.*, p. 110.
16 Frank Fletcher, *Brethren and Companions*, pp. 30f.
17 *Ibid.*, p. 152.
18 *Ibid.*, p. 99.
19 *Ibid.*, p. 154.
20 *AMD*, p. 110.
21 A. L. Irvine, *Sixty Years at School*, p. 99.
22 *AMD*, p. 158.
23 Anthony Quick, *Charterhouse, A History of the School*, p. 77.
24 *AMD*, p. 157.
25 *Ibid.*, p. 264.
26 *Ibid.*, pp. 267f.
27 Russell Page, *The Education of a Gardener*, 1935, pp. 31f.
28 June 1925 (Charterhouse archives).
29 *AMD*, p. 270.
30 Frank Fletcher, *op. cit.*, p. 127: if not the noblest the chapel is certainly the largest war memorial in England.
31 Charterhouse archives.
32 *The Greyfriar*, July 1927 (vol. viii, p. 164).
33 *Ibid.*, p. 165.

34 *AMD*, p. 216.
35 Quoted by Fletcher, *ibid.*, p. 231.
36 *Ibid.*, p. 225.
37 *The Carthusian*, July 1927 (vol. xiv, p. 251).

CHAPTER 8

1   *AMD*, pp. 74f.
2   Letter to Ralph Fletcher, 21 December 1926.
3   Edward Thring, Diary, 12 March 1869: quoted by Alicia C. Percival, *The Origins of the Headmasters' Conference*, p. 30.
4   Report of the 1906 Headmasters' Conference, p. 68.
5   *AMD*, pp. 165f.
6   *Ibid.*, p. 178.
7   Tim Card, *Eton Renewed*, 1994, p. 146.
8   Report of the 1926 Headmasters' Conference, p. 25.
9   *AMD*, p. 179.
10 *Ibid.*, p. 172.
11 *Ibid.*, pp. 166f.
12 *Ibid.*, p. 236.
13 Quoted by Fletcher, *ibid.*, p. 233.
14 W. Veale, *From a New Angle*, p. 35.
15 *AMD*, p. 237.
16 *Ibid.*, p. 278.
17 15 April 1935.
18 Quoted by Fletcher, *AMD*, p. 277.
19 *Ibid.*, p. 278.
20 *Ibid.*, p. 262.
21 George Turner's sermon at Charterhouse on the Sunday after Fletcher's death, *The Carthusian*, March 1954 (vol. xxi, p. 316).
22 'A Carthusian looks back', *The Carthusian*, December 1982 (vol. xxx, p. 20).
23 Ronald Millar, *A View from the Wings*, 1993, p. 46.
24 *AMD*, p. 265.
25 Patrick Wilkinson, quoted in a letter from Hugh Wilkinson to the author, 30 October 2003.
26 A. L. Irvine, *Sixty Years at School*, p. 87.
27 *Ibid.*, p. 88.
28 *Ibid.*, pp. 98f.

29   Letter from James Blachford Rogers to the author, 25 September
     2000.
30   *AMD*, pp. 253f.
31   Illustrations, ii, p. 4.
32   *AMD*, p. 241.
33   9 July 1912: quoted by Fletcher, *AMD*, p. 242.
34   *AMD*, p. 244: Anthony Quick describes him as 'perhaps the most
     distinguished man ever to have made a career as an assistant
     master in a public school'.
35   Sir Ronald Storrs, *Orientations*, 1937, p. 11.
36   Osbert Lancaster, *With an Eye to the Future*, 1967, p. 50f.
37   *AMD*, p. 264.
38   Irvine, *op. cit.*, p. 79.
39   R. C. Robertson-Glasgow, *46 Not Out*, p. 58.
40   'A Carthusian looks back', *op. cit.*, p. 21.
41   Quoted by Anthony Quick, *Charterhouse, A History of the
     School*, p. 107.
42   M. C. Curthoys, 'The Colleges in the New Era', *The History of the
     University of Oxford*, vol. vii, ed. M. G. Brock and M. C.
     Curthoys, p. 128.
43   Quoted by J R de S Honey, *Tom Brown's Universe*, p. 321.
44   Quoted by G L Prestige, *The Life of Charles Gore*, p. 23.
45   21 November 1934 (Lambeth Palace Library: Lang Papers,
     vol. 132, f. 177).
46   31 January 1935 (*ibid.*, f. 185).
47   *AMD*, p. 284.
48   21 March 1935 (Lambeth Palace Library: *op. cit.*, ff. 210–12).
49   23 January 1935 (*ibid.*, ff. 178–9): Claude Elliott had succeeded
     Alington as Headmaster of Eton in 1933.
50   Fletcher's handwritten reminiscences of William Temple (Lambeth
     Palace Library: W. Temple Papers, vol. 48, ff. 161–2).
51   Philip Gibbs, *England Speaks*, pp. 249f.
52   Quoted by June Rose, *Daemons and Angels, A Life of Jacob
     Epstein*, 2002, p. 193.
53   *AMD*, p. 284.
54   *Ibid.*, pp. 284f: Epstein's portrait bronzes include Churchill,
     Einstein, Nehru, Vaughan Williams and Princess Margaret.
55   See *Epstein, An Autobiography*, 1963, p. 159: the bust was exhib-
     ited in 1937 at the Leicester Galleries.

CHAPTER 9

1   Sir James Darling, *Richly Rewarding*, p. 138.
2   *AMD*, p. 282.
3   *Ibid.*, p. vii.
4   *The Times*, 22 June 1937.
5   *AMD.*, p. 44.
6   *Greece and Rome*, October 1941 (vol. xi, no. 31).
7   *Ibid.*, p. 4.
8   *The Times*, 29 October 1938
9   David Spinney, *Clayesmore, A School History*, 1987, p. 83.
10 *The Clayesmorian*, 1941.
11 Quoted by F. A. Iremonger, *William Temple*, p. 627.
12 *Ibid.*, pp. 627f.
13 *AMD.*, p. 283.
14 Quoted by W. Furness (ed.), *The Centenary History of Rossall School*, p. 45.
15 *Ibid.*, p. 21.
16 Appendix II, p. 233.
17 Fletcher quotes from a letter he received from Evelyn Abbott, the paralysed tutor at Balliol.
18 Frank Fletcher (ed.), *Virgil, Aeneid VI*, p. v.
19 Appendix II, p. 228.
20 W. Veale, *From a New Angle*, p. 68.
21 Appendix III, p. 239.

Select Bibliography

The place of publication is London unless otherwise stated

Abbott, Evelyn and Campbell, Lewis, *The Life and Letters of Benjamin Jowett*, John Murray, 1897.

Annan, Noël, *Roxburgh of Stowe*, Longmans, 1968.

——, *The Dons: Mentors, Eccentrics and Geniuses,* HarperCollins, 1999.

Arrowsmith, R. L. (ed.), *A Charterhouse Miscellany,* Gentry, 1982.

Bamford, T. W., *Thomas Arnold*, Cresset Press, 1960.

Bennett, Peter, '*Rossall Will Be What You Make It*', Rossall Archives, 1992.

Bradby, G. F., *The Lanchester Tradition*, Smith, Elder & Co., 1913.

Bradby, H. C., *Rugby*, George Bell and Sons, 1900.

Bradley, A. G. *et al*, *A History of Marlborough College* (1893), revised and continued, John Murray, 1923.

Brentnall, H. C. and Kempson E. G. H. (edd.), *Marlborough College 1843–1943,* Cambridge, Cambridge University Press, 1943.

Brock, M. G. and Curthoys, M. C. (edd.), *The History of the University of Oxford*, vol. vii, Oxford, Oxford University Press, 2000.

Carpenter, Edward, *Archbishop Fisher – His Life and Times*, Canterbury, Canterbury Press, 1991.

——, *Cantuar – The Archbishops in their Office*, Cassell, 1971.

Carter, Miranda, *Anthony Blunt, His Lives*, Macmillan, 2001.

Copley, Terence, *Black Tom, Arnold of Rugby*, Continuum, 2002.

Darling, Sir James, *Richly Rewarding,* Melbourne (Australia), Hill of Content, 1978.

Davis, H. W. C., *A History of Balliol College* (1899), revised, Oxford, Basil Blackwell, 1963.

Eardley Wilmot, E. P. and Streatfield, E. C., *Charterhouse: Old and New,* Stirling, Eneas Mackay, 1910.

Faber, Geoffrey, *Jowett: A Portrait with Background*, Faber, 1957.

Fletcher, Frank, *After Many Days: A Schoolmaster's Memories,* Robert Hale, 1937.

——, *Brethren and Companions: Charterhouse Chapel Addresses*, Robert Hale, 1936.

Fremantle, W. H. (ed.), *College Sermons*, John Murray, 1895.

Furness, W. (ed.), *The Centenary History of Rossall School*, Aldershot, Gale & Polden, 1947.

Gardner, Brian, *The Public Schools*, Hamish Hamilton, 1973.

Gibbs, Philip, *England Speaks*, Heinemann, 1937.

Gillman, Peter and Leni, *The Wildest Dream, Mallory – His Life and Conflicting Passions*, Headline, 2000.

Graves, Richard Perceval, *Robert Graves, The Assault Heroic, 1895–1926*, Weidenfeld & Nicolson, 1986.

Graves, Robert, *Goodbye to All That*, Jonathan Cape, 1929.

Gregg, Pauline, *A Social and Economic History of Britain 1760–1963*, George G. Harrap, 1950.

Haig Brown, Harold E., *William Haig Brown of Charterhouse*, Macmillan, 1908.

Hearnden, Arthur, *Red Robert: A Life of Robert Birley*, Hamish Hamilton, 1984.

Hillier, Bevis, *Young Betjeman*, John Murray, 1988.

Hinchliff, Peter, *Benjamin Jowett and the Christian Religion*, Oxford, Oxford University Press, 1987.

——, 'Jowett and Gore: Two Balliol Essayists', *Theology*, 87, 1984.

Hinde, Thomas, *Paths of Progress: A History of Marlborough College*, James & James, 1992.

Holden, W. H. (ed.), *The Charterhouse We Knew*, British Technical and General, 1950.

Honey, J. R. de S., *Tom Brown's Universe*, Millington, 1977.

Hope Simpson, J. B., *Rugby since Arnold*, Macmillan, 1967.

Iremonger, F. A., *William Temple, Archbishop of Canterbury*, Oxford, Oxford University Press, 1948.

Irvine, A. L., *Sixty Years at School*, Winchester, P. & G. Wells, 1958.

Jones, John, *Balliol College: A History* (1988), 2nd edn., Oxford, Oxford University Press, 1997.

Lockhart, J. G., *Cosmo Gordon Lang*, Hodder & Stoughton, 1949.

MacNeice, Louis, *The Strings Are False, An Unfinished Autobiography*, Faber and Faber, 1965.

Mangan, James A., 'Athleticism: A Case-Study of the Evolution of an Educational Ideology', 1976 (unpublished).

McCrum, Michael, *Thomas Arnold, Head Master*, Oxford, Oxford University Press, 1989.

Newsome, David, *Godliness and Good Learning*, John Murray, 1961.

Owen, David, *Canals to Manchester*, Manchester, Manchester University Press, 1977.

Palmer, Bernard, *A Class of Their Own*, Lewes, The Book Guild, 1997.

Percival, Alicia C., *The Origins of the Headmasters' Conference*, John Murray, 1969.

Potter, Jeremy, *Headmaster, The Life of John Pervical*, Constable, 1998.

Prest, John (ed.), *Balliol Studies*, Leopard's Head Press, 1982.

Prestige, G. L., *The Life of Charles Gore*, Heinemann, 1935.

Purcell, William, *Fisher of Lambeth, A Portrait from Life*, Hodder & Stoughton, 1969.

Quick, Anthony, *Charterhouse, A History of the School*, James & James, 1990.

Robertson-Glasgow, R. C., *46 Not Out*, Hollis and Carter, 1948.

Simpson, J. H., *Schoolmaster's Harvest*, Faber, 1954.

Stanley, A. P., *The Life and Correspondence of Thomas Arnold*, B. Fellowes, 1844.

Stedman, A. M. M. (ed.), *Oxford: Its Life and Schools*, G. Bell & Sons, 1887.

Temple, William, *Life of Bishop Percival*, Macmillan, 1921.

Thompson, E. P., *The Making of the English Working Class*, Victor Gollancz, 1963.

Veale, W., *From a New Angle: Reminiscences of Charterhouse 1880–1945*, Winchester, P. & G. Wells, 1957.

Walmsley, Robert, *Peterloo:The Case Reopened*, Manchester, Manchester University Press, 1969.

Ward, W. R., *Victorian Oxford*, Frank Cass, 1965.

Willey, Basil, *Nineteenth Century Studies*, Chatto & Windus, 1949.

Wilson, Jean Moorcroft, *Charles Hamilton Sorley*, Cecil Woolf, 1985.

——, *Siegfried Sassoon, the Making of a War Poet*, Duckworth, 1998.

Wood, Florence and Kenneth, *A Lancashire Gentleman: The Letters and Journals of Richard Hodgkinson 1763–1847*, Stroud, Alan Sutton, 1992.

Wood, Kenneth, *The Coal Pits of Chowbent*, Bolton, K. Wood, 1984.

Index